SERVICE ABOVE SELF

SERVICE
ABOVE
SELF

WOMEN VETERANS IN
AMERICAN POLITICS

ERIKA CORNELIUS SMITH

 UNIVERSITY PRESS OF KANSAS

© 2022 by the University
Press of Kansas

Published by the University
Press of Kansas (Lawrence,
Kansas 66045), which was
organized by the Kansas
Board of Regents and is
operated and funded by
Emporia State University,
Fort Hays State University,
Kansas State University,
Pittsburg State University,
the University of Kansas,
and Wichita State
University.

Library of Congress Cataloging-in-Publication Data

Names: Cornelius Smith, Erika, author.

Title: Service above self : women veterans in American
   politics / Erika Cornelius Smith.

Other titles: Women veterans in American politics

Description: Lawrence, Kansas : University Press of
   Kansas, 2022 | Includes bibliographical references
   and index.

Identifiers: LCCN 2021043905 | ISBN 9780700633227
   (cloth) | ISBN 9780700633234 (ebook)

Subjects: LCSH: Women legislators—United States—
   Biography. | Women veterans—United States—
   Biography. | United States. Congress—Biography. |
   Legislators—United States—Biography. | Veterans—
   United States—Biography.

Classification: LCC JK1030 .C67 2022 | DDC
   328.73/092—dc23/eng/20211021

LC record available at https://lccn.loc.gov/2021043905.

British Library Cataloguing-in-Publication Data is
available.

Printed in the United States of America

10 9 8 7 6 5 4 3 2 1

CONTENTS

Oath of Enlistment for Military Service

I, (NAME), do solemnly swear (or affirm) that I will support and defend the Constitution of the United States against all enemies, foreign and domestic; that I will bear true faith and allegiance to the same; and that I will obey the orders of the President of the United States and the orders of the officers appointed over me, according to regulations and the Uniform Code of Military Justice. So help me God.

Oath of Office for Congress

I do solemnly swear (or affirm) that I will support and defend the Constitution of the United States against all enemies, foreign and domestic; that I will bear true faith and allegiance to the same; that I take this obligation freely, without any mental reservation or purpose of evasion; and that I will well and faithfully discharge the duties of the office on which I am about to enter: So help me God.

When I proposed *Service above Self* to the editors at the University Press of Kansas in March 2020, I did not foresee the disruption the Covid-19 pandemic would create in our world. Needless to say, researching and writing a monograph in "Covid times" presents unique challenges. Libraries and archives closed their physical spaces in early spring 2020. Capitol Hill offices closed temporarily, and members of Congress dispersed across the country to their districts. Our community schools and college campus closed, moving to fully remote learning modalities within a ten-day period. At one very poignant moment, my elementary-school-aged children, my spouse, and I were simultaneously logged into four separate pieces of technology, accessing four separate classrooms. Did I mention we also adopted a puppy that winter?

This Covid context also presented opportunities for ingenuity and grace under pressure. Archivists at Louisiana State University and Harvard University generously offered to assist, scan, email, and advise on source material throughout the closures. Digital archives, such as those maintained by C-SPAN and the Library of Congress, and online databases became invaluable sources of material. Social media platforms used by more recent candidates, including Facebook, LinkedIn, Twitter, and YouTube provided examples of direct communication to voters, and video-conferencing technology allowed me to connect with potential interviewees for this work. Many thanks to M. J. Hegar for sharing her experiences and perspectives for this project. She is generous and inspirational—fully deserving of honorary "badass" status (see Chapter 3). Moreover, it is important to note that Hegar's story of service is one of many; to those in military, quasi-military, and intelligence roles who have served our country—past and present—I express my gratitude for your contributions and sacrifices.

As institutions tested reopening through 2020 and 2021, I reached out to archivists in hopes of continuing my research and gaining access to nondigitized materials. Fortunately, the Margaret Chase Smith Library was ready to test their new protocols in January 2021, and I became the first researcher to work in the archives midpandemic. Thank you to David Richards, Kim Nelson, and the library team for your trust and hospitality.

I cherished each day working in your beautiful conference room overlooking the Kennebec River.

Working with the University Press of Kansas (UPK) has been a seamless process, and I am grateful to David Congdon, Kelly Chrisman Jacques, and the entire UPK team for their expertise and guidance. And to my supportive peer community at Nichols College, whether you asked about progress on the manuscript or offered an intellectual space to test ideas, I appreciate you—Erin Casey-Williams, Kerry Calnan, Maryann Conrad, Bryant Richards, Heather Richards, Alan Reinhardt, Luanne Westerling, and so many others. Thank you to Bob "Kuppy" Kuppenheimer, Susan West Engelkemeyer, and Academic Affairs leadership for continuing to value and support faculty scholarship.

I am surrounded by what has been called the "formation of women." The community of BBD has helped me develop an inner strength and endurance critical to seeing this project through in Covid times—Sarah Bentley, Leia Faucher, and Erica Kesselman. Knowing that I have friends like Andee Barnes Meikamp and Jessie Brady, who are "ride or dies," makes everything possible. The Book/Fight Club with Karin and Tim Curran has provided a wonderful space to feast on good books and good food. And to Sarah Jacobs, thank you for trusting our friendship enough to read my writing—in draft form.

Last, but in no way least, my family. I have had the privilege of learning from generations of those in my family who embody the ethos of service above self in their own lives and work—Jim and Elizabeth Hurst, Hap and Joyce Cornelius, Peggy Baird Cornelius, Roger and Anna Cornelius, and Nicolette Hughes. I am indebted to Andrew Smith for his countless hours reading early drafts, providing advice, and entertaining our girls, allowing me space to write. There is no one else I would rather be with in quarantine for fifteen long months. Thanks to Wally for the many writing and stretch breaks throughout this process, and to Sophie and Phoebe, my muses, whose curiosity, spirit, and imagination inspire me every day.

SERVICE ABOVE SELF

I

Women in the service is a natural chapter in American history. It is today's acceptance of the responsibilities as well as the privileges of democracy by American women. It is a step forward in the individual and collective advancement of women.
—Margaret Chase Smith (1947)

When reflecting in later life on her lengthy political career, Margaret Chase Smith wondered if her pathbreaking experiences were a matter of destiny, a life of public service "thrust upon her."[1] The Republican "Rebel from Maine" was a woman of many firsts—the first woman from Maine elected to Congress, the first woman to win election to both the US House of Representatives and Senate, and the first woman to serve on the powerful Senate Armed Services Committee.[2] Though she was often told politics is "no place for a woman," Smith devoted her life to public service and became a steadfast advocate for women with military or quasi-military status. And like many of those servicewomen, Smith was determined to show that she was a woman who could do what a man could do "without apologizing."[3] She insisted that she was not a "woman politician," or even a "woman senator." Rather, her perspectives on politics, service, and success were shaped by her resolute belief in an American creed of individual choice and meritorious success.[4]

Smith's legacy and legislative victories created new opportunities for women in military service and public service, and her story illustrates a broader chapter of women in politics missing from the narrative of US history. *Service above Self* draws together the stories of women with military and intelligence service backgrounds who pursue elected political office. Inspired by their diverse paths to politics and the unique ways in which they communicate their experience as well as their policy positions, this work explores several important questions: What motivates servicewomen to run for office? How do they connect their military service to their careers in public service? How does a military or intelligence background allow them to negotiate or overcome gendered stereotypes about women candidates and foreign policy? The answers revealed in their individual personal and professional stories shed light on this collectively, historically significant cohort of political women.

The Second "Year of the Woman"

During an incredible year for women in politics, women with military backgrounds and intelligence experience were elected in the 2018 midterms at historic rates. The record-breaking number of women candidates running for office drew comparisons with the previous so-called Year of the Woman—1992. In both years, the country was grappling with investigations of sexual misconduct by high-profile men, a significant number of predominantly male lawmakers were retiring, and voters expressed some preference for political "outsiders" regardless of gender. When the ballots were counted in November 1992, the United States elected four women to the Senate and twenty-four women to the House.

Among the historical numbers of women running for office in 2018 were an equally unprecedented number of female military veterans and former intelligence officers. Their presence reflects the dramatic increase of women serving in the US Armed Forces. According to the US Census Bureau, in 2018 about 1.7 million, or 9 percent of veterans, were women, and that percentage is projected to nearly double to 17 percent by 2040. The number of veterans in the United States overall declined by about a third between 2000 and 2018, from 26.4 million to 18 million. Fewer than 500,000 US World War II veterans were alive in 2018, down from 5.7 million in 2000. Despite those declines, women make up an increasing percentage of veterans.[5]

In the 2018 midterm elections, nearly two hundred active-duty, reserves, and US Coast Guard veterans entered congressional races. About one-third of those running were veterans with political experience or incumbent candidates, and more than half of the candidates were nominated by the Republican Party. Of the veterans running for the House, twelve were women, marking the highest number ever. When the election results were announced in November, sixteen former servicemembers—including three women—won their races, the most "new" veterans since 2010. The number of veterans seeking political office increased slightly again in 2020. Among them were twenty-four women, doubling the number who sought election in the 2018 midterms.[6]

Though more women with military and intelligence backgrounds are seeking national political office, the larger trend in Congress has been a decline in the number of representatives with service experience. According to the Pew Research Center, less than 20 percent of the Senate and House comprised veterans in 2016, compared with about 7 percent of the overall US population.[7]

In the early 2000s, scholars identified a "generation-long decline" of military experience among those seeking national political office. As veterans of World War II and the Korean War retire and leave Congress, they are often replaced by political candidates who came of age during or after the Vietnam War and are less likely to have engaged in military service.

This generational turnover has precipitated concerns that politicians without service experience will think and behave differently than military veterans, particularly on issues related to foreign policy or defense.

With those concerns in mind, both the Republicans and Democrats engaged in vigorous recruitment of veterans of the wars in Iraq and Afghanistan to run for Congress in 2006 and 2008. These efforts continued through the 2018 midterm elections, when groups such as the Service First Women's Victory Fund worked to recruit and support female Democratic candidates with military service or intelligence backgrounds. Among the sixty-seven new Democrats in Congress in 2018, ten served in the military or worked in the intelligence field. All of them defeated Republican candidates in difficult House races, many in the thirty-one districts carried by President Donald Trump in the 2016 presidential election but now held by Democrats.[8]

Table 1.1 Members of Congress, Prior Military or Veteran Occupation

Year	US House	US Senate	Year	US House	US Senate
1953	268	71	1991	208	71
1955	277	71	1993	177	64
1959	281	70	1995	158	56
1965	316	71	1997	141	51
1967	327	72	1999	133	44
1969	327	75	2001	118	38
1971	318	80	2003	104	36
1973	322	79	2005	95	31
1975	307	81	2007	92	31
1977	299	78	2009	89	28
1979	282	76	2011	86	25
1981	264	78	2013	84	20
1983	250	79	2015	89	23
1985	232	78	2017	93	23
1987	217	72	2019	91	21
1989	210	73	2021	88	18

Source: Data on prior occupations of US representatives and senators, 83rd–117th Congresses, 1953–2021, *Vital Statistics on Congress*, Brookings Institution and American Enterprise Institute.

The "First" Candidates

Service above Self is the first synthesis of women with military, quasimilitary, or intelligence backgrounds entering political office. Identifying a form of service as *military* or *quasimilitary* involves working through a process both political and gendered.[9] Legislation formally allowing women into the military was passed in 1948, though tens of thousands had served in both world wars. Prior to the twentieth century, women such as Harriet Tubman and Mary Walker served in the Civil War as nurses, spies, and even soldiers disguised as men. During World War I women were mobilized on a large scale by the armed services, with tens of thousands serving in civilian roles under the auspices of the American Expeditionary Force (AEF) in the army, enlisting as civilian workers in the US Navy and US Marine Corps, or working in hospitals as ambulance drivers, bacteriologists, dieticians, and librarians.

Women's work in war has been more than "a simple extension" of their participation in the civilian labor force; it is also "military or quasi-military service."[10] In seeking acknowledgment of their contributions during World War I, women of the AEF adopted a new name for themselves,

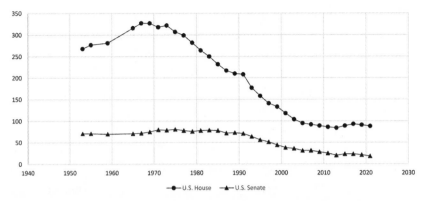

This line graph depicts the decline over time (1953–2021) in the number of representatives and senators serving in the US Congress with prior military service or veteran status. The number of US representatives with military backgrounds peaked between 1965 and 1975 and steadily declined through 2013. The number of senators with this status remained relatively constant between 1953 and 1993 and slowly declined through 2021. *Source:* Compiled from data on prior occupations of representatives and senators, 83rd–117th Congresses, 1953–2021, *Vital Statistics on Congress*, Brookings Institution and American Enterprise Institute.

servicewomen, and codified this identity in 1921 through the organization of the Women's Overseas Service League (WOSL), the first veterans' organization of women.[11] At the time, when servicewomen returned to the United States from overseas, most lacked the assistance and benefits extended to male servicemembers. With few exceptions, servicewomen were classified as civilians and therefore not entitled to benefits: no housing, no food, no insurance, no medical care, no legal protection, no pensions, and no compensation for their families in cases of death. These inequities became more apparent when women of the AEF learned that their British counterparts serving in France did have access to many of these benefits. The WOSL was formed not only to maintain social connections among women who served but also to institutionalize the memory of women's service and to provide aid—financial and otherwise—to returning servicewomen. Yet the struggle over veterans' benefits was about more than money; it was intimately connected to larger postwar struggles over workers' rights and citizenship that "defined women's civic status."[12]

Scholars have also documented the significance of women's service during World War II, both on the home front and abroad, as a turning point in US history.[13] With respect to military service, women volunteers came to be viewed "not just as a source of women's skills, but as a valuable source of high-quality personnel to meet overall manpower requirements for the massive military buildup."[14] By December 1941, more than 350,000 women served in the US Armed Forces.[15] As a result of female members of Congress creating policies and programs for servicewomen, during World War II they had their own branches of service, including the Women's Army Auxiliary Corps (later the Women's Army Corps, or WAC), the Women Airforce Service Pilots (WASP), and the Women Accepted for Volunteer Military Services (WAVES). Women served in the US Marines and in a branch of the US Coast Guard, the Women's Reserve, also known by the acronym for the US Coast Guard motto "Semper Paratus—Always Ready" (SPARs). Women were not permitted to participate directly in armed conflict, but their responsibilities often brought them close to the front lines, and their work in the US Army and US Navy medical corps could be very dangerous. Among those women not serving directly alongside the armed forces, many participated in organizations such as the American Red Cross, the United Service Organizations (USO), and the Civil Air Patrol. By the 1970s, women were permitted to enter military service academies, and nearly two decades later, after the 1988 Risk Rule was rescinded, servicewomen gained government approval to fly combat missions and serve on US Navy combat ships—though they were arguably exposed to combat prior to formal recognition of their contributions.[16] Today, women are still barred from most combat arms professions, but the percentage of women in the services is growing steadily.

This book takes an inclusive approach to identifying women who participated in or supported the US military in times of war and peace, in declared conflict and combat zones, and on missions of mercy and foreign assistance. Women veterans include those who participated in formal military institutions through active duty, reserves, or US Coast Guard service. In addition to women veterans with military or quasimilitary experience, I include in this analysis women with intelligence experience working for one of the many agencies of the US government who have sought political office. Intelligence officers play a key role in supporting military operations through information gathering and analysis, some even serving as enlisted members of specific branches of the armed services. Under specific circumstances, they work alongside or in support of the armed services when deployed abroad or to combat zones.

In 2020, seven women in the US Congress represented the largest cohort of women with military and intelligence backgrounds in national elected office in US history: US Representative Tulsi Gabbard (D-HI), US Army National Guard; US Representative Chrissy Houlahan (D-PA), US Air Force; US Representative Elaine Luria (D-VA), US Navy; US Representative Mikie Sherrill (D-NJ), US Air Force; Senator Joni Ernst (R-IA), US Army Reserve, National Guard; Senator Tammy Duckworth (D-IL), US Army Reserve, National Guard; and Senator Martha McSally (R-AZ), US Air Force. The significance and complexity of each woman's path from military to public service is a compelling story in its own right. Most of these women accomplished "firsts" in their service careers before entering the world of politics, and that has been the focus of reporting and publishing on their experiences—the first woman in Congress with military service, the first woman with combat experience, the first woman to enter a specific service academy, and so on.[17] To date, there are limited scholarly treatments of the historic contributions and military or political "firsts" of this group of pathbreaking women. Jeremy Teigen's *Why Veterans Run: Military Service in American Presidential Elections, 1789–2016* provides one of the most comprehensive analyses of veterans who enter political life; yet, his analysis includes candidates only through 2016, one election cycle before the significant spike in women veterans running for office, and focuses specifically on the US presidency.[18] Journalists have featured some of the more contemporary women in brief articles or in short biographical pieces (*Atlantic, Vogue*). M. J. Hegar released an autobiography in 2017, primarily recounting the story of her military career. Ernst and McSally published their personal and political memoirs in 2020. The popularity of these trade publications demonstrates that there is a growing public interest in the stories of these women, and by offering a scholarly analysis of the lives and political trajectories of women with military and intelligence backgrounds, both historical and contemporary, this book synthesizes divergent branches of scholarship and creates new avenues for research in US history and politics.

These famous "firsts" for women in military or quasimilitary roles marked important cracks in glass walls and ceilings that paved the way for subsequent women to enter service careers. Yet, their accomplishments represent the proverbial "tip of the iceberg," observable milestones just above the surface that indicate the presence of cultural, political, and social shifts in women's history and politics. Their presence reflects the increasing number of women entering the armed forces as well as the longer legacy of women in national public office who contributed to the nation's defense, foreign relations, and policies serving US veterans. In this book, I endeavor to balance recognition of remarkable "firsts" with their antecedents and contextualize these significant milestones in a longer narrative of US political and military history.

Service and Political Ambition

The literature on women running for political office is substantial, particularly with respect to explanations of why women choose to run (or not) and political ambition. In the 1970s, Susan Welch identified three potential factors explaining why women participated in a variety of political activities at lower rates than men: situational factors, structural factors, and political socialization. Situational factors refer to responsibilities women assume in their private lives, such as family care and household maintenance. Structural explanations focus on women's underrepresentation in demographic categories associated with high levels of participation among men. These include holding advanced degrees, having a higher income, and being employed in specific career fields.[19] The third category refers to socialization, or the idea that a gender gap in political ambition results from "long-standing patterns of traditional socialization that persist in U.S. culture."[20]

The stories of servicewomen who entered politics before September 11, 2001 (9/11) indicate that each of the factors suggested by Welch remains relevant: the women who entered office tended to be widowed, childless, or no longer parenting young children. They were often from privileged backgrounds; sometimes held professional careers before entering office; and most were socialized to politics, law-making, and campaigning because of the political careers of their parents, spouses, or other family members. However, these patterns do not fit the profile of servicewomen entering political office after 9/11, and there are potential pitfalls when employing these measures to assess women's candidacy.

Political scientists have noted with caution that a large portion of the literature explaining women's choices to run for office is based on notions of political ambition created by studying male political ambition. Barbara J. Burt-Way and Rita Mae Kelly explain, "The definition of what constitutes political ambition has typically been defined by male political career patterns and leads to the conclusion that women will be more ambitious and more successful when they attain the same characteristics as men."[21] Jennifer Lawless and Richard Fox remind readers that "the organs of government were designed by men, are operated by men, and continue to be controlled by men."[22] This is arguably true of the US Armed Forces as well.

Susan J. Carroll and Kira Sanbonmatsu (2013) and Kaitlin N. Sidorsky (2019) attempt to "consider women on their own terms."[23] This approach is based on analyzing what worked for women elected officials and then trying to understand if they must conform to the hegemonic model or forge their own pathways to elected office. This research attempts to follow the second approach, studying servicewomen who successfully sought elected office while still considering the situational, structural, and socialization factors that shaped these candidates' choices.

Collectively, the stories of these servicewomen reveal that beyond factors in these three categories, each of the women sought elected office with a broad commitment to the idea of "service"—defined in this book as an intellectual, philosophical, or personal commitment to help, aid, and benefit their local, national, or global communities. Their commitment to this work, both in their military service and pursuit of political office, was undertaken voluntarily, often with a sense of duty or responsibility. This notion of service shaped their political ambitions, preceded their entry into elected office, and often continued well after they left or lost their elected office.

Sidorsky observed a similar phenomenon in her study of women in appointed political positions: "They accepted these appointments to help others, help their families, and make a difference. Most importantly, these women pursue these appointments for an ambition unrelated to the political career ladder—yet an important ambition all the same. This ambition is both personal and professional, but to many of these appointees it is absolutely not political."[24] The women she studied believe they are taking part in politics "without being political" because they have a specific, election-centered and partisan-focused perception of what politics means. For many of the women included in my book, the initial opportunity to engage in service occurred during war and conflict. Early servicewomen volunteered in medical corps or auxiliary service, in roles such as nurse, ambulance driver, or pharmacist, to support US troops and national war efforts. Women who came of age during the cold war or war on terror entered the armed forces through military reserve forces, Reserve Officers' Training Corps (ROTC), or the service academies with a similar sense of purpose: a desire to differentiate themselves from their peers through service. Collectively, these women viewed this quasimilitary or military work as the highest calling, apolitical in nature. This concept of service underlies how my book conceptualizes what it means to study political ambition.

Political scientists have also indicated that political ambition is not static but dynamic and fluid. In their Citizen Political Ambition Studies, Fox and Lawless found that a variety of factors influences political ambition, such as family life, changes in political efficacy, and recruitment efforts.[25] Carroll and Sanbonmatsu (2013) argue for a relationally embedded model of candidate emergence, arguing that "women's decision making about office holding is more likely to be influenced by the beliefs and reaction, both real and perceived, of other people and to involve considerations of how candidacy and office holding would affect the lives of others with whom the potential candidate has close relationships." The notion is that "ambition and candidacy may arise simultaneously," for example, because of recruitment.[26] When interviewed about the decision to run for political office, many of the post-9/11 servicewomen candidates likewise shared personal stories or experiences that motivated them.

The political ambitions of women with military or quasimilitary backgrounds were further shaped and supported by the emergence of new organizations recruiting, training, and fund-raising to support political candidates, particularly female candidates, with military experience and intelligence backgrounds. New Politics, for example, was founded in 2013 and identifies itself as a "national, bipartisan organization that recruits, supports, and elects candidates who have dedicated their lives to serving our country," primarily in the military, intelligence communities, or through national service programs such as the Peace Corps and AmeriCorps. In the 2018 cycle, the organization endorsed more than twenty congressional candidates and nearly thirty state and local candidates and helped raise more than $7 million to fund campaigns.

The Approach

Service above Self focuses specifically on women running for national office, though similar analyses could be done at the state and local levels as more candidates seek political offices of all kinds. The stories in this book are divided into three parts, each section focusing on women servicemembers running for office in a specific institution of national government: the US House of Representatives, the US Senate, and the presidency. Chapters 2 and 3 begin by looking at historical and contemporary examples of servicewomen elected to the House. Female veterans posted groundbreaking electoral wins and performances in the 2018 midterm elections, expanding membership to a small caucus on Capitol Hill. Before the emergence of this new cohort, relatively few women veterans served in national political office. Chapter 2 recounts the path to national office for some of the first women with military and quasimilitary careers. Edith Nourse Rogers, Margaret Chase Smith, Mary Catherine Small Long, and several others were significant antecedents to the contemporary servicewomen candidates. Their stories collectively illustrate a longer history of women politicians with service backgrounds and the legacy of their legislative accomplishments in the twentieth century.

For this book I researched primary and secondary sources available through a variety of media. For the earliest women in service, I used archival materials from collections relevant to specific candidates. For example, Louisiana State University holds the Long papers, Harvard University holds the papers of Rogers, and the Margaret Chase Smith Library holds her collection. I combined these materials with newspaper articles, both historical and contemporary, and interviews I found in library databases. The C-SPAN archive online has a wealth of video footage available for the contemporary candidates, including early election debates, floor speeches, conference appearances, keynote addresses, and personal interviews. Current candidates and members of Congress maintain official websites, YouTube channels (which include campaign ads), and social media. Fortunately, the availability of digital content (including archival materials) made proceeding with research and investigation possible during Covid-related library closures.

As the contributions of women were recognized and institutionalized in the US military, the number of veterans and servicewomen eligible to run for public office increased. New opportunities available to women also attracted individuals who chose the military as a career rather than as a temporary form of service in a moment of national crisis. This reflects broader trends in Western militaries as they moved from a conscripted service force to an all-volunteer force in the twentieth century.[27] Examples of broad reforms include improved working conditions, revamped career paths, overhauled compensation systems and increased military pay, modernized pension plans, improved quality of life for military members and their families, and improved postservice prospects. These institutional changes (and greater access to preferred positions) made the military a more appealing professional choice for many women.

Among the impressive class of newly elected representatives entering the US House in 2018, five self-proclaimed "badass" national security women with no political experience are actively working to change voter perceptions of what it means to serve in Congress. Chapter 3 explores the professional backgrounds and path to elected office for the five "badasses" of Congress with national security backgrounds, including their issue positions and political projects and how they conceptualize and communicate their service to potential voters.

The second part of this book focuses on women elected to the US Senate: Duckworth, Ernst, and McSally. Duckworth has achieved many "firsts"—the Senate's first member to give birth while in office, its first member born in Thailand, and its first female amputee. As a wounded veteran with a Purple Heart, she has introduced or cosponsored bills protecting the rights of veterans—and she has been fearless in confronting the president over military and foreign affairs. In January 2019, when President Trump accused the Democrats of holding the military hostage over immigration, Duckworth took to the Senate floor, declaring in a now-historic speech,

"I will not be lectured about what our military needs by a five-deferment draft dodger." Chapter 4 reveals Duckworth's story, from her birth in 1968 in Bangkok, to April 2018, when at the age of fifty, she became the first female senator to give birth while holding office.

Ernst, the subject of Chapter 5, wants supporters to know that she is a mother, a soldier, and a leader. She believes she has a mandate from the voters of Iowa to take on Washington and deliver on her pledge to "Make 'em Squeal." As the first woman elected to federal office in Iowa, the first combat veteran, and now one of the first Republican women to serve on the prestigious Senate Judiciary Committee, Ernst positions herself as an "independent voice" for the people of Iowa. Service is an important part of Ernst's values—as her candidate website states, "it is who she is." Ernst served her country both in the Army Reserves and Iowa National Guard for more than twenty-three years, including leading a unit in the Middle East in support of Operation Iraqi Freedom that drove convoys through Kuwait and southern Iraq. She retired in 2015 as a lieutenant colonel in the Iowa National Guard, having served in every leadership position from platoon leader to battalion commander.

The final senator included is Arizona Republican appointee McSally. Chapter 6 explores how she emerged from traumatic moments through-out her early life to achieve academic excellence throughout high school and at the US Air Force Academy (USAFA). McSally served in the US Air Force until 2010 and rose to the rank of colonel before retiring. One of the highest-ranking female pilots in the history of the US Air Force, McSally was the first American woman to fly in combat following the end of the prohibition on female combat pilots in 1991. She was also the first female commander of a US Air Force fighter squadron. In 2001, she continued to push boundaries and sued the US Department of Defense in McSally v. Rumsfeld, challenging the military policy that required US and UK service-women stationed in Saudi Arabia to wear the body-covering abaya when traveling off base in the country. Nicknamed "Long Shot" for her electoral struggles as a political candidate, McSally was eventually appointed to a US Senate seat representing Arizona in 2018.

Chapter 7 focuses on the military and political career of US Representa-tive Tulsi Gabbard (D-HI). A Democratic military combat veteran serving Hawai'i's Second District, Gabbard was also a 2016 and 2020 presidential candidate—the first woman with military or quasimilitary service experience since Smith to actively seek a presidential nomination. Her career in US politics has also been measured by a series of "firsts"—the first state official to voluntarily step down from public office to serve in a war zone, the first woman ever to be honored by the Kuwait National Guard for her work in their training and readiness program, one of the first two female combat veterans ever to serve in the US Congress, and the first Hindu member of Congress. Gabbard is also one of the first post-9/11 veterans to run for the White House. Chapter 7 focuses on Gabbard's rapidly rising, at times controversial, profile in national politics.

Finally, the concluding chapter of *Service above Self* summarizes the lessons learned from studying candidates and identifies future areas of research. What draws these candidates from military service to public service, and how do these women connect those experiences? How do they communicate the relevance of that military service to their roles in Congress or, potentially, the White House? What types of issues or projects do they adopt after being elected to office? Do they share similarities, despite partisan and ideological differences? And how does studying these candidates help us to understand political ambition and what motivates women veterans to seek political office? Answers to these questions might help us to better understand a future in which more servicewomen write and pass the policies that govern US foreign and domestic affairs.

2

Female veterans posted groundbreaking electoral performances in the 2018 midterm elections. Their wins expanded
membership to a small caucus on Capitol Hill. Before the
emergence of this new cohort, relatively few servicewomen
campaigned for national elected office. This chapter explores the political paths of the first female service above
self candidates, defined as women who engaged in some
form of military or quasimilitary service and who, after they
were in office, advanced legislation in the areas of the military, foreign affairs, and security. These candidates served as
antecedents to contemporary political servicewomen, illus-
trating a longer history of "service first" female politicians
and the impact of their work as legislators in the twentieth
century.

Though they succeeded their husbands in office, Edith
Nourse Rogers, Florence Prag Kahn, and Margaret Chase
Smith would go on to define their political careers on their
own terms. Ruth Bryan Owen, as the daughter of William Jennings Bryan, and Mary Catherine Small Long, as a member
of the Louisiana Long political dynasty, gained experience
and exposure as members of political families. Heather Wilson followed in the footsteps of her father and grandfather
when entering the US Air Force Academy (USAFA) and pursuing a career of service through the armed forces. Whereas
Long and Helen Douglas Mankin had relatively short

congressional careers, Rogers served for thirty-five years in the House of Representatives, and Smith held office for thirty-three years, cumulatively, in the House and Senate. Each story illustrates the situational, structural, and socialization factors that influence women candidates' decisions to seek election and demonstrates the relevance of political ambition as well as personal and professional relationships in shaping women's pathways to office—and their policy priorities after they are elected.

The First Wave of Servicewomen

Owen, Rogers, and Mankin all participated in quasimilitary forms of service during World War I, known as the Great War. This war created significant economic and political disruptions in US society. It was the first war in which women were mobilized on a large scale by the armed services, with tens of thousands serving in civilian roles under the auspices of the American Expeditionary Force (AEF) in the army; enlisting as civilian workers in the US Navy and US Marines; and working in hospitals as ambulance drivers, bacteriologists, dieticians, and librarians.[1] Susan Zeiger argues in her book *In Uncle Sam's Service* that women's work at the front was much more than "a simple extension" of their participation in the civilian labor force: "It was also military or quasi-military service and therefore had profound implications for a society grappling with questions about the nature of women and their place in the public life of the nation, in wartime, and peacetime."[2] The idea of military service for women acted as a disruptor, challenging prevailing assumptions about gender differences and gender roles, which had strong implications for the way Americans thought about power, autonomy, citizenship, and civic participation.[3]

Among the thousands of women called to serve, a handful chose to continue their work in service as appointed or elected members of state and national public office. Though they followed different paths into office and pursued a variety of domestic and foreign policies after they were elected, collectively their presence, achievements, and legacies contributed to important programs for military servicemembers and veterans that paved the way for women who enlisted in the armed forces as well as future generations of servicewomen elected to Congress.

Ruth Bryan Owen

Though Owen and Rogers both pursued political office after World War I, their paths to Congress looked very different. Owen's father, the "Peerless Leader," was a national political figure and three-time Democratic presidential candidate. Her mother, Mary Baird Bryan, a lawyer admitted to the bar, served as a political advisor to her husband. Thus, Owen, born in October 1885 into a fiercely political household, was socialized to national service at a young age. She often accompanied her father to the House floor after his election to Congress, earning her the nickname "the sweetheart of the House," and in 1908 she traveled the country as his secretary during his third presidential campaign.[4] She had great respect for the work of both of her parents, at one point reflecting on her mother's accomplishments: "I would like to emulate her. She is a thoroughly feminine woman with the mind of a thoroughly masculine man."[5]

However, Owen asserted her independence from her family in 1910 when, against her parents' counsel, she divorced her first husband, artist William Homer Leavitt, and married Reginald Owen, a British officer of the Corps of Royal Engineers. In addition to the two children with Leavitt, she had two more during her second marriage, and the whole family accompanied the engineer on his international posts. The royal engineers, commonly known as the Sappers, constituted a corps of the British Army that provided military engineering and other technical support to the British Armed Forces.[6] While her husband was stationed in Egypt in 1915, Owen joined the British Volunteer Aid Detachment as a nurse to care for convalescing soldiers from the Egypt-Palestine campaign (1915–1918). Using her oratory gifts, Owen organized a volunteer entertainment troupe called the Optimists to perform for military hospitals in the region.[7]

In 1919, her husband's health began to fail, and the family moved to Miami, Florida, to be closer to her parents. She took a position as a faculty member and administrator at the University of Miami, in addition to dabbling in filmmaking, before considering politics. Her father passed away in 1925, and, carrying the torch of his political legacy, Owen sought the Democratic nomination for Florida's fourth congressional district the very next year. She narrowly lost to a six-term incumbent, William Sears, and suffered an even greater loss less than two years later when her husband passed away.

Although apprehensive about the thought of running for office again and grieving the loss of her husband, Owen could not resist the call to enter public service. Though she could sense that "there was not the friendliest feeling toward any woman taking her place in political life," Owen decided to run again for the same congressional seat.[8] In 1928, with an effective grassroots campaign, supportive newspaper editorials, and notoriety for the local relief work she provided after the 1927 Miami hurricane, she successfully defeated Sears in the Democratic primary.[9] In the general election, Owen bested her Republican opponent, William C. Lawson, and in a good-natured reference to her father's three unsuccessful bids for president remarked, "There! I am the first Bryan who ran for anything and got it!"[10]

Owen began her term of office in March 1929 as a divorcee, widow, and mother of four. But her former opponent, Lawson, contested the election results on the grounds that Owen had forfeited her US citizenship when she married the British Reginald Owen and chose to live outside the United States. Lawson claimed that she was ineligible for election to Congress because she had not recovered her citizenship under the provisions of the 1922 Cable Act, which allowed women married to foreign men to petition for repatriation upon their return to the United States, until 1925. This meant that she did not meet the seven years' citizenship requirement in the US Constitution to run for the House. In response, Owen launched a persuasive defense of her eligibility before the House Elections Committee, arguing that no American man had ever lost his citizenship by marriage, exposing the hypocrisy and deficiencies of the Cable Act.[11] The committee was convinced; Owen was sworn in at the start of the 71st Congress.

As a US representative, Owen worked on both domestic and international issues relevant to her Florida constituents. She took a special interest in issues related to children and families and established an annual program (using some of her own money) to bring high school boys and girls from her district to Washington, DC, for training as future leaders. In December 1929, after becoming the first woman to earn a seat on the influential Foreign Affairs Committee, Owen used her position to seek funding for US delegations attending international conferences on health and children's welfare.[12] Her years of international travel provided her a foundation for advocating a greater US presence on international committees and at conferences, including the Geneva Disarmament Conference in February 1932.[13] After her own experiences contesting the Cable Act, Owen also pressed US officials to abide by the resolutions coming out of the 1930 Hague Conference on the Codification of International Law regarding gender, marriage, and nationality.[14]

Owen remained in Congress until 1933, finishing her last term as a "lame duck" after losing the support of her constituents over her position in favor of temperance, and subsequently, the 1932 Democratic nomination for her seat. Yet, her career in politics and foreign affairs continued when in April 1933, President Franklin D. Roosevelt appointed her minister to Denmark—making her the first American woman ambassador. She held the position until July 1936, when she married Captain Borge Rhode of the Danish Royal Guards; in marrying Rhode she became a citizen of both Denmark and the United States and had to resign her diplomatic post. In 1949, President Harry S. Truman appointed her an alternate delegate to the UN General Assembly, and in 1954 she passed away while traveling in Denmark to accept the Danish Order of Merit from King Frederick IX, recognizing her contributions to American-Danish relations.

Edith Nourse Rogers

Rogers was the first woman elected to Congress from Massachusetts, and until 2012, she had been the longest-serving female member of Congress in US history.[15] She was given the opportunity to run for political office when her husband, a US representative, died in 1925. During her thirty-five-year House career, she authored legislation that changed the lives of American servicemen and -women, including the creation of the Women's Army Corp (WAC) and the GI Bill of Rights.

Born in Saco, Maine, in 1881, she had a world-class education because of her parents' affluence. She studied first at the private Rogers Hall School in Lowell, Massachusetts, and then in Paris, France.[16] After returning to the United States in 1907, she married John Jacob Rogers, a Harvard-educated lawyer and Republican. In 1912, he was elected to the 63rd Congress (1913–1915) and served in that role for six succeeding terms. He became the ranking majority member on the Foreign Affairs Committee and authored the 1924 Rogers Act, which reorganized the US Diplomatic Corps.[17]

In 1917, when her husband, as a member of the Foreign Affairs Committee, traveled to the United Kingdom and France to observe the conditions of the war firsthand, she volunteered with the Young Men's Christian Association (YMCA) in London and then as a "Gray Lady" (1917–1922) with the American Red Cross in France. Her work included inspecting field hospitals with women who would go on to form the Women's Overseas Service League (WOSL). As part of her work with the American Red Cross, Rogers joined a volunteer group in Washington, DC, that worked with hospitalized veterans. "No one could see the wounded and dying as I saw them and not be moved to do all in his or her power to help," she recalled.[18] This earned her the moniker "Angel of Walter Reed Hospital" and marked the beginning of what became a lifelong commitment to veterans.[19]

When the war ended, President Warren G. Harding appointed Rogers inspector of new veterans' hospitals from 1922 to 1923. She served as the president's personal ombudsperson for communicating with disabled veterans and was subsequently renewed in the position by Presidents Calvin Coolidge and Herbert Hoover. Rogers also continued to serve in her husband's congressional offices, both at home in Lowell, Massachusetts, and Washington, DC. He considered her his chief adviser on everything from policy and legislation to campaign strategy.[20] These experiences became even more significant when her husband passed away after a long battle with cancer in March 1925, in the middle of his seventh congressional term. Both the Republican Party and the American Legion urgently pressed her to enter the special election and seek her husband's seat in Congress.

Rogers was not the first congressional widow to seek her husband's seat; two Republican women from California, Mae Ella Nolan and Florence Prag Kahn, were also elected in what is sometimes called the *widow's succession* in 1923 and 1925, respectively.[21] Nolan was only the fourth woman elected to Congress and the first woman to chair a congressional committee, the Committee on Expenditures in the Post Office Department.[22] Kahn also won a special election to fill her husband's seat, but she continued to win reelection and held her membership in Congress until 1936. Kahn was not only the first Jewish woman elected to Congress but also the first woman on the Military Affairs Committee.[23] Historian Glenna Matthews argues that her remarkable success as a politician and legislator resulted from the "special character" of San Francisco's Jewish community, the political socialization and exposure Kahn received from her mother and husband, and Kahn's own personal ambition.[24] Her many accomplishments over the course of her legislative career led the Democratic *San Francisco Examiner* to call her one of the "important figures in Congress" whose "continuous and indefatigable labors" were instrumental in bringing new military facilities to the region.[25] Reflecting on her work, Kahn once remarked, "There is no sex in citizenship, and there should be none in politics."[26]

Like Kahn, within one week of her husband's passing, Rogers declared her intention to run.[27] She easily bested her chief Republican competition in the primary, former Massachusetts state senator James Grimes, by a margin of 13,086 votes to 1,939.[28] The June 30 special election appeared more daunting, however, because Rogers was competing to represent the "Fighting Fifth" district of northeastern Massachusetts, so named for its equal proportions of registered Democratic and Republican voters. She appealed to voters not just on the basis of her husband's legacy but also her familial connections to the local textile industry. Referencing both her father's business and her husband's policies, she declared, "I am a Republican by inheritance and by conviction."[29] On June 30, 1925, voters overwhelmingly went to the polls for Rogers, who earned 72 percent of the vote—handing former Democratic governor Eugene Foss the worst political defeat of his long career.[30] "I hope that everyone will forget that I am a woman as soon as possible," Rogers remarked.[31]

After she was sworn into the 69th Congress (1925–1927), Rogers set to work representing her home district on issues related to clothing manufacturing as well as foreign affairs and veterans' issues. Throughout her congressional career, Rogers was an active legislator and sponsored more than 1,200 bills, more than half on veteran or military issues. Noting her eighteen-hour work days, the press dubbed her "the busiest woman on Capitol Hill."[32] Her influence and legislative success in office were not immediate, however; in her first term, Rogers did not receive any of her husband's former committee assignments, which included the powerful Appropriations Committee as well as Foreign Affairs. Instead, she received less prestigious committee assignments, such as Expenditures in the Navy Department, Industrial Arts and Expositions, Woman Suffrage, and World War Veterans' Legislation (later renamed Veterans' Affairs). She finally won back her husband's seat on the more coveted Foreign Affairs Committee in the 73rd Congress (1933–1935), a position previously held by Owen in the 71st and 72nd Congresses.[33]

Rogers's congressional newcomer status did not dissuade her from working on significant pieces of legislation. During her first term in office, she secured pensions for army nurses and later helped create a permanent nurse corps in the Veterans Administration.[34] By spring 1930, as chair of the World War Veterans' Legislation Committee's subcommittee on hospitals, she successfully inserted a $15 million provision for the development of a national network of veterans' hospitals into the Veterans Administration Act. She did so over the objections of the committee chair, but veterans' groups applauded her diligence. "Expecting much from her, veterans always receive much," one wrote. "She never disappoints."[35]

As a US representative, Rogers adopted positions independent of those of her political party, particularly to vote on issues regarding defense, the military, or foreign affairs, when she had strong convictions. In 1937 she voted against the Neutrality Act, breaking ranks with Republicans, and in 1940 she crossed party lines to vote for the Selective Service Act, creating the nation's first peacetime draft. Doing so earned her respect from members of both parties, and this respect would be essential to the passage of one of her most significant pieces of legislation, the Women's Army Auxiliary Corps (WAAC) Act.

In May 1941, Rogers introduced legislation to create a voluntary enrollment program that would allow women to join the US Army in a noncombat capacity. She believed this proposal would give women "a chance to volunteer to serve their country in a patriotic way" as health care professionals, welfare workers, clerks, cooks, messengers, military postal employees, chauffeurs, telephone and telegraph operators, and hundreds of other capacities.[36] President Roosevelt signed the WAAC Act into law in May 1942, creating a corps of up to 150,000 women. Nearly one year later,

President Franklin D. Roosevelt signs the GI Bill in the Oval Office on June 2, 1944. Edith Nourse Rogers—longtime member of Congress from Lowell, Massachusetts, representing the Fifth District—sponsored and helped to draft this landmark piece of legislation. *From left:* Bennett "Champ" Clark, J. Hardin Peterson, John Rankin, Paul Cunningham, Edith N. Rogers, J. M. Sullivan, Walter George, John Stelle, Robert Wagner, Scott W. Lucas, and Alben Barkley. *Source:* FDR Presidential Library Photo Collection.

that measure was replaced by Rogers's WAC Act, which granted official military status to those volunteers. These legislative milestones opened the way for other uniformed women's services in the US Navy (Women Accepted for Volunteer Military Services, or WAVES) and the US Air Force (Women Airforce Service Pilots, or WASP). The recognition of servicewomen's contributions and institutionalization of their roles laid a foundation for the future integration and recruitment of women in both the armed services and intelligence fields.

Yet, Rogers's work did not end with these legislative achievements. Recalling the difficulties of demobilization after World War I and the challenges facing veterans coming home, Rogers fought to create programs that would ease the transition for returning servicemen and -women after World War II. By 1944, Rogers was the ranking minority member of the World War Veterans' Legislation Committee. She sponsored legislation providing college tuition benefits for veterans and low-interest home mortgage loans. Later referred to as the GI Bill of Rights, the provisions became law in June 1944.

Her work continued throughout the 82nd Congress (1951–1953), when she spearheaded the Veterans Re-adjustment Assistance Act of 1952, extending the provisions of the GI Bill to Korean War veterans.[37] As the scope of her work on behalf of veterans grew, Rogers also proposed the creation of a cabinet-level Department of Veterans Affairs. The proposal was not adopted in her lifetime but eventually came to fruition in 1989.

Embodying the spirit of her motto, "Fight hard, fight fair, and persevere," Rogers returned to the House by increasingly large electoral victories, eclipsing those of her husband, in her subsequent seventeen reelection campaigns. The American Legion, recognizing her work on behalf of veterans, made her the first woman awarded the Distinguished Service Cross. Rogers became a congressional institution and was never seriously challenged for reelection. In 1950, on the twenty-fifth anniversary of her first election, GOP colleagues hailed her as "the First Lady of the Republican Party."[38] Rogers continued to serve until 1960, when three days before the 1960 primary election, during her nineteenth congressional campaign, she passed away from pneumonia.

Helen Douglas Mankin

Although Mankin's service in the House was brief, she was able to accomplish an important goal: bringing national attention to issues facing poor and disenfranchised voters in her home state of Georgia. She was born in September 1896 in Atlanta, and her parents were teachers who had studied law together at the University of Michigan. Her mother, Corrine Douglas, became a teacher when the family moved to Georgia, where state laws prevented women from taking the bar exam. Her father, Hamilton Douglas, eventually founded the Atlanta Law School. As committed reformers, her parents opened their home to visitors such as Jane Addams and former president and Supreme Court justice William Howard Taft.[39] This exposed a young Mankin to progressive ideas about poverty, inequality, and opportunity.

Following the paths of both her grandmother and mother, Mankin attended Rockford College in Illinois. She entered law school but suspended her studies following the outbreak of World War I, when she joined the American Women's Hospital (AWH) Unit No. 1 in France.[40] In February 1918, the Red Cross had allowed the AWH to set up its first hospital in Luzancy, France, which gave women physicians the authority to provide medical care to civilians and members of the military without the supervision of men from either the US or French Armed Forces.[41] The AWH also agreed to provide medical and surgical services for communities aided by the American Committee for Devastated France (ACDF), a civilian relief organization created by Anne Murray Dike and Ann Morgan, the youngest daughter of financier J. Pierpont Morgan.[42] In April 1919, the physicians, nurses, and ambulance drivers of the hospital in Luzancy received honorary French citizenship and the distinguished Medaille de Reconnaissance from the French government.[43]

Mankin, like other women who enlisted in quasimilitary health-care services at the time, not only concerned herself with delivering aid to the AEF but also wanted to use war service to advance the status of women. Mankin served as an ambulance driver for more than a year before returning to her legal studies and graduating from Atlanta Law School in 1920. The following year, Georgia admitted her to the bar along with her sixty-one-year-old mother when the state legislature lifted the ban on women. Mankin's political career began at the state level, first through her work on the mayoral campaign of I. N. Ragsdale and then in her work as the appointed chair of the Georgia Child Labor Committee, where she unsuccessfully lobbied the state legislature to ratify a proposed constitutional amendment eliminating child labor.[44] In 1936, she won a seat in the state legislature, where she served for a decade advocating for educational, electoral, labor, and prison reforms. When US Representative Robert Ramspeck resigned from the House at the end of 1945, Mankin entered the race for the February 1946 special election. The only woman in the crowded contest for the three-county district seat, which included Atlanta and Decatur, Mankin won the backing of Governor Ellis Arnall, women's groups, and the Congress of Industrial Organizations (CIO).[45] Her determination to pursue voting reforms, seen in her support for a constitutional amendment to abolish the poll tax, earned her the solid backing of Black voters.[46] Though Black people were barred from voting in primaries, they were eligible to participate in special elections and helped Mankin secure an electoral victory on February 12, 1946. In celebrating her victory, Mankin reflected, "I earnestly believe that the election of a woman from this State to the House of Representatives will mean to the rest of the country another note of progress out of the South."[47] Yet her election and diverse coalition of support made her a target for Southern segregationist politicians. Former Georgia governor Eugene Talmadge derided her election, mocking "the spectacle of Atlanta Negroes sending a Congresswoman to Washington."[48]

During her brief time in national office, Mankin represented the concerns of her constituents in domestic affairs and supported internationalist foreign policies.[49] Between the special election in February 1946 and the Georgia Democratic primary of July 1946, Mankin's opponents devised a series of strategies to undermine her reelection. She lost the Democratic primary, and though she worked diligently to secure a position on the ballot, she lost each of her legal appeals. Mankin chose to remain in the race as a write-in candidate despite strong opposition from white supremacy groups, including threats and reports of voter fraud. When the election results were finally counted, she earned 38 percent of the vote but lost to her opponent by a significant margin. She challenged the results in the House Administration Committee's Subcommittee on Privileges and Elections, but the subcommittee rejected her charges.[50] This marked the end of her battle for the 1946 election, and a fiercely disappointed Mankin remarked, "I was written in and counted out; they stole my seat in Congress."[51] Mankin unsuccessfully attempted to regain her seat in the 1948 election but remained active in politics until her death in July 1956. She worked on the presidential campaign of Adlai Stevenson and stridently fought to eliminate the county unit system, which had derailed her own political career.

The Second Wave of Servicewomen

Whereas Owen, Rogers, and Mankin each participated in quasimilitary service during World War I, their contemporary Margaret Chase Smith chose to take another path; her interest in foreign affairs and armed services came after her election to office with the outbreak of World War II. For another future US representative, Long, service during World War II meant joining the US Navy at age twenty and serving at its hospital in Corpus Christi, Texas. The efforts of these women were recognized and supported by advocates in Congress, many with service experience themselves, who worked to further institutionalize the roles of women in the armed services and diplomatic corps.

Margaret Chase Smith

Smith was twenty years old when the AEF deployed to a training area near Verdun, France. Unlike women who engaged in quasimilitary volunteer service during World War I, she chose to enter the workforce. Born in December 1897, in Skowhegan, Maine, the oldest of six children, to George Emery, the town barber, and Carrie Murray Chase, a waitress, store clerk, and shoe factory worker, she graduated from Skowhegan High School in 1916 and set straight to work as a teacher, a basketball coach, and a telephone operator. She eventually became an office manager for a wool mill and a staff member of the *Independent Reporter*, a small weekly newspaper owned by Clyde Smith. Her interest in business led her to cofound the Skowhegan chapter of the Business and Professional Women's Club in 1922, and from 1926 to 1928 she served as president of the Maine Federation of Business and Professional Women's Clubs.

In 1930, she married Clyde Smith, an accomplished local Republican politician.[52] Her interest in politics grew, and she was eventually elected to the Maine Republican State Committee, where she served for six years. In 1936, her husband was elected to the US House for the 75th Congress (1937–1939). They moved to Washington, DC, and she managed his congressional office, insisting on compensation for her work. She handled his correspondence, conducted research, and helped write his speeches. She also served as treasurer of the Congressional Club, a group of wives of members of Congress and cabinet members.[53]

Her husband suffered a heart attack in 1938, and while he recovered in Washington, DC, Smith traveled frequently to Maine—giving speeches, visiting with state party officials, appearing before the Maine Republican Convention, and addressing constituent concerns. She developed a voice of her own that would become even more critical in spring 1940, when her husband once again fell ill with a serious heart condition. Realizing his health would prevent him from seeking reelection, he persuaded her to run for his seat in the next general election. Before his death in April 1940, he reassured supporters, "I know of no one else who has the full knowledge of my ideas and plans or is as well qualified as she is to carry on these ideas or my unfinished work for the district."[54] Smith declared her candidacy for the special election to serve out her husband's unexpired term in the 76th Congress (1939–1941).[55] She won the Republican special primary by a greater than ten-to-one margin, and no Democratic challengers entered the race for the June 3 special election, ensuring her election as Maine's first female US representative.[56]

In the general election of 1940, Smith ran on a platform of military preparedness, an issue at the forefront of her constituents' minds. With Maine's 230 miles of coastline just 1,420 miles west of the United Kingdom, its residents were cognizant of the bombing campaign against London in fall 1940 as well as the threat of German submarines along the US shoreline. Smith's constituents supported her desire to expand the US Navy, which boosted the shipbuilding economy in districts across the state. She portrayed herself as a political moderate who, in contrast to liberal feminists, would work within the established order.[57] Following the success of her 1940 campaign, Smith was reelected to three succeeding congressional terms with relatively little challenge, consistently defeating her opponents with 60 percent or more of the vote.[58]

As a new US representative in 1940, Smith was assigned to the War Claims, Revision of the Laws, and Invalid Pensions Committees, along with the Election of the President, Vice President, and Representatives in Congress Committee.[59] Through her persistent lobbying in Congress, Smith earned a position on the more prestigious Naval Affairs Committee. It actually came as a compromise after her strategic request for the distinguished Appropriations Committee. Smith enjoyed recalling, "When I asked for a committee, I asked for Appropriations, knowing that I would not get it." She clarified, "I asked for it because that was the thing to do in those days. You didn't expect to get what you asked for, so you would ask for something that was impossible. . . . And Naval Affairs was what I wanted; I didn't want Appropriations. . . . I think I was smart."[60] After the Legislative Reorganization Act of 1946 merged disparate committees with military jurisdictions, Smith was also assigned to the Armed Services Committee.

Serving on the Naval Affairs and Armed Services Committees, Smith was able to award shipbuilding projects to Maine. She became an expert on military and national security matters, leading to her participation in an investigation of the construction of destroyers and inspection of bases across the globe. She made a 25,000-mile tour of bases in the South Pacific during the winter of 1943–1944 and became the first and only civilian woman to sail on a US Navy ship during World War II.[61] Going one step further, Smith participated in a trip to observe the postwar reconstruction in Europe, North Africa, and the Middle East. Her interest in foreign affairs and support for the policies of President Truman earned her consideration as a candidate for undersecretary of the navy in 1945 and for assistant secretary of state in 1947.[62]

On the Armed Services Committee, Smith also worked on behalf of women in the armed forces. With a wartime peak enrollment of about 350,000 during World War II, women were still considered volunteers for the armed services and did not receive any benefits.[63] Smith used her leadership position on the Armed Services' Subcommittee on Hospitalization and Medicine to pass legislation assigning regular military status to navy and army nurses in 1947. Her colleagues in the House were "more comfortable accepting the change of status because it covered women in traditional, 'angel of mercy' roles."[64] The Women's Armed Services Integration Act, which permanently included all servicewomen in the military, easily passed the Senate. Smith faced a greater challenge pushing the bill through the House, where opponents of the legislation amended it over Smith's lone dissenting vote, significantly diminishing servicewomen's rights and benefits by limiting them to reserve status.[65] When the House passed the amended version, Smith appealed to her friend Secretary of Defense William Forrestal, who offered his full support for the original form of the bill. The House conferees acquiesced, and legislation granting women regular military status passed on July 2, 1948.[66] President Truman signed the bill into law ten days later, just weeks before his executive order desegregating the armed services.[67]

When Senator Wallace White of Maine, the Republican majority leader, announced he would not seek reelection, Smith entered the 1948 primary

President Harry S. Truman signs a bill to establish the permanent Army Nurse Corps and Navy Nurse Corps, April 16, 1947. *From left*: Margaret Chase Smith, coauthor of the bill; Colonel Florence A. Blanchfield, superintendent of the Army Nurse Corps; Lieutenant Commander Ruth B. Dunbar, assistant superintendent of the Navy Nurse Corps; Major Helen Burns, director of Dieticians, US Army; and Major Emma E. Vogel, director of physical therapy, US Army. *Source*: Margaret Chase Smith Library and Archives, Skowhegan, Maine.

election for the open seat. Smith traveled throughout the state, promoting her legislative achievements with the slogan "Don't trade a record for a promise."[68] Voters addressed her as "Margaret," evidence of her intimate campaign style.[69] Supported by an active corps of women volunteers across the state, Smith emerged successfully from the primary and the general election, earning more than 70 percent of the vote in the latter.[70] Smith's election to the Senate marked the first time a woman won election without the widow or appointment connection and the first time a woman served in both chambers of Congress. She was reelected three more times to the Senate by comfortable majorities.[71]

Although Smith entered the Senate with years of legislative experience, she was still new to the chamber and was assigned to less prestigious committees during her first term. When Republicans briefly regained control of the Senate in the 83rd Congress, however, Smith was assigned to two prominent committees on which no woman had served before, the Appropriations and Armed Services Committees. The positions allowed her to once again influence shipbuilding projects and develop expertise on the military and national security, eventually leading to her inspection of military bases in the South Pacific. She also gave up her seat on the Government Operations Committee for an assignment on the Aeronautical and Space Sciences Committee in the 86th Congress (1959–1961)—a particularly influential committee position as the space race with the Soviet Union began to accelerate. Smith maintained her seats on these three more prestigious committees for the remainder of her Senate career. She held aggressive positions on issues of foreign policy, frequently criticizing John F. Kennedy's administration for its diplomatic management of international affairs. After the Berlin Crisis of 1961, she accused President Kennedy of lacking the resolve to use nuclear weapons against the Soviet Union, chiding from the Senate Floor, "In short, we have the nuclear capability but not the nuclear credibility."[72]

Smith's active legislative agenda and reputation for independent positions made her a Senate institution. From June 1, 1955, to September 6, 1968, she cast 2,941 consecutive roll-call votes.[73] In January 1964, she announced her candidacy for US president and sought the nomination of the Republican Party. "I have few illusions and no money, but I'm staying for the finish," she noted. "When people keep telling you, you can't do a thing, you kind of like to try."[74] Smith embarked on a strong grassroots campaign during the primary election, and despite losing every Republican contest, in 1964 she achieved yet another milestone as the first woman to have her name put in for nomination for the presidency by a major political party at the Republican National Convention.[75]

In 1972, Smith lost her bid for reelection to a fifth consecutive Senate term. Although she was considering retirement, claims by her challengers that the seventy-four-year-old Smith was too old to serve motivated her to run yet again. After leaving office, she returned to her hometown of Skowhegan and oversaw the construction of the Margaret Chase Smith Library, the first of its kind to focus its collection on the papers of a female member of Congress. In 1989, President George H. W. Bush awarded her the Presidential Medal of Freedom, the nation's highest civilian honor. For more than three decades, Smith served as a role model for women aspiring to national politics. Although she strongly believed women should assume political roles, Smith refused to make her gender a central issue of her campaigns and service. "If we are to claim and win our rightful place in the sun on an equal basis with men," she once noted, "then we must not insist upon those privileges and prerogatives identified in the past as exclusively feminine."[76]

A Gap in Representation

Rogers passed away in 1960, and Smith lost her last election in 1972. From 1972 until Long's election in 1985 and Heather Wilson's election in 1998, there were no servicewomen elected to national office. This gap resulted from many factors, including limited opportunities for women to engage in military service as a career choice, a broader "generation-long decline" of military experience among legislators serving in Congress, and a smaller pool of candidates with veteran status seeking national political office.[77]

Mary Catherine Small Long

Historians consider Long the first female military veteran elected to Congress, though she was not seated until the 99th Congress, in 1985. Born in Dayton, Ohio, in 1924, she served as a hospital corpsman and pharmacist's mate, a member of the WAVES, during World War II. In 1942, President Roosevelt signed legislation authorizing the US Navy to accept women into the Naval Reserve as commissioned officers and enlisted personnel, effective for the duration of the war plus six months. After Rogers introduced a bill in Congress to establish WAAC in 1941, the Senate Naval Affairs Committee recommended legislation to create a women's reserve for the US Navy parallel to that of WAAC the next year. This expanded opportunities for women to engage in service with the US Navy, and by September 1942, another 108 women were commissioned as officers in the WAVES, selected for their educational and business backgrounds.[78]

After marrying Gillis Long in 1947, Long received a bachelor's degree from Louisiana State University (LSU) in 1948. Her husband was a decorated World War II veteran and member of one of Louisiana's most powerful political families as a distant cousin of controversial Louisiana political boss Huey Long and Senator Russell Long.[79] After graduating LSU, Long expanded her political resume by working as a staff assistant to Senator Wayne Morse of Oregon and US Representative James G. Polk of Ohio and then by serving as a delegate to the Democratic National Convention.[80] She became a member of the Louisiana Democratic Finance Council as well as the state party's central committee while raising two young children.

Her husband was first elected to the US House in 1962 from a central Louisiana district that included Baton Rouge. His support for civil rights legislation during his first term in Congress cost his reelection when defeated by his openly segregationist cousin, Speedy Long.[81] After this defeat, he served in President Lyndon B. Johnson's administration for two years before returning to private law practice and unsuccessfully campaigning for governor of Louisiana twice. When Speedy Long retired from office in 1971, Gillis Long once again entered the race for US representatives and won his seat back. He continued serving for six consecutive terms, becoming one of the most respected figures in the Democratic Party until his sudden passing in 1985.[82]

During her husband's legislative career, Long put her own political experience to work on his behalf, campaigning as a surrogate, canvassing the district to hear constituent issues, and acting as an informal adviser to him. Later she remarked, "You couldn't have found a wife that was more active than I was."[83] His heart condition slowed his electoral activities during his later years in the House, necessitating her frequent trips back to the district for grassroots campaign work. Throughout her husband's political career, she recalled campaigning more than the candidate himself: "I feel thoroughly at home with campaigning, I've done it so much."[84]

When Long's husband passed away in 1985, the Democratic Party immediately turned to her to run for his vacant seat. "From the very minute Gillis died, I was under terrific strain to run," she recalled. "One person called me at 3 a.m. that morning and said, 'You have to run.' At the wake I had two people give me checks for $1,000 each."[85] She was not the first widow of the Long family to be approached about succeeding her husband in office. After Huey Long's death in 1935, his wife, Rose McConnell Long, was appointed to serve in the US Senate. She went on to win the special election on April 21, 1936, and served the remaining months of her husband's term, though she declined to run for reelection to a six-year term in November 1936. She was the third woman to serve in the Senate and the first from Louisiana.

Cathy Small Long declared her intention to run for her husband's seat two weeks after his passing.[86] In her campaign, she had the advantage of name recognition and pledged to remain consistent with her husband's legislative interests. She reminded voters of her familiarity with the House: "I don't have to start from scratch. I already know the way Congress works."[87] She received strong support from wives of other US representatives who came into the district to campaign on her behalf.[88] Her strategy was effective, and she defeated her closest opponent by more than a two-to-one margin, with 56 percent of the vote, and carried all but one of fifteen parishes in a special election on March 30, 1985.[89] "The biggest change in my life is not Congress," she told a reporter shortly after taking office. "It was the death of my husband."[90]

After being sworn in as a US representative in April 1985, Long worked to advance the same agenda her husband did and dispel notions that she was a one-termer: "I would not have run if I didn't want to stay," she told a reporter. "Of course, I'm going to run again. It was part of the decision I made at the time."[91] She took a strong interest in legislation that would have economic or environmental impact on her home district as well as adopting positions critical of President Ronald Reagan's administration's foreign policy. This included voting against aid to the Nicaraguan Contra rebels, working to secure aid for Nicaraguan refugees, and supporting economic sanctions in opposition to the South African apartheid system.[92] Yet, citing personal reasons and the financial burden of substantial campaign debts from her special election, Long decided not to run for another term in 1986. "The decision was not an easy one. I sought this seat to carry on my husband's work. I would love to continue the job, but the weight of my current debt jeopardizes the possibility of a credible campaign in 1986. I believe it better for me to step aside now to give all others the opportunity to pursue this job."[93]

Heather Wilson

On October 7, 1975, President Gerald R. Ford signed legislation permitting women to enter the US service academies, and the following year, 157 women entered the USAFA in the class of 1980. Although they were still excluded from combat roles and vessels or aircraft engaged in combat missions, their rigorous studies prepared them to participate to the best of their abilities in national defense. In 1980, 66 percent of the women in the first coeducational classes graduated—comparable with 70 percent of the men, whose attrition rate because of academic failure was twice that of women.[94]

Wilson entered the USAFA just two years after the institution began accepting women, determined to become a pilot like her grandfather and father before her. Born in December 1960 in Keene, New Hampshire, Wilson not only graduated the USAFA with distinction but also received a Rhodes scholarship to study at Oxford University and earned a doctorate in international relations. She continued to serve in the US Air Force until 1989, when she joined the National Security Council (NSC) as director for European Defense Policy and Arms Control. In 1991, she married attorney Jay Hone, and they settled in New Mexico to raise their three children. Wilson began consulting and from 1995 to 1998 served as the secretary of the New Mexico Children, Youth, and Families Department.

When US Representative Steven H. Schiff, from Albuquerque, announced he would not run for reelection in 1998, Wilson made her first run for Congress.[95] Wilson resigned her state cabinet post and entered the Republican primary, winning endorsements from Schiff and Senator Pete V. Domenici, who lent her several trusted aides and called her "the most brilliantly qualified House candidate anywhere in the country."[96] Schiff lost his battle with cancer in March 1998, triggering the state to call a special election in June. Wilson not only won the Republican primary that spring but also the special election in a competitive three-way race. She was sworn in to office on June 25, 1998, as the first Republican woman to represent New Mexico in Congress and only the second female US representative from the state following Georgia Lusk, elected in 1946.[97]

Wilson served in the House until 2009, facing increasingly tough electoral challenges in her home district.[98] She was first assigned to the Commerce Committee (later renamed Energy and Commerce), including

US Representative Heather Wilson (R-NM) raises her glass of orange juice in celebration after she declared her victory in the First District race at her campaign headquarters on November 9, 2006, in Albuquerque, NM. *Source:* Photo by Jake Schoellkopf, AP Photo.

its Subcommittees on Telecommunication, Energy, and Air Quality and Environment and Hazardous Materials as well as the Permanent Select Committee on Intelligence. But she left the latter assignment during the 107th Congress (2001–2003) for a seat on the prestigious Armed Services Committee, primarily because it offered her the opportunity to oversee personnel and infrastructure issues at two installations in her home district: Kirtland Air Force Base and the Sandia National Lab. In the 109th Congress, Wilson left the Armed Services Committee and returned to the Permanent Select Committee on Intelligence, where she chaired its Subcommittee on Technical and Tactical Intelligence.

Her committee work and legislative agenda earned Wilson a reputation as a moderate Republican with the tendency to take positions independent of her party. Though she was fairly moderate on social issues, she became a leading Republican voice in the House criticizing the US bombing campaign in Kosovo. Expressing deep reservations about the war, she flatly stated in an interview, "It's been screwed up from the first day."[99] She voted down an amendment that would have banned adoptions by gay parents in the District of Columbia and strongly opposed a plan by the

Republican leadership to move management of the nuclear weapons program (largely based in New Mexico) from the Department of Energy to the Pentagon.[100] In 2006, Wilson also led efforts to create greater congressional oversight of the executive branch's terrorist surveillance programs.[101]

In 2008, Wilson chose not to seek reelection to a sixth term in the House and to pursue an open Senate seat soon to be vacated by Domenici. She lost the Republican primary, and her congressional term concluded in January 2009. Wilson made a second run for the Senate in 2012, when Senator Jeff Bingaman decided to retire, and although she did win the Republican nomination, Wilson lost the general election to Democrat Martin Heinrich 51 percent to 45 percent.[102] In March 2017, President Donald J. Trump nominated Wilson secretary of the US Air Force, and she served in this position until she resigned in May 2019 to become president of the University of Texas–El Paso.[103]

Conclusion

Unlike her predecessors, Wilson was able to enter the armed services as a profession, not just in response to a specific war or conflict. Her political career developed independently of her marriage based on her own credentials, ambition, and record of prior service. In many ways, her path represents the changes institutionalized and normalized by earlier women in quasimilitary, military, or congressional service. And like those women, Wilson's election and contributions forged pathways for the next cohort of post-9/11 servicewomen.

The economic, political, and social disruptions of wartime created new opportunities for the women I discuss in this chapter to develop proficiency in military and defense policy. That proficiency provided them the credibility to advocate in Congress on issues of foreign policy and defense, areas of government traditionally viewed as the jurisdiction of their male colleagues. For those who entered quasimilitary or military service, their careers with the armed forces socialized them to one of the most masculine institutions in US history. The "first" servicewomen forged new pathways through their quasimilitary and military service, their subsequent election to national office, and their legislative work for future generations of women seeking careers in public service.

3

When twenty-seven new women won seats in the House and Senate in 1992, political analysts dubbed it the Year of the Woman. In 2018 that record was shattered, and for the first time more than a hundred women were elected to the House—just over a century after the first woman was sworn into Congress in 1917. Among this impressive class of new representatives, five self-proclaimed "badass" national security women with limited political experience are actively working to change voter perceptions of what it means to run as a woman in the Democratic Party. In this chapter I explore the professional backgrounds and path to public office for women candidates with military and intelligence backgrounds in the 2018 and 2020 elections.

Representatives Mikie Sherrill (New Jersey's Eleventh District) and Elaine Luria (Virginia's Second District) accumulated a combined three decades of military service in the US Navy, deploying and leading over the Pacific and Atlantic Oceans, in Europe as well as the Middle East, before launching congressional campaigns for the 2018 midterm elections. Another "badass," US Air Force veteran Chrissy Houlahan (Pennsylvania's Sixth District), parlayed her military experience into higher education—an engineering degree from Stanford—and then served with Teach for America as a chemistry teacher before entering politics as a self-described "leader driven by the spirit of service." Each

From left, members elect Elissa Slotkin (D-MI), Mikie Sherrill, (D-NJ), and Chrissy Houlahan (D-PA), attend the new member room lottery draw for office space in the Rayburn Building on November 30, 2018. *Source:* Photo by Tom Williams, *Congressional Quarterly Roll Call* via AP Images.

of these dynamic women successfully tied their military service overseas to a vision for serving their constituents at home.

US Representatives Elissa Slotkin (Michigan's Eighth District) and Abigail Spanberger (Virginia's Seventh District) served the interest of national security as Central Intelligence Agency (CIA) officers. Slotkin was recruited for a career in intelligence shortly after 9/11 and rose from a Middle East analyst to a member of the National Security Council (NSC) staff under presidents George W. Bush and Barack Obama. Spanberger transitioned from a career in federal law enforcement to the intelligence community and then left her position in Langley, Virginia, to run for office—though she maintained her role as a Girl Scout leader. Slotkin and Spanberger claim firsthand knowledge of national security and defense issues in a way that few politicians, male or female, are able to, and demonstrate service in their communities. Like Sherrill, Luria, and Houlahan, these "badasses" bring new voices to committees and legislation related to veteran's affairs and foreign policy—voices hard to ignore given the women's unique experience.

The "Badasses" of the 116th Congress

Representative Mikie Sherrill

Born in Alexandria, Virginia, in January 1972, Rebecca Michelle "Mikie" (pronounced "Mikey") Sherrill grew up along the East Coast of the United States. Family legend has it that she earned the nickname "Mikie" around the age of two, long before her military service.[1] Sherrill grew up listening to her grandfather's stories about his time in the armed forces during World War II. As a pilot shot down over France, he was rescued by the French Resistance.[2] His stories of adventure and service inspired ten-year-old Mikie to dream of becoming a pilot.[3] Her father suggested that she apply to the US Naval Academy during her senior year at South Lakes High School in Reston, Virginia, and by that time restrictions on women entering service academies had been lifted.[4]

Sherrill graduated from the US Naval Academy in Annapolis, Maryland, in 1994 and continued to serve on active duty in the US Navy for ten years. She entered flight school and trained to become an H3 Sea King helicopter pilot, graduating flight school with the first class of women eligible for combat. In 2000, she was based at Naval Air Station Corpus Christi, and from there she flew missions throughout Europe and the Middle East, including participating on the battle watch floor during the US invasion of Iraq and working as a flag aide to the deputy commander in chief of the US Atlantic fleet.

A self-described "child of the Cold War," Sherrill studied to become a policy officer on Russia during her years of service.[5] She earned a master of science degree in global history from the London School of Economics and Political Science in 2003 and a certificate in Arabic from the American University in Cairo in 2004. During this time, Sherrill achieved the rank of lieutenant and received the nomination for promotion to the rank of lieutenant commander, though she left the US Navy just before obtaining her permanent promotion.[6]

In 2003, coinciding with her decision to leave the US Navy, Sherrill applied to Georgetown University for law school. Toward the end of her studies, she worked as an associate at the firm of Kirkland and Ellis in New York, where she continued work after graduating law school in 2007.[7] Sherrill and her husband, Jason, another US Naval Academy graduate, also celebrated new additions to their family during this time; the couple currently has four children.[8] Living in Montclair, New Jersey, Sherrill split her time between her legal profession and coaching girls' lacrosse as well as managing her son's baseball team.

After leaving Kirkland and Ellis, Sherrill joined the staff of the US attorney for the district of New Jersey and worked as an outreach and reentry coordinator. Coordinators promote statewide crime prevention strategies by working to reduce recidivism and support formerly incarcerated individuals through rehabilitation and reintegration back into their communities. In 2015, Sherrill served as an assistant US attorney for the district of New Jersey, where she was responsible for prosecuting federal cases and advising law enforcement on investigations.[9] In spring 2016, after serving one year, Sherrill left the US attorney's office and entered the field of criminal justice reform.[10]

Although she enjoyed her work in the field of criminal justice reform, the November 2016 election inspired Sherrill to choose a different path of service. Reflecting on her career in the military and defense, she shared in an interview that it burdened her "to see things that I hold dear being attacked."[11] She lamented attacks on Gold Star families, prisoners of war (POWs), women, minorities, the US Constitution, and the federal court system. "I really felt strongly that I had to act *again*," she explained. In spring 2017, she made the decision to run for Congress from the Eleventh District of New Jersey and formally launched her campaign on May 11, 2017.[12] Her candidacy generated enthusiasm and support from organizations such as VoteVets, EMILY's List (a political action committee that supports pro-choice Democratic women running for office), and the *New York Times* editorial board.[13] "Mikie's background is something that's unique and exciting for the time that we're in. She's a veteran. She's a former prosecutor. She's taking on a sitting Republican incumbent and is ready to be a leader of her community," said Julie McClain Downey, the national director of campaign communications at EMILY's List.[14]

The Republican incumbent Downey referenced was twelve-term US

Representative Rodney Frelinghuysen, who served as chair of the powerful House Appropriations Committee. But Frelinghuysen announced in January 2018 that he would not seek reelection, leaving an open seat in November 2018.[15] Several stories speculated about the reasons for his decision. The district lines had been redrawn after the 2010 census, including large portions of Essex County and the northern portion of Montclair. Though Frelinghuysen was elected several times following the redistricting, President Donald Trump only narrowly carried the district by a single point in the 2016 election.[16] Some even suggested that Sherrill's strong candidacy and momentum influenced Frelinghuysen's choice.[17]

Sherrill emerged as the clear winner of the Democratic primary in June 2018, earning more than 77 percent of her party's vote in a five-way contest.[18] She raised nearly $3 million during the primary election and more than $8.4 million during the 2018 midterm election cycle, shattering fundraising records.[19] In the November election, Sherrill campaigned against Republican Jay Webber, a member of the New Jersey General Assembly once highlighted by *Time* as one of the "40 leaders under 40" because of his rising profile in US politics.[20] During her campaign, Sherrill used language and images that emphasized her lifetime of service, primarily in her military roles. Though she remained critical of President Trump, she also positioned herself as a moderate voice: "When I was a helicopter aircraft commander and people were entering the helicopter I never said, 'OK, I'm only taking Democrats on this mission, or I'm only taking Republicans on this mission.' I couldn't have told you the political preference of most of the people in my squadron. But I knew they were all Americans, and we were going to get our mission accomplished."[21] This message proved effective in her district, and on November 6, 2018, Sherrill emerged with the winning share of the vote, defeating Webber by fourteen points (183,684, or 56.8 percent, to 136,322, or 42.1 percent).[22]

As a first-term US representative, Sherrill continued to emphasize her bipartisanship, sharing with constituents that she worked "hard to find partners in Congress that share common mission."[23] She served as first-year whip for the New Democrat Coalition and was assigned to the Armed Services Committee and the Science, Space, and Technology Committee. She also chaired the Environment Subcommittee for the Science, Space, and Technology Committee. Beyond her committee roles, Sherrill gained national attention when she coauthored an editorial with other new Democratic US representatives in support of formal impeachment hearings for President Trump. Citing the importance of preserving "the checks and balances envisioned by the Founders" and the need to "restore the trust of the American people in our government," the seven new Congressmembers with national security backgrounds, including Representatives Gil Cisneros, Jason Crow, Houlahan, Luria, Slotkin, and Spanberger argued, "everything we do harks back to our oaths to defend the country" and "these new allegations are a threat to all we have sworn to protect."[24] In an emotional interview about the decision to draft the opinion piece, Sherrill shared: "I think it's important that we remind people of the sacrifices that have been made for the Constitution and for what we believe in." It feels, Sherrill said, like a "1776 kind of fight."[25]

Sherrill campaigned for reelection to represent New Jersey in Congress in 2020, and she defeated Republican nominee Rosemary Becchi, a tax policy lawyer and consultant, by a margin of 141,930 (58.6 percent) to 100,146 (41.4 percent). Once again, Sherrill raised significant funds for her campaign, $6 million, compared with Becchi's $1.3 million.[26]

Representative Chrissy Houlahan

Houlahan is a third-generation veteran who grew up idolizing pioneering astronaut Sally Ride and action hero Indiana Jones.[27] Andrew C. A. Jampoler, her father, was born in Poland to a Jewish family and fled the country as a child to escape the Holocaust.[28] The Jampoler family, including Houlahan, born in June 1967, lived on US naval bases across the country while Jampoler served as a naval aviator. His job flying P-3 Orion antisubmarine reconnaissance planes meant the family would always be along the water. By the time she was a teenager, Houlahan was a certified scuba diver, an open-water swimmer, and a budding marine biologist.[29] Stories of her grandfather and father's experience as pilots inspired Houlahan to envision herself as a pilot someday. More specifically, she envisioned exploring space as an astronaut, following in the path of her childhood hero Ride. If Ride went to Stanford University, so would she. If Ride was an engineer and a pilot, she would become one too.

When Houlahan was ready to graduate from high school and commit to the next stage of her education, her father advised her to consider the

US Air Force: "And so my dad actually advised that there were more pilot slots in the Air Force than there were in the Navy. And that at the time, certainly, it was better for women and their opportunities in the pilot seat to be in the Air Force rather than in the Navy. And that's one of the biggest reasons why I went into the Air Force."[30] With the help of an Air Force Reserve Officers' Training Corps (ROTC) scholarship, Houlahan earned her bachelor's degree in industrial engineering from Stanford University in 1989, though the university was not a welcoming place for military students. In an interview with Jeffrey Mervis of *Science*, Houlahan shared that because the military was not welcome on Stanford's campus when she arrived there in 1985, every Friday she and twenty other university undergraduates would "pile into cars and drive 40 kilometers to San Jose State University for daylong training."[31] The schedule of engineering classes led to frequent absences for ROTC students participating in training. "So, R.O.T.C. meant you were basically missing one-third of your classes, for 4 years," she recalled. "And that made it pretty hard to be a very good student."[32] This contributed to the dwindling numbers of cadets participating in ROTC, eventually leaving only four, with Houlahan as the sole female student.

As Houlahan neared graduation, the US Air Force offered her the opportunity to participate in its highly competitive pilot training, but she turned it down. She had just started dating the man who would become her future husband, and she chose a path that better suited the life she envisioned for herself. After graduating from Stanford, Houlahan continued to serve for three years on active duty at Hanscom Air Force Base in Bedford, Massachusetts. The close proximity to the Massachusetts Institute of Technology (MIT) enabled her to pursue a master's degree in technology and policy while also working as a project manager on air and space defense technologies.[33]

With three years of active service in the US Air Force, Houlahan achieved the rank of captain and chose to enter inactive reserve. She joined her husband in managing the sports apparel company AND1 and used her business and engineering training to help turn the company into a major brand. The company provided employees forty hours of paid community service annually, which Houlahan devoted to supporting women and girls of color in science, technology, engineering, and math (STEM) fields. The time she invested in working with public schools and school-aged children inspired Houlahan to enroll in a continuing education program at the University Pennsylvania and eventually apply to work as a chemistry teacher with Teach for America, an on-the-job training program that placed her at Simon Gratz High School in north Philadelphia. Though these teachers normally participate in the program for two years, Houlahan left her position after one year to join the Springboard Collaborative, a nonprofit based in Philadelphia that aims to improve literacy by creating a year-round learning environment for students that extends into the home and community, where she served as president and chief operating officer (COO) and chief financial officer (CFO).[34]

The election of President Trump in 2016 inspired Houlahan to change course once more. She expressed concerns in an interview while campaigning: "I was raised to respect the democratic process, and the will of the people, and whoever is your commander in chief. And this was the first time that I felt I couldn't do that."[35] She organized a bus trip to the Women's March in Washington, DC, but she felt like she was not doing enough.[36] She determined that the best option to effect real and immediate change would be to enter the race for Congress, specifically for Pennsylvania's Sixth District. When asked about why she decided to run for national office in her first election, rather than a local position, Houlahan replied, "I don't have time for that. The stakes are too high, and I think I'm qualified."[37]

Houlahan methodically studied the district map and aggressively raised funds. In January 2018, the Pennsylvania Supreme Court tossed out a gerrymandered map by the state's Republican-led legislature that apportioned all eighteen congressional seats in Pennsylvania. Representative Ryan Costello, a Republican, was the only incumbent to retain his district number, but the redrawn district map was significantly more compact and Democratic than before. Houlahan earned the Democratic nomination, running unopposed in the primary and receiving endorsements from EMILY's List, VoteVets, the Human Rights Campaign, local unions, and other Democratic-leaning organizations. At the same time, Costello dropped out of the race a week after the March filing deadline, leaving Greg McCauley, a tax lawyer and first-time candidate, the only eligible Republican nominee. Houlahan raised more than $4 million to fund her campaign, whereas McCauley raised a mere $300,000.[38]

In the general election, Houlahan defeated McCauley by a wide margin, 177,704 votes (58.9 percent) to 124,124 (41.1 percent), becoming the first woman ever elected to Pennsylvania's Sixth District and the first Democratic candidate in 160 years.[39] As a first-term US representative, she was assigned to the Armed Services Committee, the Foreign Affairs Committee, and the Small Business Committee. In addition, she joined the Women in STEM Caucus, the Honor and Civility Caucus, the For Country Caucus, the Veteran's Education Caucus, the Congressional LGBT Equality Caucus, the Sustainable Energy and Environment Coalition, and the New Democrat Coalition. She made history in May 2019 with the launch of the Servicewomen and Women Veterans Congressional Caucus, of which she serves as chair and cofounder alongside Representatives Tulsi Gabbard (D-HI), Luria (D-VA), and Sherrill (D-NJ).[40] In 2020, Houlahan once again received the Democratic nomination, was unopposed in the primary, and was reelected as the representative for Pennsylvania's Sixth District by a margin of 199,504 votes (54.7 percent) to 165,408 (45.3 percent).[41]

Representative Elaine Luria

Luria was born in August 1975 in Birmingham, Alabama. Her grandparents and parents were active in their local communities, from working to start a Reform Jewish congregation in Jasper, Alabama, to leading the National Council of Jewish Women, Hadassah, the Temple Emanu-El Sisterhood, and the Birmingham Jewish Federation.[42] Luria has credited her family's legacy of service and leadership as inspiring her own path.[43]

Although both of her grandfathers served in the US Navy, Luria was not committed to the idea until she experienced the US Naval Academy Summer Science and Engineering Seminar, a high school program on the historic campus in Annapolis.[44] That was the moment she knew a career in the navy was for her, and after graduating from Indian Springs School in 1993, she applied and was accepted to the US Naval Academy. In 1997, she graduated with a double major in physics and history and a minor in French, in addition to completing surface warfare division officer training and Tomahawk land attack missile launch officer training.[45] She became one of the first women to attend the US Naval Nuclear Power School, where she received training on shipboard nuclear power plant operation and maintenance of surface ships and submarines in the US nuclear navy. Eventually, Luria would go on to earn her master of science degree in engineering management from Old Dominion University while deployed to Japan and stationed aboard the flagship USS *Blue Ridge*.[46]

The USS *Blue Ridge* was one of six ships on which Luria would serve during her two decades in the US Navy. Her assignments also included five deployments to the Middle East, Mediterranean, and Western Pacific areas of operation and two assignments forward-deployed to Japan on the destroyer USS *O'Brien* and the aircraft carrier USS *Harry S. Truman*. After she was promoted to lieutenant, she became a flag aide to the commander of the US Seventh Fleet. She was then deployed on the destroyer USS *Mason*, the nuclear-powered USS *Enterprise*, and as an executive officer of the guided missile cruiser USS *Anzio*. From 2014 until her retirement in 2017, Luria then commanded Assault Craft Unit Two, a combat-ready unit of 400 sailors that supported amphibious forces along the East Coast of the United States.[47] Under her leadership, the group supported "five Amphibious Ready Group deployments to the Mediterranean and Middle East areas of operations, humanitarian assistance to Haiti during Hurricane Matthew relief, multi-national exercise Cold Response in Norway, and support for United States Marine Corps assets in Honduras and Panama."[48] She is credited as one of the first women in the US Navy's nuclear power program and among the first women to serve the entirety of her career on combatant ships.[49]

In addition to earning distinction as a female commander stationed aboard combat ships, Luria's Jewish identity proved an important form of representation during her service. Although there is a large Jewish community at the US Naval Academy, Luria says that was not the case on the six ships on which she served. In an interview with Terri Dennison, Luria shared how she managed several times to help coordinate Passover Seders and volunteered to serve as a lay leader. On one particularly memorable Passover after the September 11, 2001 (9/11), attacks, stationed thousands of miles from home on an aircraft carrier in the Middle East, Luria recalled, "We're going through the Haggadah . . . having our little makeshift Seder there while we're launching and recovering aircraft that are striking terrorist targets in Afghanistan."[50] When asked if it was difficult being female and Jewish in the US Navy, she responds without hesitation, "I believe that over the decades, that the Navy has been a step ahead of society in terms of integration and acceptance. The Navy embraces diversity. I never felt that I was treated differently."[51]

In 2005, Luria married Commander Robert Blondin, who retired after more than twenty years of naval service and holds a graduate degree from Old Dominion University.[52] They welcomed their first child, Violette, in September 2009.[53] As Luria continued active service in the US Navy, she and her husband also started their own business, Mermaid Factory, in 2013. The venture started as a "block of clay on her kitchen table" but quickly grew into a social enterprise that celebrated the iconic symbol of Hampton Roads, Virginia.[54] The couple opened a storefront location in Virginia Beach in 2015, where visitors can stop and paint their own mermaids. A portion of the cost of each figure sold is donated to organizations supporting youth and the arts, including ForKids, the Norfolk Public Library, and the Chrysler Museum.[55]

On June 1, 2017, Luria retired from the US Navy at the rank of commander. Within six months, on January 8, 2018, she launched her campaign to represent Virginia's Second District in Congress.[56] When asked about her decision to enter a career in politics, Luria explained, "My daughter just turned nine. In 10 years from now, she will have her first opportunity to vote in a presidential election. I don't want her to ask me that question in ten years, 'What did you do in this trying time?'"[57] Luria garnered just more than 62 percent of the vote, defeating educator Karen Mallard in the June 2018 Democratic primary.[58]

Her opponent in the November general election, Republican incumbent and former navy SEAL Scott Taylor, won his first term in 2016 with more than 60 percent of the vote, though President Trump only carried the district by a narrow margin.[59] The state of Virginia has become more reliably left-leaning in national elections, voting for every Democratic presidential candidate since 2008.[60] The Democratic Party also gained seats in the Virginia House of Delegates election in 2016, and the Democratic candidate for governor, Ralph Northam, won the district by four points the following year.[61] Luria's status as a veteran was considered a "political plus" in Virginia's Second District, which includes Hampton Roads, all of Virginia

Beach, Williamsburg, and portions of Norfolk and Hampton. According to her campaign website, the district is home to several military facilities, including the world's largest US Navy base, one of the highest concentrations of veterans, and the largest number of female veterans nationwide.[62]

Though both Second District congressional candidates raised just more than $4 million heading into the November 2018 general election, Luria emerged from the close race as the winner, with 51 percent of the vote, compared with Taylor's 49 percent (139,571 to 133,458, respectively).[63] Luria won six of the district's nine county-level jurisdictions, including all but one of the district's five independent cities and Taylor's hometown of Virginia Beach.[64] Luria was sworn into the 116th Congress on January 3, 2019, and assigned to the Armed Services Committee and the Veterans' Affairs Committee. She also led the Veterans' Affairs Subcommittee on Disability Assistance and Memorial Affairs and served as vice chair of the Armed Services Subcommittee on Seapower and Projection Forces.[65] Of all members in the House Democratic Caucus, she served the longest on active duty in the armed forces.

Luria identifies herself as a "security Democrat"—a nickname used by Democrats with national security experience—and in September 2019 joined other first-term party members in support of impeachment proceedings against President Trump in their editorial in the *Washington Post*.[66] In 2020, Luria announced her campaign for reelection and once again faced former representative Taylor in the general election. She won a second term with 51.6 percent of the vote, compared with Taylor's 45.8 percent (185,733 to 165,031, respectively).[67]

Abigail Spanberger

Spanberger, born in Red Bank, New Jersey, in August 1979, represents Virginia's Seventh District. Her family relocated from the Garden State to Short Pump in Henrico County, just outside Richmond, Virginia, when she was a teenager. As a child, she listened in fascination to her Ecuadorian babysitter speaking in Spanish to her own grandchildren, and this inspired her love of languages.[68] She attended J. R. Tucker High School's Spanish immersion program, where she was active in Spanish, drama, forensics, and debate. As a high school student, she also worked as a page for Senator Chuck Robb (D-VA) and studied abroad in Grenoble, France.

Spanberger graduated with a bachelor of arts degree in French language and literature and a minor in foreign affairs from the University of Virginia.[69] Afterward, she earned a master of business administration (MBA) in a dual program offered by Purdue University's Krannert School of Management and the GISMA Business School in Germany.[70]

Upon returning from her graduate studies abroad, Spanberger worked as a waitress, then as a substitute teacher, before receiving a full-time position as a federal postal inspector. In interviews about her time in Washington, DC, she shares that her work as a postal inspector consisted mainly of coordinating with District of Columbia police and Maryland state police on drug, money laundering, and white powder investigations after 9/11. During this time, she married Adam Spanberger, whom she had known since high school.[71]

Though she received a job offer from the Central Intelligence Agency (CIA) in 2002, it took nearly four years for her to pass a background check and final clearance to work for the agency.[72] As a case officer, she traveled and lived abroad collecting intelligence, managing assets, and overseeing high-profile programs in service to the United States. Although she is unable to speak openly about her work for the CIA, Spanberger has shared in interviews that during her eight years of service she gathered intelligence about nuclear proliferation and terrorism.[73]

In 2014, Spanberger left her position with the CIA and moved back to Henrico County with her husband and three children. She began her private sector career with EAB (formerly Royall and Company), a consulting firm that works with higher education institutions to build more diverse student bodies, increase graduation rates, and reduce financial barriers to student success. In 2017, Spanberger was also appointed by Governor Terry McAuliffe to serve on Virginia's Fair Housing Board, a body that works to prevent housing discrimination and expand access to affordable housing.[74]

The politics of the 2016 election and movement to repeal the remaining policies of the Patient Protection and Affordable Care Act (ACA) motivated Spanberger to consider running for Congress. In one interview, she shared that her decision was shaped by conversations with a close friend whose daughter suffered from a genetic disorder. He feared his daughter might lose access to the care she needed or the costs of her treatment might drive the family into bankruptcy without the protections of the ACA. Spanberger realized that "any fear or apprehension I had related to publicly campaigning, or putting myself out there . . . that was absolutely nothing compared to the fear that my friends feel when they think about what the future holds for their daughter."[75] She committed to running when the Republican majority in Congress voted to repeal the ACA.[76]

Spanberger officially announced her candidacy for Virginia's Seventh District in July 2017. The district, which includes portions of the northern suburbs of Richmond and exurban territory surrounding Fredericksburg, was represented by Republican incumbent and Tea Party member Dave Brat. Brat gained national attention when he defeated House Majority Leader Eric Cantor in the 2014 Republican primary and went on to win the general election that November. He was the first challenger to defeat a House majority leader incumbent since the creation of the position in 1899.[77]

Throughout her campaign, Spanberger emphasized her CIA credentials and that she was "more than just a pencil pusher."[78] "I worked to recruit people to commit espionage on behalf of the United States," she explained, and this impressed audiences who came to hear her speak.[79] In the June 2018 Democratic Party primary, Spanberger earned 73 percent of the vote, more than any other candidate running in the Virginia primaries that year.[80] This generated further momentum for her campaign, which raised more than $7.2 million through the 2018 election cycle, compared with Brat's $3.3 million.[81]

Despite out-fund-raising her opponent by a margin of two-to-one, Spanberger narrowly won the general election in November by a margin of 6,600 votes (176,079, or 50.3 percent, to 169,295, or 48.4 percent).[82] Her election broke a thirty-six-year winning streak for the Seventh District held by the Republican Party. After she was sworn into Congress in January 2019, Spanberger was assigned to the Agriculture and Foreign Affairs Committees, including the Subcommittees on Asia, the Pacific, and Nonproliferation and Europe, Eurasia, Energy, and the Environment. She also serves as chair of the Conservation and Forestry Subcommittee. In 2020, Spanberger campaigned for reelection against Republican state delegate

Nick Freitas. She raised more than $7.8 million, compared with Freitas's $3.1 million, and won reelection with 230,893 votes (50.8 percent) to 222,623 votes (49.0 percent).[83]

Representative Elissa Slotkin

Though Slotkin was born in New York City in July 1976, she spent much of her early childhood on her family's farm in Holly, Michigan. In interviews she proudly shares the story of her family's immigrant heritage, particularly that of Hugo Slotkin, who entered the United States at Ellis Island.[84] After becoming established in Detroit, Michigan, the Slotkin family created its own business, Hygrade Meats, in 1949, and the company grew as it supplied famous brands, such as Ball Park Franks, first sold at Tiger Stadium.[85]

Slotkin was a strong student in high school. Her interest in international development inspired her to apply to Cornell University's College of Agriculture and Life Sciences, where she earned a bachelor of arts in rural sociology in 1998.[86] After graduation, she remained in New York and decided to pursue a master's degree at the Columbia School of International Affairs. The 9/11 attacks occurred during her first week of graduate classes, which shifted her academic focus toward national security policy: "That terrible day changed the trajectory of my life. I decided that after graduate school, I would join the intelligence community and work to prevent future terrorist attacks against the United States."[87] She added training in Arabic from the American University in Cairo to her course of study in 2001. To supplement her income and graduate studies, Slotkin also worked as a community organizer for Roca as a Swahili language translator for Harbor Area Early Childhood, as a grant writer at Isha L'Isha ("Woman to Woman" in Hebrew), and as a political affairs intern with the US Department of State.[88]

By the time she finished graduate school, Slotkin knew what she wanted from her career. "When the dust settled, I really knew then that my interest in public service would be more focused on national service."[89] The CIA reached out to recruit Slotkin as an analyst, then intelligence briefer, when she finished her master's degree in 2003.[90] After working as a senior assistant to the director of National Intelligence in 2005, she was invited to lead a CIA assessment team from 2006 to 2007 during Operation Iraqi

Freedom (later named Operation New Dawn). During one of her three tours of duty, Slotkin also met her husband, Dave Moore, now a retired US Army colonel and Apache helicopter pilot.[91]

In 2007, Slotkin served as the director for Iraq on the NSC at the White House. She worked for President Bush as a member of his national security staff and was asked to stay on when President Obama took office in 2009.[92] After spending two years as a senior adviser on Iraq for the State Department, Slotkin brought her expertise to the Department of Defense (DOD), first as a senior adviser, then as a chief of staff to the assistant secretary for International Security Affairs, and finally as a principal deputy undersecretary and assistant secretary of defense between 2011 and 2015. She remained at the DOD until January 2017, overseeing defense policy in Africa, the Middle East, and Europe.

The election of Trump in 2016 was not the only motivating factor in Slotkin's decision to leave the White House. Her mother, Judith, was diagnosed with ovarian cancer. To complicate matters further, Slotkin's mother had allowed her insurance to lapse and needed financial assistance to help cover the costs of her treatment. In one interview, Slotkin shares of her mother's condition: "She was lying on an MRI gurney and they made us write a check for $8,000 before they would treat her."[93] Her mother passed away before the provisions of the ACA went into effect, and Slotkin recalls US Representative Mike Bishop (R-MI) celebrating his vote against the historic health care reform bill at the White House. Slotkin shares, "In the military, this is called dereliction of duty. We decided to fire him that day."[94]

She announced her candidacy for Michigan's Eighth District seat in the House in July 2017 and defeated a Michigan State University criminal justice professor in the August 2018 Democratic primary with 70.7 percent of the vote.[95] Through the general election in November, Slotkin raised more than $7.4 million, compared with the incumbent Bishop's $3.3 million.[96] When the votes were tallied, Slotkin defeated Bishop by a margin of 172,880 votes (50.6 percent) to 159,782 (46.8 percent) and became the first Democrat to represent the district since 2001.[97]

As a first-term US representative, Slotkin was assigned to the Armed Services and Homeland Security Committees, including the Subcommittees on Intelligence, Emerging Threats, and Capabilities, Readiness,

Counterterrorism, and Intelligence, and Cybersecurity and Infrastructure Protection. She stood for reelection in 2020 against challenger Paul Junge, a Republican with experience in law, as the Fox 47 television news anchor in Lansing, and in the Trump administration's US Citizenship and Immigration Services division.[98] Slotkin ran unopposed in the Democratic primary and, once again, raised impressive campaign funds, $8.3 million, compared with Junge's $1.9 million.[99] She received 50.9 percent of the vote (217,922) to Junge's 47.3 percent (202,525) in the November 2020 general election, earning a second term in Congress.[100]

Honorable Mentions, or Near "Badasses"

Amy McGrath

Amy McGrath was born in Cincinnati, Ohio, in June 1975, the youngest of three children. Her father, Donald, worked as a high school English teacher, and her mother, Marianne, was a psychiatrist, notably one of the first women to graduate from the University of Kentucky's medical school. McGrath was determined as early as the seventh grade to become an aviator, when she was inspired by a school project on World War II. She decided she did not want to become just any pilot but a fighter pilot.[101] Though she had three uncles who previously served in the US Marines, family trips to Wright-Patterson Air Force Base, home of the world's largest and oldest military aviation museum, encouraged her love of fighter jets.

As she studied fighter jets and aviation in the US military, McGrath came to the realization that fighter jet pilot and combat positions were not open to women. At twelve years old, she wrote to the US Naval Academy to find out how soon women would be allowed to fly in combat. An official from the academy phoned McGrath and her family with news that deflated the ambitious young aviator. He did not believe women would be allowed to fly anytime soon. This was 1987; President Gerald R. Ford had just desegregated the male-only US service academies in 1975, and the US Air Force Academy (USAFA) graduated its first class of female cadets in 1980.

Young McGrath interpreted the limitation as a challenge, and it only enhanced her determination to become a fighter pilot. She wrote to her US representatives and senators, including Senator Mitch McConnell, to ask them about the policy that restricted women's opportunities to fly. Neither senator responded, and her US representative responded, "Women are precious commodities and must be protected. . . . Do something else and good luck."[102] McGrath then wrote to every member of the House Armed Services Committee and received a response only from Representative Patricia Schroeder (D-CO), who encouraged her to continue following her passion and confirmed that Congress was working on the issue.[103]

Throughout high school, McGrath excelled as a student and as an athlete, competing in soccer, basketball, and baseball. In her senior year, she received an appointment to the US Naval Academy, and by the time she graduated, Congress lifted the Combat Exclusion Policy, which banned women from becoming fighter pilots.[104] At the academy, McGrath studied political science and served as the director of the Foreign Affairs Conference. She was commissioned as a US Marine officer and completed flight school in 1999, and she was assigned as a F/A-18 weapons systems officer to Marine All-Weather Fighter Attack Squadron 121. Unfortunately, she did not meet the eyesight requirements necessary to become a pilot.[105]

It is worthwhile to note that McGrath could have flown for any branch of the armed services at that point in time. In *Band of Sisters*, the authors note, "Traditionally, the F-18 has been one of the least popular aircraft for female aviators to fly because of its aggressive role in combat—dogfighting, air-to-air combat, and dropping bombs."[106] Moreover, the path to becoming a US Marine fighter pilot arguably requires some of the most rigorous and physical ground training of the military branches.[107] When McGrath arrived at her F-18 training squadron, she was held up by the commanding officer for nearly four months until another female officer arrived and they could begin training together.[108] The commander believed he was doing the right thing and being supportive of McGrath, given how tough the environment was for women and new trainees at the time. However, McGrath and other servicewomen frequently object to these types of accommodations on the grounds that they single out female servicemembers who want to be part of the squadron and community and that they signal to other male aviators that women are unable to handle the training on their own. Women in military service reiterate that they believe for a unit to work, "everyone has to be equal."[109]

In March 2001, McGrath and another female aviator, Jaden Kim, joined the Green Knights, becoming the first women in the squadron. Following the 9/11 attacks, the Green Knights deployed to Manas, Kyrgyzstan, approximately 650 miles from the northernmost border of Afghanistan. On the first mission to Afghanistan in March 2002, McGrath became the first female US Marine to fly as a backseat weapons system operator in an F/A-18 in combat. Kim became the second woman when she flew in April 2002. McGrath participated in a total of fifty-one combat missions as part of her six-month deployment, supporting Operation Enduring Freedom in Afghanistan. She continued to support multiple operations in the Middle East, deployed to Kuwait in support of Operation Iraqi Freedom in 2003, and deployed to Afghanistan again from 2005 to 2006. After receiving corrective LASIK eye surgery, McGrath was eventually able to become a front-seat pilot from 2004 to 2007.[110] She fulfilled her childhood dream of landing on an aircraft carrier, and in 2007, after being promoted from captain to major, she was deployed to East Asia. In total, McGrath flew more than 2,000 flight hours and more than eighty-nine combat missions throughout her military career.[111]

McGrath returned to the United States in 2011 and was assigned as a congressional fellow in Representative Susan Davis's (D-CA) office in Washington, DC. At the time, Davis was a senior member of the Armed Services Committee and chair of the Subcommittee on Military Personnel. McGrath served as a defense and foreign affairs adviser for the year she worked in the congressional office. Following her time as a congressional fellow, McGrath worked as a US Marine liaison to the Department of State and the US Agency for International Development (USAID).[112] She earned a graduate certificate in legislative studies from Georgetown University and a master of arts degree in international and global security studies from Johns Hopkins University. These advanced degrees and her wealth of firsthand experience enabled McGrath to teach political science as a senior instructor at the US Naval Academy from 2014 to 2017.

After twenty years of service, McGrath chose to retire from the military in 2017 at the rank of lieutenant colonel and pursue a career in public service, entering the Democratic congressional primary for Kentucky's Sixth District. Her campaign announcement video, shared on August 1, 2017, gained national attention and more than 1 million views on YouTube.[113] In the advertisement, McGrath shares her personal story, directly challenges

Amy McGrath, Democratic candidate for US Senate, speaks to the media at Bluegrass Airport in Lexington, Kentucky, on November 3, 2020, before flying herself to several campaign events around Kentucky. *Source:* Photo by James Crisp, AP Photo.

both Senate Majority Leader McConnell and her future opponent, incumbent Andy Barr (R-KY), and tells the audience that running for Congress is her "new mission." Her campaign made a special effort to establish rural field offices and reach out to rural voters. She received national endorsements from prominent elected Democrats, including Representative Seth Moulton (D-MA), a veteran, and political action committees (PACs) supporting veterans such as VoteVets and With Honor.[114] Though she won her party's nomination, she eventually lost the November midterm election in 2018 to Barr by a margin of 51 percent to 47.8 percent.[115]

Less than one year later, on July 9, 2019, McGrath took to Twitter to announce that she was entering the race for US senator from Kentucky in 2020. This meant she would challenge McConnell, who had served in the Senate since 1985 and who had ignored her letter about women aviators in combat thirty-three years prior. Her announcement generated significant enthusiasm and financial support, raising $3.5 million during the first week.[116] McGrath once again emerged with the nomination of the Democratic Party, earning a plurality of the primary vote. She received endorsements from Kentucky's Democratic governor, Andy Beshear, Kentucky newspapers, and national Democratic Party leaders.[117] By October 2020, her campaign raised more than $88 million, nearly 40 percent more than McConnell's $55 million.[118] In the end, McConnell still defeated McGrath, 1,233,074 votes (57.8 percent) to 816,184 (38.2 percent).[119]

Gina Ortiz Jones

Although she was born in Arlington, Virginia, in 1981, Gina Ortiz Jones was raised as a first-generation Filipina American 1,600 miles to the west in San Antonio, Texas. Her mother, Victoria Jones, emigrated from the Philippines, earned a teaching certificate, and worked multiple jobs as a single parent to raise Jones and her sister. Jones learned from her mother that education and service could lead to better opportunities, so she worked hard in school. She graduated as one of the top students in her class at John Jay High School in San Antonio and earned a ROTC scholarship to fund her studies at Boston University.[120] While there, Jones completed bachelor's degrees in economics and East Asian studies, then a master's degree in economics.

In 2003, Jones drew on her service experience and academic background when applying to the US Air Force, where she received a position as an intelligence officer. This was an ideal opportunity for Jones to continue her service, save one personal challenge. As a teenager, Jones shared with her mother that she identified as a lesbian. The military policy of Don't Ask, Don't Tell, in force from February 1994 until September 2011, prevented Jones from disclosing her sexual orientation during her service as an Air Force ROTC student and while on active duty in the US Air Force.[121]

Jones deployed to Iraq and achieved the rank of captain after three years, but her military service was disrupted when she abruptly returned home to Texas in 2006. Her mother had been diagnosed with cancer. When Jones finished her term of active service, she continued to work on issues of national security, intelligence, and defense as a civil servant for the federal government.[122] This included advising on operations in Latin America and Africa, on military operations that supported South Sudan's independence referendum, and serving in the "Libya Crisis Intelligence Cell."[123] She served as the senior adviser for trade enforcement and later as a director for investment at the Office of the US Trade Representative, where she oversaw the review of foreign investments to determine whether they posed potential national security risks.[124] During her years as a civil servant, Jones also became a Council on Foreign Relations term member and a member of the Truman National Security Project Defense Council. She earned a second graduate degree, this time from the US Army School of Advanced Military Studies. In 2013, she established the Leadership Through Service Scholarship at Boston University, an annual award that recognizes student excellence in the classroom and service to the surrounding community.

In 2016, during President Obama's second term in office, Jones was appointed to her position in the Office of the US Trade Representative, part of the executive office of the president. As a civil servant with experience serving under Republican and Democratic presidents, Jones remained part of the office when President Trump entered the White House in 2017. However, within six months of the new administration taking office, Jones resigned her position and shared with media outlets that she had deep concerns: "The type of people that were brought in to be public servants were interested in neither the public nor the service. . . . That, to me, was a sign that I'm going to have to serve in a different way."[125] Jones returned to San Antonio and made the choice to run for political office. When asked about her decision to campaign without prior political experience, Jones explained, "There's just a point where you just ask yourself the question, 'Can I afford not to do this?' I think like a lot of women, you're done assuming that somebody is going to do for you that which you can do yourself."[126]

Jones was the first Democrat to announce a challenge to Representative Will Hurd, the Republican incumbent representing the Twenty-Third District.[127] The district, which stretches from San Antonio to El Paso, is considered one of the most competitive in Texas. Given the tendency to swing back and forth between the two parties, it is "a regular target of both national Democrats and Republicans."[128] When Hurd, a former clandestine CIA officer, won reelection in 2016, it was the first time an incumbent held on to the seat for a second term in eight years.

The March 2018 Democratic Party primary for the Twenty-Third District was incredibly competitive, and though Jones earned 41 percent of the vote, she did not meet the threshold to earn the party's nomination.[129]

She emerged from the May runoff with a clear majority and faced Hurd in the general election. As in many 2018 races, the candidates broke fundraising records; Jones raised more than $6 million, compared with Hurd's $5 million.[130] Despite endorsements from EMILY'S List, VoteVets, the Asian American Action Fund, the Equality PAC, and national attention on the race, Jones lost the race by fewer than 1,000 votes.[131]

This close electoral defeat inspired Jones to enter the race again. In May 2019, she launched her second campaign, and surprisingly, Hurd announced in August 2019 that he would not seek reelection in 2020.[132] The open seat generated significant interest among Republican candidates in the party's primary. Following a primary runoff election, Tony Gonzalez, a US Navy veteran who served for nearly twenty years, won the party's nomination. Though Gonzalez had no prior experience serving in political office, he did previously serve as a DOD legislative fellow in Senator Marco Rubio's (R-FL) office. Jones, once again, raised more than $6 million for her campaign, compared with Gonzalez's $2.2 million.[133] Despite significantly higher turnout in the 2020 race, Jones once again lost the election, 135,415 (46.5 percent) to 147,496 (50.7 percent).[134]

M. J. Hegar

Born in March 1976 in Connecticut, Mary Jennings (M. J.) Hegar remembers witnessing, as a four-year-old girl, her biological father pushing her mother, Grace, through a plate-glass door while her ten-year-old sister tried to intervene.[135] Hegar's mother moved her daughters to Cedar Park, Texas, a few years after this violent episode when she received a threatening phone call from the girls' father.[136] Hegar's mother then married David Jennings, a Vietnam veteran who became a father figure to Hegar.

After settling into her new life in Texas, Hegar excelled in school. She played tennis, soccer, volleyball, and basketball and ran track; participated in cheerleading and marching band; and became class president in her first year of high school.[137] At a young age, Hegar determined she wanted to be a combat pilot, the closest thing available to what it might feel like piloting the Millennium Falcon.[138] This drove her to be "the absolute best" at everything she attempted, in an effort to build the highest qualifications for entering the US Navy. When it came time to apply for a ROTC scholarship, she experienced her first taste of discrimination toward women in military service. Her high school mentor wrote a "scathing description of her leadership ability, discipline, and drive" designed to sink her application. According to her memoir, when confronted with the letter, her mentor explained that the armed services was "no place for a woman."[139] Undeterred, Hegar was accepted to the University of Texas–Austin and chose to pursue the Air Force ROTC.

Though she suffered injuries during training that would plague her for the rest of her military career, as well as the untimely loss of her stepfather, Hegar succeeded in the ROTC. She assumed the role of vice wing commander of Detachment 825 in the Air Force ROTC and deputy commander of the Arnold Air Society, a cadet fraternity.[140] Though she failed to earn a pilot slot upon completing ROTC, Hegar attended Aircraft Maintenance Officer's training when she was commissioned into the US Air Force in December 1999 because she believed it was the best path toward becoming a combat pilot. Initially serving at Misawa Air Base in Japan, she was later stationed at Whiteman Air Force Base in Missouri, where she worked on the F-16 Fighting Falcon and B-2 Stealth Bomber. Outside of her military training, Hegar also earned her civilian pilot's license.

In 2003, Hegar made the difficult decision to leave the US Air Force after an abusive gynecological exam by a flight surgeon the previous year; to her knowledge, no action was ever taken against the doctor.[141] But her next opportunity to train and serve came in March 2004, when she was offered the opportunity to pilot the A-10 Warthog with one national guard unit or pilot the Combat Search and Rescue (CSAR) HH-60G Pave Hawk helicopters with a different national guard unit. She chose to join the New York Air National Guard for pilot training to fly CSAR, and during her first two deployments to Afghanistan during Operation Enduring Freedom, flew more than a hundred missions, including medevac missions in combat zones.[142] Hegar also served as a pilot with the California National Guard, participating in search-and-rescue missions, wildfire suppression flights, and marijuana eradication missions. She was a trainer with the Counterdrug Task Force in San Jose from 2007 to 2011.[143]

During her third tour of Afghanistan in July 2009, Hegar, her copilot, and the onboard combat search-and-rescue team were shot down near Kandahar.[144] Though women were technically barred from ground combat at the time, the government policy did not prevent Hegar from receiving shrapnel wounds in her arm and leg as a result of Taliban ground fire during the mission, taking additional heavy fire as her helicopter was forced to make an emergency landing, or returning fire as she strapped herself to the skids of a US Army helicopter that flew her away from the violent combat scene.[145] In addition to her shrapnel wounds, Hegar also sustained a serious back injury from the hard emergency landing. She was awarded the Purple Heart in December 2009 and the Distinguished Flying Cross with Valor in 2011, one of a select few women to receive this award after Amelia Earhart did.[146]

Following the 2009 mission, Hegar's lingering back injury medically disqualified her from flying as a combat pilot for the Air National Guard. Though she hoped to stay engaged in combat support, the Ground Combat Exclusion Policy prevented her from even applying to ground combat positions, for example, as a special tactics officer.[147] She returned to Texas in 2010 and entered the private sector, first working as a program manager in the health-care field and then as a consultant for Dell.[148] She earned her executive MBA from the University of Texas–Austin, occasionally teaching for the university and mentoring cadets in the Air Force ROTC as a member of its Advisory Committee.

Hegar once again found herself in the national spotlight when a conversation with her stepdaughter about women serving in the military prompted her to accept the American Civil Liberties Union's (ACLU) invitation to join a lawsuit opposing the US military's Combat Exclusion Policy. Alongside former US Army staff sergeant Jennifer Hunt, US Marine Corps captain Zoe Bedell, US Marine Corps first lieutenant Colleen Farrell, and the Service Women's Action Network (SWAN), Hegar sued US Secretary of Defense Leon Panetta, challenging the Combat Exclusion Policy as unconstitutional and arguing that it rendered the US military less effective.[149] Though the lawsuit failed to overturn the policy, the DOD still chose to repeal the exclusion in January 2013.[150]

Hegar's experience advocating against the impractical exclusion policy, becoming a new mom, and witnessing the politics of the presidential election of 2016 inspired her to enter public office.[151] Like other candidates with service and security backgrounds seeking the Democratic nomination, Hegar felt that election security issues, cyber threats, and increasing Russian aggression presented a serious threat to the US Constitution,

Democratic US Senate candidate M. J. Hegar, *left*, shows her tattoo to supporters during her election night party in Austin, Texas, on March 3, 2020. *Source:* Photo by Eric Gay, AP Photo.

which she had taken an oath to defend during her military service.[152] In July 2017, she announced her intent to run for the Democratic nomination for Congress in the Thirty-First District. In her short-form political ad, "Doors," Hegar described not only her distinguished military career and civilian life at home as a working mom but also the lack of responsiveness of representatives in Washington, DC, when she tried to advocate on behalf of women in the military. The viral ad began with the vivid memory of domestic violence from her early childhood and followed Hegar as she escorts potential voters through a series of doors that lead to the halls of Washington: "And I went to D.C. to lobby Congress. But door after door was slammed in my face."[153] The video ends by connecting her opponent, incumbent Representative John Carter (R-TX), to the closed doors: "Apparently being a constituent and a veteran wasn't enough to get a meeting. I guess I also needed to be a donor."[154] Despite raising more than $5 million, compared with Carter's $1.8 million, Hegar finished second in the November general election, earning 136,362 votes (47.7 percent) to Carter's 144,680 (50.6 percent).[155]

Less than six months later, Hegar announced that she was running for election again—this time for the US Senate. The Democratic Party last held a US Senate seat in Texas in 1994, and Hegar had to challenge Senator John Cornyn (R-TX). She finished first in the March 2020 Democratic primary with 22.37 percent of the vote and won the July runoff against Texas state senator Royce West.[156] She received endorsements from prominent figures in the national Democratic Party, including Obama, and raised more than $24 million through the general election.[157] Despite Hegar's strong debate performances and an extensive grassroots campaign, Cornyn won reelection with 5,669,704 votes (53.8 percent) to her 4,606,710 (43.7 percent).[158]

Conclusion

Women with military and intelligence backgrounds running for office in the second Year of the Woman in 2018 are descriptively different from those who served before 9/11. The majority of these women candidates are married, not widowed, and raising families—a point they emphasize in their political communications and introductions to potential voters. Several candidates do not come from elite families or privileged backgrounds. Many, including those who self-identify as middle class, entered ROTC or military service to access scholarships and fund their college studies. None of the candidates were socialized into politics through family members serving in office, though they are often related to or know someone with a background in military service or civic leadership.

The candidates also share a similar understanding of "service" as women with military or related backgrounds who ran for office prior to 9/11. They believe service entails a commitment to helping, aiding, or benefiting their local, national, or global communities. This translates not only to defending one's country through participation in the armed forces but also national security policy, corruption in government, and protecting the most vulnerable citizens through veteran and health-care policy reform. After the Year of the Woman in 1992, the women elected to Congress helped shape the passage of bills such as the Family and Medical Leave Act and the Violence Against Women Act. In 2018 and 2020, servicewomen candidates, like women running for midterm election more broadly,

From left, US Representatives Mikie Sherrill (D-NJ), Abigail Spanberger (D-VA), Elissa Slotkin (D-MI), and Chrissy Houlahan (D-PA) ride to the Russell Building after a group photo of House Democrats in the Capitol Visitor Center who will wear white to the State of the Union Address to highlight women's agendas on February 5, 2019. *Source:* Photo by Tom Williams, *Congressional Quarterly Roll Call* via AP Images.

expressed that they were motivated to do so because of Republican threats to eliminate health-care protections under the ACA.

These candidates also conform to Kaitlin Sidorsky's observation that some women in public service are motivated by a political ambition "both personal and professional, but . . . it is absolutely not political."[159] The servicewomen I discuss in this chapter share personal stories about the issues that motivated their decisions to run, grounded in fighting to protect or rectify harm done to those around them (family members, friends, veterans, and women in the military). There is little evidence that the motivation to run stems from a desire to elevate their personal political profiles or is strictly grounded in partisan politics. Rather, they express a desire to step up and act when duty calls.

4

After Tammy Duckworth was born in 1968 in Bangkok, Thailand, her family eventually relocated to Hawai'i, where she attended high school and college. Duckworth was deployed to serve in the Iraq War in 2004 and lost both of her legs when her helicopter was struck by a rocket-propelled grenade (RPG). She became an advocate for veterans and eventually served as the director of the Illinois Department of Veterans Affairs in 2006. Three years later, President Barack Obama appointed her assistant secretary in the US Department of Veterans Affairs (VA). In 2012, Duckworth was elected as a US representative representing the Eighth District in Illinois. A rising star in the Democratic Party, she was elected a US senator in 2016, becoming the first woman with disabilities and the second Asian American woman in the Senate. In April 2018, at the age of fifty, Duckworth became the first senator to give birth while holding office.

1968: The Year That Rocked the World

Most historians view 1968 as the year that defined the 1960s. Eldridge Cleaver wrote in Soul on Ice, "The destiny of the entire human race depends on what is going on in America today." The year began with a growing counterculture, broke apart with racial violence, and brought the end of Lyndon B. Johnson's presidency and the collapse of the cold war consensus.

Historian Mark Lytle argues that the escalation of war in Vietnam, combined with this series of events, marked a "deterioration of the prosperity that had been an essential ingredient in the optimism that inspired both the vision of American [sic] as the [sic] both the leader of the free world in its struggle against Communism and the belief that Americans possessed both the will and the means to eliminate social injustice at home."[1]

During this defining historical moment, on March 12, 1968, Ladda "Tammy" Duckworth was born in Thailand. Her mother, Lamai Sompornpairin, of Thai and Chinese descent, met her father, Franklin Duckworth, a US Army veteran, while he was stationed in Thailand during the Vietnam War. The official US military presence in Thailand started in April 1961, when an advance party of the US Air Force arrived at Don Muang Royal Thai Air Force Base at the request of the Thai government to establish an aircraft warning system. The number of US troops grew rapidly with the expansion of the Laotian civil war and the Vietnam War. At the height of the conflict, some 50,000 US military personnel were stationed throughout Thailand.[2]

Her father was forty years old when Duckworth was born, and his career soon transitioned from service in the US Army to work with the UN refugee program. The family, including Duckworth's brother, Thomas, moved from Thailand to Singapore and eventually Indonesia and Cambodia. Her itinerant childhood allowed her to develop trilingual fluency in Thai, Indonesian, and English, attend international schools with diverse peers, and witness historical events unfolding across Southeast Asia. The Duckworth family moved from Cambodia in spring 1975, for example, just two weeks prior to the Khmer Rouge seizing control of the country.[3] As an adult, she later recalled her mother "taking me as a very little kid to the roof of our home in Phnom Penh, Cambodia, to look at the bombs exploding in the distance. She didn't want us to be scared by the booms and the strange flashes of light. It was her way of helping us to understand what was happening."[4]

Her family settled in Hawai'i when Duckworth was sixteen, though their situation was far from paradise. They were in dire financial straits. Her father was laid off and at nearly sixty years old had a difficult time locating full-time employment. Potential employers often dismissed his application because he was "overqualified." Duckworth was less convinced: "Those are the words for 'you're too old.'"[5] To survive, the family moved into a pay-by-the-week motel and relied on public assistance. She later recalled, "We'd use the food stamps for baloney and white bread, praying it would last the week," and she sold flowers from a plastic bucket on the side of the road to contribute to her family's income.[6] These experiences shaped her views on poverty in the United States. In a 2018 interview with *Vogue*, she explained, "I never worked as hard as when we were at our poorest," she says. "So, I felt if we could end up there, anyone could."[7]

Though Duckworth has not explicitly shared stories or memories of personally facing discrimination, she was keenly aware of broader social anxiety regarding her parents' biracial relationship when she first moved to the United States. Marriage between a servicemember and his bride represented more than a commitment between two individuals in love, particularly with the opening of permanent bases in both Europe and Asia. Susan Zeiger writes that after World War II, international marriages were symbolic of "the nation's ability to woo and win the admiration of foreign others in the context of the emerging Cold War."[8] Interracial couples were viewed through the lens of cold war politics, with foreign or nonwhite wives often stigmatized as "prostitutes and economic 'parasites.'"[9] In her *Vogue* interview Duckworth observed, "Being Amerasian, post–Vietnam War, people just assumed you were the child of a GI and a prostitute. I was so lucky my parents were married, and I had an American passport."[10] American leaders and society had little interest in emphasizing the happy endings, both personal and political, these unions signified, compared with those of prior international conflicts.

Yet, Duckworth credits her mother for not allowing the family's challenging circumstances to affect her academic work; she graduated from high school with honors and subsequently earned a bachelor of arts in political science from the University of Hawai'i in 1989. This academic foundation, along with her international experience and trilingual abilities, allowed her to apply to the master's program in international affairs at George Washington University with the ambition of becoming an ambassador.

An "Equal Risk"

In her quest to become a Foreign Services officer, Duckworth joined the Reserve Officers' Training Corps (ROTC) and became a commissioned officer in the US Army Reserve in 1992. She felt it was a practical choice: "I figured I should know the difference between a battalion and a platoon if I were going to represent my country overseas someday."[11] Duckworth believed that military experience would support her professional goals and allow her to continue work that aligned with the values imparted by her parents:

> My parents have always taught us that you need to give something back for all the great stuff we get for being Americans. I know that sounds really corny, but I grew up overseas. My father worked for the United Nations refugee program, so I was exposed to a lot of refugees and developing countries. And he worked for a short time in Indonesia with the housing estates for ex-patriots. But I grew up in Asia and in a lot of countries that had authoritarian regimes or were fighting the communists, Vietnam, and Cambodia, and all those kinds of places. So being an American was not only something that was important to me, but it was actually vital to the quality of life that I had. When I came back and we moved back to the states to live, it was very clear to us the difference in standards of living and what you could do here that you couldn't have done overseas.[12]

Duckworth's early exposure to the political instability and conflict of Southeast Asia during the cold war, and the helping hand up in the form of public assistance provided by the US government during her family's economic struggles, instilled a sense of duty, responsibility, and gratitude that fundamentally shaped her perspective on service.

It did not take long before Duckworth "fell in love" with the military.[13] In interviews, she reflects on the decision as "a calling that was out there that [she] did not realize she wanted to fulfill."[14] Beyond the camaraderie and sense of purpose, Duckworth also met her husband, Bryan Bowlsbey, in the armed forces and found a passion for flying helicopters. In 2004, she trained as a Black Hawk pilot, one of only a handful of jobs with combat potential for women. Although the first group of young women pilots became pioneers in 1943, the members of the Women's Airforce Service

Pilots (WASP) were not considered military pilots until 1977, when Congress recognized their status as veterans of World War II. As I noted previously in this book, women began entering Air Force pilot training in 1976 and fighter pilot training in 1993, when the secretary of defense lifted the ban on women serving as pilots of combat aircraft.[15] In April 1993, President Bill Clinton ordered the services to open combat aviation to women and to investigate other opportunities for women to serve. In response, Secretary of Defense Les Aspin ordered the services to "permit women to compete for assignments in aircraft including aircraft engaged in combat missions."[16] Later that year, Congress repealed 10 U.S.C. 6015 (the Combat Ship Exclusion), opening most US Navy combatant ships except submarines to women. As a result of these and other policy changes, the number of positions open to women increased substantially. Positions open to women in both the US Navy and US Marines increased by about 30 percent.[17] Before the policy changes took effect in 1993, 67 percent of positions in the military were available to women; by 1997, 80.2 percent were available.[18]

Though institutional barriers were lifted to allow women greater opportunities, Duckworth and her female colleagues still faced gendered obstacles in their attempt to serve. In her foreword to *Band of Sisters: American Women at War in Iraq*, she explains her hesitation to be identified as "a woman anything": "A generation of women had already pushed through, breaking down the barriers in Army aviation. Like any group of people, some were outstanding Soldiers, while others simply used their gender to gain an unfair advantage."[19] Duckworth believed that the actions of the latter group, though she does not identify specific examples, made it very difficult for her to earn the respect and trust of her male colleagues. She felt as though she and her female colleagues in the military had to prove they were just as qualified and competent "all over again—this time, by being as tough and gender-neutral as possible."[20] She applied this philosophy when choosing among training opportunities and occupations during her time with the US Army. As a female soldier, Duckworth was not required to select a combat role among her ten preferences. Her male colleagues, however, were required to include three combat roles in their selection of ten possible occupations. She felt that the exception for women created an unfair selection system, and it was her responsibility to accept an equal level of risk to that of her male colleagues. Equality for women in the military was not only about opportunity and choice but also responsibility and duty. This view ultimately shaped her strategic choice to include aviation, a combat role open to women, among her preferences.[21]

Beyond the politics of combat, stories of her early years of service include her attempts to build rapport with her unit by serving hot cocoa before training exercises. "I got a lot of shit," she recalled of her time as the first female platoon leader of her unit. Pilots often called her "mommy platoon leader," challenging her attempts to fit in with her male colleagues in a hypermasculine environment.[22] In these situations Duckworth maintained her focus on the Soldier's Creed, always placing the mission first and refusing to accept defeat. Reflecting on the challenges of navigating gender politics in the military, Duckworth and many of the other women interviewed for Band of Sisters state that their mission is "not about being the first female anything. It's about not wanting to be average."[23]

As a member of the US Army Reserve, Duckworth attended flight school, later transferring to the Army National Guard and serving in the Illinois Army National Guard in 1996. Her ethos of service extended beyond the armed forces to her civilian work. She worked as a staff supervisor at Rotary International headquarters in Evanston, Illinois; served as a coordinator of the Center for Nursing Research at Northern Illinois University; and enrolled in a doctoral program in political science. Rotary International, also known as the Rotary Club, is an international service organization whose stated purpose is to bring together business and professional leaders to provide humanitarian service and to advance goodwill and peace around the world. In her own words, Duckworth described the mission this way: "The goal of Rotary Clubs around the world is to do community service and to improve the lives of people in their local community. Their motto is 'Service above Self.'"[24]

Duckworth's studies and civilian service were disrupted when she was deployed to Iraq in 2004 as part of Operation Iraqi Freedom. In her role as a pilot, Duckworth flew more than 120 combat hours during her eight months in Iraq without incident.[25] That would change on November 12, 2004. As she copiloted a UH-60 Black Hawk helicopter alongside Chief Warrant Officer Daniel Milberg, insurgents launched an RPG. The RPG struck the helicopter cockpit, eviscerating Duckworth's lower limbs and severely burning Milberg. The copilots struggled to regain control of the helicopter, Duckworth frantically trying to push the pedals before she realized the real problem: "The pedals were gone, and so were my legs."[26]

The story of Duckworth's injury in the helicopter incident on November 12 has taken on mythological qualities. Published accounts describe the scene with cinematic drama, "straight out of *Saving Private Ryan*," or embellish the details with some inaccuracy, writing that "even while losing consciousness, she still . . . save[d] her team by flying the helicopter to safety."[27] Although these descriptions give the story a more romantic, heroic tenor, they smooth over the gruesome elements of what Duckworth endured. She lost half of her blood, and her right arm remained barely attached to her body. Surgeons in Baghdad amputated what remained of her right leg just below the hip and her left leg just below the knee. These losses marked the beginning of a grueling process of recovery for nearly thirteen months at the Walter Reed Army Medical Center in Washington, DC. As she battled through the agonizing pain, Duckworth would focus on the clock and count to sixty as each minute expired. She shares that she initially recited, "One dead Iraqi, two dead Iraqis, three dead Iraqis."[28]

Duckworth's service and sacrifice earned her the dubious honor of being the first American female double amputee from the Iraq War. She received a Purple Heart on December 3, 2004, an honor she shared with her father, and was promoted to major two weeks later. During her time at Walter Reed, which she affectionately referred to as the "amputee petting zoo," Duckworth was visited by numerous politicians. She felt that some members of Congress, such as Arizona Republican John McCain and Kansas Republican Bob Dole, expressed a genuine interest in the care and recovery of "wounded warriors," whereas others appeared more interested in staging a photo opportunity for their upcoming campaigns. In a 2018 interview, Duckworth credits conversations with these veteran statesmen as influencing her eventual decision to seek public office: "You know, my heroes were John McCain, Daniel Inouye, Bob Dole—the greats, those who served and, after their service in the military, often with significant personal sacrifice, found a different way to serve their nation."[29]

But before ever considering a career in public service, Duckworth expressed a strong desire to remain in the army and resume her career in aviation. When asked during her recovery about why she felt so strongly about remaining in the military, she responded:

The explosion didn't change who I am. I want to continue to serve. It's just part of me. . . . It's just how I chose to—choose to serve. I sincerely believe we should all give something back to our communities. Not everybody has to become a soldier. You know, you can volunteer at your church or at the school or at your local hospital, but I feel very strongly that for everything we have in this country, we should give a little something back of yourself. I just choose to serve being a soldier.[30]

Duckworth was not about to let "some guy with an RPG who got lucky" end her opportunity to serve.[31] By May 2005, she was back in the cockpit of a Black Hawk at Fort Belvoir, Virginia. Though she was unable to demonstrate enough strength and control in her prosthetics to fly combat missions once again, she continued to serve as a lieutenant colonel in the Illinois Army National Guard until she retired in October 2014.

An Advocate for Veterans

Because increasing numbers of injured veterans were returning home from Iraq, the media took interest in Duckworth's story. In addition to an in-depth interview with C-SPAN, Duckworth was featured on morning talk shows, in fashion magazines, and in blogs. Talk radio's Laura Ingraham gushed over Duckworth, her "new hero."[32] On Blackfive, a veterans' blog and forum, one contributor remarked: "A most admirable, intelligent, impressive individual, American Patriot, and lady! If she ran for political office, she has my vote! Gee, I hope she is Republican!"[33]

During her time at Walter Reed, Duckworth was the highest-ranking amputee; compared with the other residents in the hospital, Duckworth had, on average, almost fifteen additional years of military service. She drew on her experience and seniority to advocate on behalf of wounded veterans she met during her recovery. This included spending time on the phone with Senator Dick Durbin (D-IL), with whom she had developed a professional relationship, and testifying before congressional hearings on concerns over military health care. She contacted the Department of Veterans Affairs and members of Congress on behalf of veterans who needed assistance with insurance payments, billing, or other areas of personal concern. This advocacy exposed Duckworth to the complexity and inefficiency of veterans' health care. She became frustrated with "politics" and felt that servicemembers were not well represented in Congress. Durbin responded by challenging her to think about running for a congressional seat herself. On December 14, 2005, a determined Duckworth left Walter Reed hospital against the recommendations of her medical team and began her first congressional campaign at 7:00 a.m. on December 15.[34]

The Fightin' Dems

Duckworth was one of sixty military veterans nominated by the Democratic Party for congressional office in 2006. Nicknamed the "Fightin' Dems," the "Capitol Brigade," the "Blue Force," and the "Security Dems," these veterans were part of an organized coalition led by former senator Max Cleland (D-GA), a Vietnam veteran who chartered Veterans for a Secure America. This recruitment strategy by the Democratic Party was shaped by conversations about the historically low number of veterans serving in Congress (at less than 25 percent in 2006 compared with nearly 73 percent of House and Senate members in the early 1970s) as well as growing criticism of the George W. Bush administration and Iraq War.[35] Arguing that the veterans would serve on the "front lines of democracy," the Democratic National Committee sharply criticized the president: "We all know the current administration doesn't hesitate to stand in front of the troops when it comes to a photo-op, but never stands behind them when it comes to providing the armor necessary to fight in Iraq, or the benefits promised when they return home."[36] The Fightin' Dems' website provided interested supporters information about the Democratic Council for Veterans and Military Families, individual candidate profiles, an interactive map, and a link for campaign contributions.

In addition to support from the national party and fund-raising, political campaigns require intense energy and investment by candidates. Duckworth often worked sixty to seventy hours per week despite the fact that for nearly two months of her campaign she remained tethered to an IV that had to be changed every six hours to continually administer a crucial antibiotic. Yet, in her consistently positive perspective, Duckworth credits the intense travel schedule with providing her additional opportunities to improve her gait and grow comfortable using her new prosthetic devices. Alternating between the prosthetics and her wheelchair, Duckworth found that she enjoyed kitchen-table talks with potential voters the most: "I learned to sit down and talk and have great discussions with people."[37] In debates with her Republican opponent, Peter Roskam, she referred to herself as an "independent voice" with no ambition of becoming "just another Washington politician."[38]

To introduce Duckworth to Illinois voters, her campaign raised and spent $4.5 million, compared with Roskam's $3.4 million.[39] Most of Duckworth's funding came from individual contributors: $3.7 million or 82 percent of contributions. Individual contributions amounted to about 55 percent of Roskam's funding, or $1.9 million. Most of Duckworth's campaign funds went to advertising, sharing her political positions as well as her powerful personal story. She chose not to run a single negative advertisement, though the Republican and Democratic National Committees and outside groups engaged in significant negative messaging.

Throughout the campaign, Roskam criticized Duckworth for failing to participate in public debates. Although she agreed to participate in four of the twelve requested debates, she expressed concern that he was proposing "dozens of debates in random places, including one in a hall accessible only by spiral staircase."[40] Roskam countered, "My sense is if she's afraid to debate me in the district, heaven help her when she steps onto the House of Representatives' floor in Washington, D.C."[41]

Perhaps the most difficult moments came when the political action committee (PAC) of the Veterans of Foreign Wars of the United States (VFW) organization and former senator Dole, a man Duckworth greatly respected for both his military and public service, chose to endorse her opponent. Although endorsements do not win elections, they are certainly powerful in specific electoral contexts—candidate positions on the Iraq War were a central issue in the 2006 race. The VFW PAC decision to endorse Roskam caught Duckworth by surprise, and she quickly called together a press conference in response. Flanked by local veteran supporters angry with the organization's decision, she shared her disappointment, noting that the VFW had never reached out to ask her to fill out a questionnaire, which typically happens prior to organizational endorsements.[42] Several members of the local VFW spoke out against the decision, tearing up their membership cards in protest. Despite Duckworth's disappointment, she chose not to sever her relationship with the organization because she supports its mission, like that of other veterans' organizations, above the politics: "It's sad because it shouldn't be about party politics. It should be about who do you think is going to fight for what you believe in."[43]

The race garnered significant attention in national media, and Duckworth's political profile was rising. *Glamour* magazine even dubbed her "the patriot" whose "strength is an instinct" in its 2006 "Women of the Year" feature.[44] In most polls, Duckworth appeared tied or leading Roskam by as many as fourteen points going into the last week of October.[45] Speaker of the House Nancy Pelosi provided a cheering endorsement on Election Day: "Let's hear it for our candidates all across the country—our Fighting Dems, our vets who are running! . . . All across the board these candidates have excellent credentials, great ideals, and they are, again, fighters for the future. Let's hear it for our candidates!"[46] But in the end, Duckworth lost the race to Roskam by a margin of nearly 4,000 votes, at 91,382 (51.35 percent) to 86,572 (48.65 percent), respectively.[47] Of the sixty Fightin' Dems candidates nominated, only five successfully won seats in the House; Jim Webb was elected to represent Virginia in the Senate. In his analysis of the 2006 election, Jeremy Teigen noted that although the Democratic veteran candidates were the most salient in 2006, Republican veteran candidates enjoyed higher vote shares that year on average.[48] These larger trends were no comfort to Duckworth, who, crushed by the loss, "sat in a bathtub and cried for three days."[49]

In 2006, Election Day fell ten days before her "alive day," which gave her perspective on her loss. Despite being devastated, she shifted her outlook to celebrating the gift of life. "What's losing an election when you could have lost your life on this day two years before?"[50] Duckworth did not have to wait long for her next service opportunity. Three days after she lost the election, Governor Rod Blagojevich called to offer her a position as director for the Illinois Department of Veterans Affairs. As a member of the governor's cabinet, she would oversee a $105 million budget and 2,000 employees across the state agency and get the chance to create real change in the lives of Illinois veterans.

Over the next few years, Duckworth continued her duties with the National Guard and her role as director of the Illinois Department of Veterans

Affairs, where she launched a hotline for suicidal veterans and helped improve access to health-care payments and work for veterans. Beyond mandates from the governor, Duckworth was inspired to create these programs not only based on what she learned from wounded soldiers at Walter Reed but also from her own father's struggles to find steady, full-time employment upon returning to the United States.

Duckworth's signature program from her time as director was the 24/7 veteran's crisis hotline. A 2008 study by the RAND Corporation found that approximately 18.5 percent of servicemembers who returned from Afghanistan and Iraq have post-traumatic stress disorder (PTSD) or depression, and 19.5 percent report experiencing a traumatic brain injury during deployment.[51] The same study, along with others published at the time, found that roughly half of those who need treatment for these conditions seek it, but only slightly more than half who receive treatment get minimally adequate care. When veterans call in to the Illinois hotline, they are immediately connected with a trained, professional counselor (with a master's degree, at minimum). They receive a limited assessment while on the call and then are referred locally for treatment. Following the call and referral, the state agency then tries to support the caller to gain access to federal benefits. One of the important policies adopted by the hotline response group is privacy. If callers do not want to disclose an issue to the federal government out of concern that it might jeopardize their career while serving, the state of Illinois bears the full cost of treatment and keeps the condition confidential.[52]

Outside of the crisis hotline, studies analyzing the impact of the tax credit program and expanded health-care options in Illinois show mixed results.[53] Under the tax credit program, for every veteran they hired, companies were eligible to receive a $600 credit. State records show that in Duckworth's first year, only twelve firms took advantage of the program, and only eleven received credits in year two. With respect to the Illinois Veterans Care health program, the Illinois Department of Healthcare and Family Services reported that the average annual enrollment in Veterans Care during Duckworth's first year was only twenty-seven veterans. The next year, that number increased to eighty-two, and during her final year at the agency, average enrollment was ninety-nine. Though these enrollment numbers are low, the real controversy came from Governor Blagojevich's promises that the program "will help up to 9,000 veterans in Illinois" who fell between the cracks of not making enough money to afford private health insurance but making too much money to qualify for a federal health-care insurance program. Statements and memos to this effect were often sent from the governor's office without coordination or comment from Duckworth's office.[54]

Duckworth spent three years serving as the director of the Illinois Department of Veterans Affairs before being tapped by newly elected Obama for a position as an assistant secretary to the US Department of Veterans Affairs in 2009. It was the right time to leave the executive branch in Illinois because Governor Blagojevich had just been arrested and charged with conspiracy to commit mail and wire fraud and one count of soliciting bribes the month prior. Duckworth's approach to the federal agency was consistent with her approach as an administrator in Illinois; she was "all about admitting our failures" to address the culture of "hiding its problems."[55] In her short time as an assistant secretary, she worked to increase services for homeless veterans and created the Office of Online Communications, staffing it with experienced military bloggers who could help address day-to-day questions from younger troops.

A True Hero

When asked in the 2008 interview whether another political run was a possibility, Duckworth carefully responded that she was "keeping her options open." For Duckworth, this meant that any choice to run again would have to be for the right reasons: "I did not want to be a senator or a Congressperson, and I was running because I wanted to inject something into the debate. If I were to run again it would have to be for good reason. It cannot just be for the office because, frankly, I am not interested in that."[56]

Her first opportunity came in the 2012 election for Eighth District of Illinois, when she campaigned against staunch fiscal conservative incumbent Joe Walsh (R-IL). Dubbed a "firebrand Tea Party icon," Walsh began his career as a social worker focused on expanding educational opportunities and job skills training in the Chicago area. He was first elected to Congress in 2010 as part of the Tea Party wave, defeating three-term incumbent Melissa Bean. Unfortunately for Walsh, a significant portion of his district was redrawn during Democratic control of the Illinois legislature. The 2011 redistricting created some of the most notoriously gerrymandered districts in the United States.

This context led to a bitter contest between Walsh and Duckworth in the 2012 general election. At a July 2012 campaign event, an exasperated Walsh accused Duckworth of politicizing her military service: "My God, that's all she talks about. Our true heroes, the men and women who served us, it's the last thing in the world they talk about."[57] Duckworth responded in turn, "The Congressman has said himself that he went to Washington to be a poster child for the Tea Party. To scream from the mountaintops. And there's not been a crackpot Tea Party idea that he hasn't embraced."[58] Despite distancing himself from establishment Republicans, Walsh raised more than $2 million for his 2012 campaign. Additionally, third parties spent nearly $1.5 million to support his campaign and another $4.7 million to oppose Duckworth. Duckworth was able to raise $5.3 million, with relatively little in the way of outside spending supporting her campaign.[59] On Election Day, Duckworth defeated Walsh with 55 percent of the vote, 121,298 votes to 100,360, respectively.[60] She became the first woman with a disability to be elected to the US House of Representatives and the first member of Congress born in Thailand.

During her brief tenure in the House, Duckworth served on the Armed Services Committee, including its Subcommittees on Tactical Air and Land Forces and Oversight and Investigations; the Committee on Oversight and Government Reform; and for a brief period, the Select Committee on Benghazi. She was supportive of previous efforts to reform the Department of Veterans Affairs, such as the Veterans' Choice and Accountability Act of 2014, which increased the availability of care outside of the department's health-care system for eligible veterans, and the bipartisan Clay Hunt Suicide Prevention for American Veterans Act, which she coauthored. Named for a decorated US Marine veteran who struggled with PTSD, the bill was designed to reduce military and veteran suicides and improve access to quality mental health care. The bill passed both the House and Senate unanimously and was signed into law by President Obama. Duckworth also introduced the bipartisan Troop Talent Act of 2013 to help servicemembers transition to civilian life by making it easier for them to turn the skills they learned in the military into the credentials

As the former assistant secretary, US Department of Veterans Affairs, Tammy Duckworth waves to delegates at the Democratic National Convention in Charlotte, North Carolina, on September 4, 2012. *Source:* Photo by Lynne Sladky, AP Photo.

and licenses needed for similar civilian fields. In her legislative work, Duckworth often found common ground with moderate Republicans on veterans' and military issues.

In addition to supporting legislation on behalf of veterans and the military, she backed legislative initiatives championed by the Obama administration and other Democrats, including the Patient Protection and

Affordable Care Act (ACA). In 2016, she joined the House floor sit-in against gun violence staged by Democrats, hiding her cell phone inside her prosthetics to avoid having it confiscated.[61] The decision demonstrated keen political instincts because the Democratic members came to rely on their own mobile devices to stream the protesting when House Republicans called a recess and stopped the official broadcast.

In 2016, Duckworth made the decision to challenge incumbent Mark Kirk (R-IL) for the US Senate. Writers for the *Chicago Tribune* called it "one of the nation's most bitter and expensive" political races that year.[62] Despite their divergent political views, the two candidates shared many common qualities—veterans of the military with compelling stories of recovery after physical injury. In 2012, Kirk suffered a stroke and underwent neurosurgery. He spent a year in rehabilitation and recovery, returning in January 2013 for the first time since his stroke. Vice President and President of the Senate Joe Biden escorted him up the Capitol steps in time for the start of the 113th Congress. As a moderate Republican, Kirk often spotlighted veterans' care and national security as central issues of concern. Duckworth hoped to initially keep the focus on her key policy priorities and issues, explaining to voters, "I do not care who you voted for. Let's talk about what we need to do to make America as strong as she once was because that is what we will—that is why I put on the uniform was to defend democracy."[63]

As the race grew more competitive, tensions between the candidates escalated—and so did the rhetoric. The National Republican Senatorial Committee sent out a message via Twitter, later deleted: "Tammy Duckworth has a sad record of not standing up for our veterans."[64] Duckworth's team promptly used the quote in a fund-raising pitch. At a particularly low moment of the campaign, during a televised debate on October 27, 2016, Duckworth referenced her ancestors' past service in the US military. Her father could trace his family lineage and history of military service back to the Revolutionary War. Kirk turned to Duckworth, seated to his right at the shared table, and responded, "I'd forgotten that your parents came all the way from Thailand to serve George Washington."[65] The clip went viral and circulated in national media outlets. Organizations such as the Human Rights Campaign withdrew their support for Kirk and called his statements "deeply offensive and racist."[66] As the incumbent, Kirk raised nearly $12 million compared with Duckworth's $16.3 million. Outside spending added another $3 million in support of Kirk and $1.9 million in opposition to Duckworth.[67] With 3 million votes (54.9 percent), Duckworth defeated the "most imperiled incumbent Republican in the Senate" and placed Democrats in control of both Illinois Senate seats.[68] Along with Kamala Harris, elected in 2016, and Mazie Hirono, elected in 2012, she is one of the first three female Asian Americans to serve in the US Senate.

As a senator, Duckworth has served on the Small Business and Entrepreneurship Committee; the Commerce, Science, and Transportation Committee, including its Subcommittee on Aviation Operations, Safety, and Security; the Environment and Public Works Committee; and most recently, the Armed Services Committee. She is also a member of the congressional Asian Pacific American Caucus, along with servicemember Representative Tulsi Gabbard (D-HI). Duckworth made national headlines twice in 2018. The first time occurred in January, when she responded to a statement made by President Donald Trump on Twitter accusing the Democratic Party of putting "unlawful immigrants" ahead of the military. The federal government had recently shut down when the Senate could not agree on a funding bill. Duckworth took to the Senate floor to address the president's comments directly:

> I spent my entire adult life looking out for the well-being, the training, the equipping of the troops for whom I was responsible. Sadly, this is something that the current occupant of the Oval Office does not seem to care to do—and I will not be lectured about what our military needs by a five-deferment draft dodger. And I have a message for Cadet Bone Spurs: If you cared about our military, you'd stop baiting Kim Jong Un into a war that could put 85,000 American troops, and millions of innocent civilians, in danger.[69]

The president did not directly respond to Duckworth's statement.

The second time occurred just a few months later when Duckworth became the first US senator and one of only ten women across both chambers to give birth while serving in Congress. When Duckworth learned that her career flying in combat was over, she and her husband, Bryan, decided to start a family. They struggled to conceive, so they sought help from a fertility doctor recommended by the Department of Veterans Affairs. After eight unsuccessful years, Duckworth took a friend's advice to seek a second opinion from a notable fertility specialist in Chicago. In 2014, less than two years after working with her new specialist, Duckworth gave birth to the couple's first child. After turning fifty, she gave birth to their second child, Maile, in 2018. In sharing these struggles, Duckworth disclosed that she had discovered that the fertility specialist recommended by the Department of Veterans Affairs worked with a Catholic facility that did not approve of fertilizing embryos outside the body, the technique that ultimately made it possible for Duckworth and Bowlsbey to conceive.[70] In an interview with *Vogue*, she shared her frustration: "What bugs me to this day, is that she never said, 'You need to go to a different kind of facility.' I was educated! I was the director of Illinois Veterans Affairs. I didn't do my due diligence, so what about those other families?"[71]

Duckworth's identity as a mother has become intertwined with her work as a senator. In a statement issued shortly after Maile's birth, she wrote: "As tough as juggling the demands of motherhood and being a Senator can be, I'm hardly alone or unique as a working parent, and my children only make me more committed to doing my job and standing up for hardworking families everywhere."[72]

Her perspective as a working mother inspired Duckworth to work with other senators to pass a bipartisan resolution allowing children under the age of one onto the Senate floor. Unlike in the House, there is no electronic mechanism for floor votes; each senator must indicate his or her decision to clerks in person. The "new parents" rule change allowed Duckworth to be present for votes and to breastfeed her infant daughter as needed. The change passed the Senate without much complaint, though some senators grumbled to reporters after the fact: "What if there are 10 babies on the floor of the Senate?" asked eighty-four-year-old Senator Orrin G. Hatch (R-UT).[73] The senator's office later issued an apology and clarifying statement, but his remark invokes broader gender and generational tensions in the Senate, where an increasing number of diverse, young, female colleagues are pushing for change on some of its traditions. Still, the positive and persistent Duckworth dressed Maile in her tiny duckling onesie and a coordinating green blazer, wrapped her across her chest, and rolled onto the Senate floor to cast a vote, joking that it was important her infant daughter's apparel "doesn't violate the Senate floor dress code."[74]

Senator Tammy Duckworth (D-IL), with her baby Maile Pearl Bowlsbey, goes to the Senate floor to vote on Capitol Hill in Washington on April 19, 2018. *Source:* Photo by Manuel Balce Ceneta, AP Photo.

She also took her advocacy on behalf of new mothers beyond the Senate floor to include expanding access to nursing facilities in airports. As a mother who frequently travels, Duckworth realized that airports offered limited private space for nursing; many mothers were forced to use bathrooms when other spaces were not available. Along with Stephen Knight, a Republican member of the House representing California's Twenty-Fifth District, Duckworth introduced the Friendly Airports for Mothers (FAM) Act. The new law, signed by President Trump in October 2018, requires that all large- and medium-sized airports provide clean, private, nonbathroom space in each terminal for the expression of breast milk. The area must be accessible to persons with disabilities; available in each terminal building after the security checkpoint; and include a place to sit, a table or other flat surface, and an electrical outlet.[75]

In the first years of her Senate term, Duckworth received high marks not only from supporters and Democratic colleagues but also from institutions evaluating her effectiveness as a legislator. According to the Center for Effective Lawmaking (CEL), a joint partnership between the University of Virginia Frank Batten School of Leadership and Public Policy and Vanderbilt University, Duckworth achieved a Legislative Effectiveness Score (LES) of "Exceeds Expectations" as a first-term senator in the 115th Congress (2017–2018). Among the forty-eight Democratic senators in the 115th Congress, Duckworth's LES ranked eleventh. Specifically, the universities credited her with passage of "three of her 45 proposed bills into law, including the Veterans Small Business Enhancement Act of 2018."[76]

Conclusion

In 2011, sculptor Don Morris unveiled his completed work to the Mount Vernon, Illinois, community. With support from the Daughters of the American Revolution and local organizations, Morris crafted a statue with two female figures to honor women veterans and servicemembers. On the right is Molly Pitcher brandishing her stick and rammer ready to load the cannons of the Revolutionary War. On the left, a resolute Duckworth looks out toward the horizon, ready to take flight. The sculpture and monument are one of only a few in the world dedicated to female veterans, connecting women who served in the past with those who serve in the present.

When asked about the role of women servicemembers in today's military, Duckworth does not equivocate:

> Our military can no longer exist and perform its duties and its missions without its female servicemembers. Not going to be able to do it. Female servicemembers are so integrated into the military, so critical and vital to all functions of the military, from combat service support to combat support, to direct combat, that we could not go to war as a nation, we could not defend America, without our women.[77]

Duckworth wants Americans and their leadership to recognize that "America's daughters are fully capable of doing their jobs and fighting for freedom."[78] She has never had the desire to be recognized as the "first female anything," only to be credited with equal competence when warranted and allowed to assume an equal level of risk when required.

Her rising political profile also earned Duckworth consideration as a running mate for Democratic presidential nominee Biden in the 2020 election. Jon Soltz, chair of VoteVets, which has close ties to Duckworth and supported her candidacy in 2016, observed that Duckworth and Biden have much in common, especially because both have suffered horrendous tragedies. "If Joe Biden is looking for somebody who will be a loyal partner we can trust, who hasn't attacked him, who helps bring the base along but also protects our majority and helps us take back the Senate, who is consistent with him on policy positions, Tammy Duckworth would be a phenomenal choice," Soltz said.[79]

Though Duckworth was not selected for the 2020 ticket, her position on the short list of candidates among other high-profile women indicates the potential for her to play a leading role in US politics in the coming years. She acknowledges that she "stands on the shoulders of the women before me who broke through," creating new opportunities in both the military and public service.[80] And like those women, Duckworth is breaking new paths for generations of servicewomen who will follow. In Duckworth's own words:

> It has been a long road to recovery. But life does go on. Sometimes it takes dealing with a disability—the trauma, the relearning, the months of rehabilitation therapy—to uncover our true abilities and how we can put them to work for us in ways we may have never imagined. It's not about what we lost. But it's about the way our eyes have been opened to new talents and new abilities that we can now put to use in building productive and rewarding lives.[81]

Her optimism, intensity, tenacity, and determination enabled her to break barriers and challenge long-standing assumptions about women in combat, politics, and parenthood.

5

Joni Ernst wants voters to know that she is a mother, a soldier, and a leader. She believes that she has a mandate from the voters of Iowa, where she was born and raised among Hawkeye farming communities, to take on Washington, DC, and deliver on her pledge to "Make 'em Squeal." As the first woman elected to federal office from Iowa, the first combat veteran, and now one of the first Republican women to serve on the prestigious Senate Judiciary Committee, she draws on her experiences as a farmer, a soldier, and a mother to shape her conservative perspective on US politics and government.

Farmer

In the introduction to her memoir, *Daughter of the Heartland*, Ernst describes herself as "Farmer, Soldier, Mother, and Senator." Born in Red Oak, Iowa, in July 1970, Ernst has spent most of her life in the heartland. With the exceptions of her military deployments and current work in the nation's capitol, she has lived in or near Montgomery County, Iowa. Her grandparents owned a farm north of Stanton, and her parents, the Culvers, continued that tradition, growing soybeans and corn and raising hogs. Their family belonged to the main church in Stanton, the Mamrelund Lutheran Church, which Ernst still attends today.

Like most kids growing up in the rural Midwest, Ernst and her siblings participated in agricultural community organizations such as the Future Farmers of America (FFA), and they helped their family and neighbors on local farms. But the 1980s were a challenging decade for the small, family-owned farm. In 1979, an embargo by the Union of Soviet Socialist Republics (USSR) led to a sharp decline in US exports, more than 20 percent between 1981 and 1983.[1] Yet, agricultural production during that same period set record highs, and by the early 1980s, commodity prices fell sharply. Farm debt across the United States grew to $215 billion by 1984, double the amount for 1978. The problem was further compounded by the fact that interest rates in the United States had risen to nearly 21 percent, and the Federal Reserve adopted monetary policies that caused farmland value to drop by almost 60 percent.[2] This led to a farm recession, particularly for those in the Midwest who carried substantial debt. As if the economic circumstances were not dire enough, a drought swept through the southeastern United States in 1986 and continued through the Midwest in 1988.

During these difficult years, Ernst's parents sought outside sources of income when their farm struggled; her father did construction work on the side, and her mother worked first as a secretary for their church, then for a local car dealer, and eventually in the office of the Montgomery County treasurer in Red Oak. Beyond her own family's financial struggles, Ernst recalls, "in the face of hardship, the community came together."[3] In her memory and her experience, when members of the community struggled, other farmers or families offered support with a simple, "Don't worry. We've got this."[4]

Although community efforts might have ensured that crops were harvested and livestock tended, they offered only limited support for mental health. The economic hardships, seasonal isolation, exposure to hazardous agricultural chemicals and working conditions, and other workload pressures of farming contribute to a high rate of depression among farmers. Mike Rosman of the National Agriculture Safety Database also argues that certain character traits and social values among farm families perpetuate higher rates of mental health issues and suicide, including a "willingness to take risks, very high conscientiousness about work, [and] great capacity to persevere in the face of adversity and self-reliance."[5] When they suffer stress, most farmers work harder and keep their problems to themselves instead of reaching out for mental health support.

Ernst witnessed this growing up during a difficult decade in Iowa, and in 2018, along with Senator Tammy Baldwin (D-WI) and others representing midwestern states, she cosponsored FARMERS FIRST legislation to invest federal dollars in expanding access to mental health services to farming communities.[6]

Ernst credits her experiences growing up on a farm as the training ground for both her military service and public service careers. "On the farm, every person is part of a larger purpose," she writes.[7] The commodities they grow and their culture of relying on other members of the community rather than government-supported social safety nets made her feel as though her family was contributing to the larger nation, right from her farm in the southwestern corner of Iowa. This ethos also guided her decision to enroll at Iowa State University (ISU) and study psychology after high school. Ernst was a strong student, a self-described "bookworm," and she was also part of the first generation in her family to attend college.[8] She recalls that she did well in her first semester at ISU but that her relationship with her first serious boyfriend, from Stanton, was becoming increasingly unhealthy. Ernst has publicly shared that the issues escalated to the point of sexual assault when her boyfriend raped her during a visit home from college in her second semester. Embarrassed and traumatized, Ernst reached out to a sexual assault counseling center hotline but chose not to report the rape to authorities. The experience affected her focus, her academic performance, and her daily activities. Like many other farmers in Iowa plowing through the 1980s, she tried to bury her discontent. "Internally, I struggled, but I acted as if everything was okay."[9]

Though Ernst was privately struggling, it was not long before a new opportunity would change the course of her personal and professional journey. A friend of her mother's shared an advertisement in the Iowa Farm Bureau Spokesman recruiting participants for a two-week agricultural exchange with Ukraine.[10] The initiative was sponsored by the Iowa Peace Institute (IPI) in Grinnell, a nonprofit organization established in 1986 in response to the farm economy crisis. Educators, business leaders, and government officials in Iowa wanted to address cold war tensions and global conflict that threatened Iowa's agricultural economy. They initially focused on international peace-building projects, such as facilitating encounters between conflicting groups and hosting international visitors and interns from Bulgaria, Cameroon, Ghana, Japan, Russia, and other countries. The IPI hoped its efforts would not only foster cross-cultural understanding but also allow international groups to experience Iowa communities and build relationships with Iowa businesses. In 2003, the IPI was moved to Grinnell College as part of the foundation for the Peace Studies program (now Peace and Conflict Studies).

The IPI sponsorship of cross-cultural exchanges also supported larger national discussions about agricultural policy and thawing tensions with the Soviet Union. Working groups from the United States and Soviet Union met in Washington, DC, from September 1987 onward, where they negotiated two-year cooperative exchange programs in the areas of agricultural materials, science, and information. This planning process continued through 1989, as the House Committee on Appropriations Subcommittee on Rural Development, Agriculture, and Related Agencies held hearings about the promise of supporting US-USSR foreign exchange programs.[11] Organizations representing farmers and agricultural interests paid careful attention to these programs, encouraging their members at the annual convention of the American Farm Bureau Federation to think in terms of world markets. During the congressional hearings, Representative Jamie Whitten (D-MS) testified that his state, for example, was about to send thirty-one teams to the Soviet Union on foreign exchange: seventeen of those teams were specifically in the field of agricultural research and technology; fourteen were involved with economic issues.[12] The two- to three-week programs were open to US Department of Agriculture (USDA) officials; university researchers, faculty, and students; representatives from the private sector; and members of farm communities. Under the Science and Technology Cooperation (STC) Division agreement, each country would fund its own participants, a "sending-side-pays" agreement that covered costs of travel and in-country accommodations.[13]

For a student experiencing a personal crisis, the opportunity to travel 5,500 miles from Stanton, Iowa, to Lozuvatka, Ukraine, provided a much-needed change of scenery. Ernst decided to write the essay application and "go for it." She wrote about "the importance of keeping an open mind and learning to work together regardless of the differences" between the United States and Ukraine. Ernst was selected, along with eighteen others from Iowa, to live and work on collective farms alongside their host families. With a limited orientation and no familiarity with the language or culture, they travelled from Des Moines to Moscow with their Russian-English dictionaries and a student-translator from Georgetown University.[14]

The exchange students, including Ernst, arrived in what historians have described as a "politically volatile republic." The Soviet Union promoted russification policies to continue asserting its influence throughout the 1980s, and nationalist Ukrainian leaders pushed back with language laws that recognized Ukrainian as the official state language. The Chernobyl nuclear power reactor exploded in 1986, sending shock waves through the region, and mass protests swept from Kyiv to Lviv in 1988. Mikhail Gorbachev's policy of *perestroika* was never fully implemented in Ukraine in practice, and the Soviet state still owned nearly 95 percent of industry and agriculture in 1990. The economy stagnated in the late 1980s, and mine workers began to spontaneously strike in summer 1989.[15]

Despite the simmering tensions, Ukraine was a strategic location for an agricultural exchange between the United States and the Soviet Union. Recognized as the "nation's breadbasket," it held special agricultural importance with the USSR.[16] Ukraine, which in 1989 "held only 15 percent of the arable land area and 4.6 percent of the total agricultural land area, in the same year produced 26 percent of Soviet grain output, 53.3 percent of sugar beet output, 26.7 percent of potato output, and more than 20 percent of livestock production."[17] According to agricultural and land reform studies, the country possesses "one-third of the world's chernozem (black earth) soils, and these account for one-third of the total agricultural land area in Ukraine."[18] These natural resources, combined with its strategic geographic position and population of 50 million people in 1989, made Ukraine "one of the most critically important republics" in the Soviet Union.

To reach their destination, Ernst's group flew to Moscow, traveled fourteen hours by train to Kyiv, and then traveled from Kyiv to the "May 1st Collective Farm" in Lozuvatka.[19] Working side-by-side with her Ukrainian host family, Ernst contrasted her new surroundings with her life in the United States and shared her perspective on her home culture with Ukrainian groups as part of discussion panels. Questions about US democracy and governance led Ernst to believe "a fundamental shift" was happening across the Soviet Union.[20] The following year, her family hosted members of the Ukrainian exchange families in the United States and introduced them to life in Iowa. Ernst emphasizes, "The whole experience changed me. . . . I decided I couldn't take my freedom for granted as I always had. I think the seeds of my future public service were sown in the awakening that came from that exposure to a wider world."[21]

Soldier

When Ernst returned from her exchange journey to the Ukraine, her renewed confidence gave her the strength to separate from her abusive boyfriend and seek new opportunities to expand her horizons at ISU. With the encouragement of some of her friends in the Reserve Officer's Training Corps (ROTC), she enrolled for classes in military science. She enjoyed the military subjects and felt that she found a community of students with similar values; Ernst signed a contract and earned a two-year ROTC scholarship covering all her expenses at ISU.[22]

Her family expressed some reservations about her decision. Her father had briefly served in the Iowa Army National Guard as a mechanic and felt that the military would prevent Ernst from growing as an individual. Undeterred, Ernst completed her two years of ROTC at ISU, including basic training at Fort Knox, in Kentucky. The intense program included demanding physical training (PT) exercises, disorienting chemical training in mission-oriented protective posture (MOPP) suits, marksmanship, and tedious chores to help maintain the women's barracks. Drill sergeants shouted at her and her colleagues as they worked through these preparatory activities, in some cases bringing other cadets to tears as they were barraged by profanities. Ernst believes this experience not only prepared her to tolerate military life out in the field but also shaped her own vision of leadership. "I swore to myself that I would never be like either one of those individuals—the drill sergeant, harsh and unyielding; or the cadet, weeping and shamed in the face of adversity," she wrote.[23]

Ernst met her first husband, Gail, during her time at ISU. Nearly two decades her senior when they met, Gail was a supervisor with the Ranger Challenge Team, a divorcé, and father of two. They shared a military lifestyle, balancing Gail's orders to relocate to different military bases across the country with her own continuing service in ROTC, graduate studies in public administration at Columbus College, and efforts to build a professional career in the civilian workforce.

One of Ernst's first positions after completing her master's degree was providing career and professional counseling to soldiers transitioning from the military to civilian life. According to the Pew Research Center, "While more than seven-in-ten veterans (72%) report they had an easy time readjusting to civilian life, 27% say re-entry was difficult for them— a proportion that swells to 44% among veterans who served in the ten years since the Sept. 11, 2001, terrorist attacks."[24] These difficulties might include preparing to enter the workforce, creating structure, dealing with ambiguity, adjusting to a different pace of life, and gaining access to services. By helping soldiers with résumé writing, career coaching, professional wardrobes, and networking, Ernst felt as though she was providing a "valuable service."[25] She continued this work when her family relocated to Columbia, South Carolina, and she was able to secure a similar position with Midlands Technical College—only this time, she applied her skills to assisting long-term unemployed adults with transitions into new careers.

Mother

During the first six months of Ernst's first pregnancy, her spouse was on assignment in Saudi Arabia. She was working full time in her position at Midlands Technical College and actively participating in her reserve unit in Fort Jackson. At times, Ernst felt lonely, and she chose to spend her time at a local Department of Veterans Affairs (VA) nursing facility. When Gail returned from overseas, they relocated for his Ranger Camp assignment at Eglin Air Force Base in western Florida. Ernst recalls that she had the chance to meet her new doctor once before she gave birth to Libby.[26] Like many first-time mothers, Ernst was excited about the arrival of her beautiful daughter, but she also struggled with breastfeeding and long nights of caring for her colicky newborn. Gail worked long hours, and despite support from her "military family" and a parenting community of officers' wives and enlisted women, Ernst struggled privately, sharing, "Fortunately, I got through it."[27]

When Gail retired from the military, Ernst and her family moved back to Red Oak, and she transferred from the Reserves to the Iowa National Guard. Ernst writes that, unlike her choice to join ROTC or the Reserves, her decision to become part of the National Guard "wasn't about getting college benefits or even about being heroic. I understood the risks and didn't take them lightly." The National Guard allowed Ernst to continue to serve on a part-time basis and pursue a civilian career; it also meant the possibility of deployment. She accepted these risks because she had "a desire to give back and be part of something" that differentiated her from everyone else.[28]

Ernst started her work with the National Guard as a supply officer for a battalion and then moved to the 1168th Transportation Company, which supported the logistical needs of other companies. By 2002, she earned a promotion to company commander.[29] Although Ernst was incredibly proud of earning the position, it meant more time and responsibilities with the National Guard, which would further divide her attention from her family. She also recognized the challenges of assuming a leadership role in a majority male military company in which she was the only woman officer. She was the first female company commander of that particular unit and observed that the lack of other women officers meant she needed to develop her own leadership style. Women serving in leadership roles often face what is known as the *double bind*. If a female leader acts in a strong and assertive manner or exhibits "masculine" traits, she might be judged or seen as abrasive and not well liked. If she acts in a nice, caring, supportive way or exhibits "feminine" traits, she might not be well respected or seen as a leader.[30] As an institution, the military fosters an environment in which masculine characteristics are the norm, and this can lead to a tremendous dilemma for women.[31] The pressure to exhibit effective leadership within the armed forces, where it is critical for mission success, is particularly high. Military leaders provide purpose, direction, and motivation while operating to accomplish the mission; in field operations, this can be a matter of life or death.

Ernst recognized these challenges and struggled with whether she should try to emulate the leadership styles of the other commanding officers she observed and trained under, or if she should craft a more authentic leadership style that represented her unique position as a female company commander. Even the colonels who promoted her admitted, "I just didn't know how to mentor a woman."[32] Ernst discussed the issues of gender and mentorship years later with a noncommissioned officer (NCO), the first female who went into the infantry for the National Guard, and the NCO explained, "I don't need somebody to tell me how to be a woman. I already know how to do that. I need somebody to teach me how to be an infantryman."[33] Ernst echoed these sentiments, later writing, "I told him (one of the colonels) that it wasn't that I needed a woman mentor. I just needed to know how to be a leader. I think a lot of men get too wrapped up in gender in the military. The way I saw it, a soldier is a soldier. It doesn't matter your gender. You still have the same job to do."[34]

Initially, Ernst chose to adopt a more assertive leadership style, writing that she "learned quickly that because it was such a boys' club, I would have to be assertive. I was still nice, but all business."[35] But as she grew more comfortable in her role as a commander and built a rapport with both men and women in her company, she transitioned to a more authentic leadership style, in which she felt comfortable leveraging her gender and role as a mother:

> In fact, being a woman could be an advantage. Taking care of my troops was an instinct. They were very much like part of my family, and some of the younger kids were almost like my children. I wanted the best for them. I wanted them to behave. I wanted them to work hard. I encouraged them when they needed encouragement. I disciplined them when they needed discipline.[36]

Ernst's philosophy of leadership was tested in the field when the 1168th Transportation Company deployed during the Iraq War. In January 2003, Secretary of Defense Donald Rumsfeld announced that the United States would increase troop presence in the Middle East, though Ernst notes that there were several hints or indications throughout fall 2002 that this increase was coming. The company received its alert notification, and in February 2003, its 183 soldiers went to Camp Dodge to begin administrative processes and preparations.[37] These citizen-soldiers, sent to Iraq by the Iowa National Guard through 2007, were one group of the nearly 10,000 troops, serving in support roles such as logistics, operations, and medical services. According to reports, by the time the war started in Iraq, the number of National Guard and reserve troops on active duty was 188,592, the "largest reserve call-up" since the 1991 Gulf War.[38]

Before deployment, Ernst's company received eight weeks of training at Fort McCoy, an army installation on 60,000 acres in Monroe County, Wisconsin, near the Iowa border. Because the National Guard troops would be deployed to combat zones, the training was rigorous; they needed to be as prepared as fighting forces, including receiving an introduction to Iraqi customs and intercultural training.

When Ernst and her company arrived in Kuwait on April 18, 2003, the scene was "pure chaos."[39] Thousands and thousands of US troops packed into Camp Wolf, a staging post in the central region of Kuwait on the grounds of Kuwait International Airport. Ernst's company was originally attached to a company going to Iraq through Turkey, but the route through Turkey never received formal approval by the Turkish government.[40] The US government requested access to use Turkish airspace and Turkish bases for launching the military campaign to attack northern Iraq. However, on March 1, the Turkish Parliament passed a resolution that only allowed the United States authorization to fly aircraft over Turkey. It did not allow the United States to use aircraft based in Turkey or to use Turkish territory for refueling.[41] As an alternative, between 2003 and 2004 Camp Wolf became the launching point for most military personnel and supplies headed to northern Iraq in support of Operation Iraqi Freedom.[42] The staging post was not equipped to support the layovers of tens of thousands of troops for weeks at a time. They slept nearly on top of each other in massive tents without access to showers or hygiene facilities. Although it was April, the region was extremely hot, with average temperatures well above 85 degrees Fahrenheit. Troops were constantly on the move, particularly in the transportation and logistics division. They worried about everything from scorpions in their combat boots to explosives and ambushes. Ernst recalls, "The whole Army was learning in the field, because this was a very different kind of battlefront."[43] The company from Iowa eventually settled at Camp Arifjan, located south of Kuwait City. Divided into seven zones, the installation is built to accommodate elements of the US Air Force, US Navy, US Marine Corps, and US Coast Guard in addition to National Guard and Reserve units that provide support. It is the largest army post in Kuwait and was built with funding and support from the government of Kuwait.

During this fluid, evolving, often volatile context, Ernst was responsible for the morale, discipline, and service of her company. She and her company happened to be assigned to the South Camden Yards, an international camp that also included about 500 Ukrainian soldiers.[44] Ernst was assigned the position of "mayor" at Camp Camden Years, which meant she was responsible for all the logistics. Reflecting on her position as a company commander and then mayor of the sizable subcamp, Ernst found being a woman in a war zone "both gratifying and challenging." As mayor, she had more access to communication technology and could try calling home to talk to Libby and her husband, but the technology was "rudimentary," and it was difficult to build a connection with her then three-year-old daughter over the phone.[45]

She was also conscious of the ways in which her gender as well as her status as a citizen-soldier affected her relationships and authority with troops outside of her own company. In recalling an issue of blatant sexual harassment, Ernst explained that her company was freestanding and did not have a battalion commander. This meant she had to attend briefings for the area support group they were attached to in Iraq. During those meetings, a commander from another battalion would wink at her and give her suggestive looks. She recalls that initially "it was annoying, but no big deal." After the meetings, though, he would catch up to her and "start a very insistent pitch." The commander became so persistent and aggressive that a male first sergeant from her company intervened when he observed the behavior. This frustrated Ernst, who later wrote, "I realized that even though I was a commander, I was vulnerable just for being a woman, and that infuriated me. What right did some commander have to take advantage of his rank to harass me?"[46]

This lack of respect from other commanders also signaled to troops that this behavior toward women in the military was acceptable. In yet another example, Ernst recalls a run-in with a group of soldiers who "would hang out around the female shower trailer, taking pictures every time the door opened." She called them out on their behavior, and they ignored her, even though she outranked them. Angry and embarrassed, Ernst was forced to call on a maintenance sergeant from her team, "a big, burly guy," to enforce her orders.[47]

Ernst believes that her experiences as a woman in the armed forces, including those described above, provide her perspective both as a military leader and a future public servant. By traveling dangerous, unpredictable transportation routes while deployed to northern Iraq, she learned about the importance of up-armoring vehicles and the necessity of properly fitting, potentially life-saving body armor for men and women in combat zones. Body armor designed for men in combat did not fit women well, and poorly fitting body armor was among the leading causes of injury for women in war zones. Without her on-ground experiences and perspective, she might not have been prepared later to introduce the Female Body Armor Modernization Act (2019), along with Senator Tammy Duckworth, Senator Martha McSally, and Senator Richard Blumenthal, and made it a point to address this inequity later in her public service career.[48]

After Ernst completed her service requirements in Iraq and returned home to Red Oak in April 2004, she continued to navigate gendered perceptions of women's role in the military. There were misconceptions about her role in Iraq—as a member of a support unit, a woman, and a transportation specialist: "I was a combat veteran, but some people didn't see me that way."[49] At a ceremony she attended shortly after returning home, a member of the Women's Auxiliary League of the Veterans of Foreign Wars (VFW) invited her to join their organization. When she stated that she would just join the VFW, the woman responded, "You can't do that. The VFW is only for men."[50] Yet, in similar ways to how she applied lessons from combat to advocate for women in the military, Ernst felt that her gender and her identity as a mother allowed her to serve as a citizen-soldier in authentic ways. After she was back in Iowa, as a military leader in the National Guard, she had the responsibility of notifying next of kin in the area when a loved one passed away in the line of duty. She shares a particularly memorable moment in her memoir when she was able to empathize with the mother of a soldier killed abroad. The chaplain accompanying her shared, "I was really moved by the way you sat and cried with that mother, as a mother yourself, and that you took the time to look at her pictures."[51]

Ernst's status as a citizen-soldier in the National Guard, performing a supportive role in transportation and logistics, was also misunderstood or devalued both by civilians and other members of the military. Some Americans perceived the National Guard as a strictly domestic force and did not realize the extent to which troops were deployed to Kuwait and Iraq between 2003 and 2007. After they were overseas, some infantrymen felt their work was more important or valuable because of their branch designation or combat engagement. Ernst describes the ways in which she and other members of the National Guard, upon returning home to Iowa, struggled with feelings of isolation and lack of supportive services. A key difference between citizen-soldiers of the National Guard and other areas of the military is its members go their separate ways, back to civilian jobs, when they return. Members of other divisions of the military, depending on their status, stay together as a unit. Given the disbursement of National Guard members, particularly in rural areas with low population density, some soldiers returning home felt isolated: "In those years, we were pretty much left on our own to deal with any emotional issues. The mental health screenings were perfunctory." Ernst struggled with these issues personally and witnessed it in members across her company. In turn, she vowed to try to find ways to support men and women at home in Iowa as she had done in the field: "I didn't know yet that this support would come from the path of government service."[52]

Conservative

When Ernst's family moved back to Red Oak following Gail's retirement from the military, she became "nominally involved" with the county Republican organization and in local government. She writes that her parents had voted Republican, but she did not consider herself political or a partisan while growing up. Her first opportunity to engage in electoral politics as a candidate arose while she was still deployed to Iraq; the local Republican Party approached her family to see if she might be interested in running for county auditor when she returned home. At the center of county operations, the county auditor has oversight of the financial records for all coffers in the county. This includes maintaining financial records, preparing the budget, scheduling public hearings, and paying bills.

In Montgomery County, the person in this position also serves as commissioner of elections and is responsible for real estate transfers.

The auditor serving at the time, Connie Magneson, held the position for twenty-four years, and by the time of the election, the office was the site of significant controversy. Magneson had a volatile personality and was at one point accused of assaulting the female county supervisor after a budget meeting.[53] Needless to say, she was a tough political opponent. Ernst sought advice from friends at ISU involved in state politics, as well as Kim Reynolds, someone who considers her "ideal for public service."[54] After talking it over with friends who had experience in local politics, Ernst felt more prepared to enter the race when she returned from Iraq in April 2004. She saw the "call of public service in government as a natural step." It was more than a career or a temporary position; like her military service with the National Guard, "it was an expression of patriotic duty."[55]

Ernst won the election against Magneson and served as county auditor for six years before considering her next political move, candidacy for the Iowa Senate.[56] Friends in local politics once again encouraged her to run and pursue the open seat, but her family situation weighed heavily on her decision not to enter the race. Ernst was a survivor of domestic violence and discloses a serious physical episode in her memoir. After the incident, Ernst wondered about "her own culpability" in the violence and fretted over her family's privacy. Concerned that "in this small town, it would have taken about five minutes for word to get out" if she went to the hospital, she felt obligated to conceal the situation as a "soldier, a leader of men and women" with a "brave face befitting my public image."[57]

Reynolds won the race to represent the Forty-Eighth District in the Iowa Senate in 2008, and in 2010 she was tapped to run as lieutenant governor with Terry Branstad. When the seat came open a second time, Ernst's friends and colleagues in the Republican Party tried to recruit her once again. Beyond the volatile relationship with Gail, Ernst shares that her identity as a mother was a primary consideration in whether she should run the second time: "The timing isn't great. Libby's in elementary school now, and I should stick closer to home."[58] On the one hand, the capitol building in Des Moines is a two-hour drive from Red Oak. With sessions running from January to April, Monday through Thursday, winning election meant Ernst would have to spend significantly more time away from home. On the other hand, knowing that Libby would see her mother's leadership in public service helped convince Ernst to take the leap: "I hoped she would come to see me as a model for what was possible for women."[59]

She won the special election for Reynolds's seat in January 2011 with 67.5 percent of the vote.[60] After redistricting, she won the newly drawn Iowa Senate Twelfth District in 2012, unopposed.[61] The structure of the Iowa Senate is informal, with only fifty members in the upper house. Senators do not have designated individual office space unless they occupy a leadership position and must work from the floor of the Senate chamber. Their staff consists of one clerk each, and most senators handle their own correspondence and schedule their own meetings. Ernst enjoyed the informal context and eventually earned a position as the assistant minority leader in the upper chamber, a partisan role working with the minority leader to advance the party's agenda in the legislature.

Ernst drew attention from Iowa media during her first year in the Iowa Senate when she took a strong position in support of the proposed 2011 Stolen Valor Act. The bill initially mirrored a 2006 federal law that made it a crime to falsely represent one's military service. Following suit, the Iowa bill made it a criminal offense to falsely claim receipt of military honors, decorations, or medals, with enhanced punishments for more distinguished medals.[62] When Senate Majority Leader Mike Gronstal expressed concerns about free speech, Ernst issued an impassioned defense of the proposed law:

> We are calling this the Stolen Valor Act because that is exactly what we are attempting to stop—the theft of honor earned in wartime by everyday Iowans who went above and beyond the call of duty. I understand that some of my colleagues from across the aisle are concerned that this act would infringe upon the right to free speech. I cannot begin to comprehend your hesitation in this specific instance.[63]

She acknowledged their concerns regarding free speech but felt that the law did not infringe upon individual rights and likened the act of falsely representing one's service to false claims associated with identity theft, slander, and intellectual property theft. During debate, she also invoked her own record of service to further add credibility to her position: "You cannot possibly know the devastation of war simply by watching *Platoon* or *Saving Private Ryan*. You cannot know what it feels like to lose a life that you are charged with, or what it is to take a life. Even as a veteran, I do not know those things, and I do not want to know."[64] In response, the Democratic majority leader accused Ernst of making remarks that were "a bit extreme."[65] In the end, Iowa passed legislation making it a crime to impersonate a decorated military veteran, and the federal government followed suit with a parallel federal bill, also named the Stolen Valor Act, signed into law by President Barack Obama in 2013.

Following these early moments in the spotlight, Ernst continued to balance her career in public service with her military service, and she was able to take on greater positions of leadership in both venues. In addition to being assistant minority leader in the Iowa Senate, Ernst was promoted to battalion commander for one of the combat sustainment support battalions in the Iowa National Guard. She was content serving in both capacities until 2014, when Senator Tom Harkin (D-IA) announced his retirement. Though Ernst was tempted to pursue the open seat, she initially felt that "the opportunity rightly belonged to Kim Reynolds, if she wanted it."[66] But Reynolds planned to seek reelection as lieutenant governor alongside Governor Branstad in 2014. With Reynolds's blessing and the support of her family, as well as endorsements from other Republicans, Ernst announced her candidacy for the US Senate.

On the steps of the Montgomery County Courthouse in Red Oak, Ernst introduced herself to voters in what would become her signature refrain: "As a mother, soldier, and conservative, these Iowa values are what I hold dear. And they're threatened by the failed values of Washington."[67] Ernst's identity as a woman seeking the open seat was significant. She was the only woman to enter the race from either political party; at least four men entered the field.[68] If her candidacy was successful, she would be the first woman elected to represent Iowa in either house of Congress.

Moreover, Ernst emphasized her gender and openly spoke about her identity as a mother when introducing herself to potential voters or when framing public policy positions. This approach became popular among female candidates between 2014 and 2018, as observed by journalist Annika Neklason: "Moms are not only seeking political seats, but seeking them explicitly, and proudly, as moms; in this year's election cycle, motherhood has become an asset to be flaunted in progressive campaigns, resolving a decades-old tension for women seeking to enter electoral politics."[69] Although visual and verbal appeals to motherhood have always been a part of US politics, Susan Carroll of the Center for American Women and Politics believes that they might have new relevance in the current political climate. At a political moment in which voters are seeking authentic, "outsider" candidates, Carroll argues that these female candidates use their experience as mothers "to seem authentic and to really say, 'Well, these politicians in Washington are totally out of touch. They just don't understand your lives, and I do. I'm here struggling with the same issues and confronting the same issues as you.'"[70] This approach to political authenticity was at the very heart of Ernst's "Mother. Soldier. Conservative, in an Iowa-sort-of-way" campaign.

To help with her messaging, Ernst hired a veteran Republican strategist, Todd Harris. In one of their working interviews, she shared stories about her childhood—growing up on a farm and castrating hogs. Harris was both dumbfounded and fixated by Ernst's hog castration story. He took time to search YouTube videos about the process.[71] They kept coming back to the connections between Ernst's conservative message on cutting Washington spending ("pork") and her Iowa, political outsider identity ("farmer"), and they decided to test the message at an upcoming debate with her Democratic opponent, Bruce Braley. She threw out the prepared line, "Well, you know, I grew up castrating hogs, so I know how to cut pork," and the audience roared with laughter.[72] They produced the ad titled "Make 'em Squeal," showing Ernst standing in front of hog pens: "I'm Joni Ernst. I grew up castrating hogs on an Iowa farm. So, when I get to Washington, I'll know how to cut pork"—and a hog squeals.

The ad generated significant national name recognition for Ernst. She recalls a moment the day after the ad aired: "I was walking into a library in Des Moines for an event when I got a text from the campaign: 'Oh, man, Jimmy Fallon played your ad on the *Late Show*.' Then, a second text: 'Stephen Colbert talked about your ad on his show.'"[73] Colbert, in his character as a conservative talk show host, said, "Joni, you had me at castration. Folks, it does not matter what else she stands for. I am pulling for her whole hog, or whatever is left of the hog when she's done with it.'" But he also embedded jokes and commentary about her identity as a woman candidate: "I mean, while the other little girls were reading *Charlotte's Web*, Joni was out back with ten-snips making a soprano out of Wilbur," and, "Folks, when it came time to play with Barbies, Joni took one look down Ken's pants and said, 'My work here is done.'" [74] Ernst recalls watching the clip, and it made her laugh. [75]

Daytime shows and morning programs such as *Good Morning America* featured the ad as part of their reporting on the election. Almost over-night, Ernst became the "'Make 'em Squeal' lady" or "the pig lady." [76] She was struggling to raise money and polling in second place to Mark Jacobs in February 2014, prior to the national attention generated by the ad. [77] Two months later, a Suffolk University poll showed her with a narrow lead and momentum. [78] Although her porcine-themed ad helped her establish a presence in a crowded five-way primary race, it would not be enough. She needed to continue refining her conservative message to appeal to Repub-lican primary voters in Iowa. Her second campaign ad, "Shot," featured Ernst on her Harley Davidson motorcycle as well as scenes of her engaged in staged target practice. The narrator reminds viewers that "Joni Ernst is not your typical candidate." It introduces her as "Conservative Joni Ernst. Mom. Farm girl. And a Lt. Colonel who carries more than just lipstick in her purse." The ad reinforces her identity as a political outsider who will take on establishment politics and dismantle the health-care policies of the Obama administration.

By May 2014, Ernst was labeled a "strong front-runner" in the Republi-can primary. [79] Creative political ads introduced Ernst to local and state au-diences. She drew endorsements from high-profile Republicans such as Mitt Romney and Sarah Palin early in the race. [80] As poll numbers shifted, she drew criticism and attacks from her opponents. Jacobs, the former CEO of Reliant Energy and a Republican primary candidate, created the website JoniErnstExposed.com and put out a statement shortly before the primary accusing Ernst of being "AWOL" from the state legislature and missing some votes: "There are work horses. There are show horses. And then there are no-show horses. Joni Ernst missed 42 percent of the votes in the Iowa Senate this year. And now she wants a promotion?" [81] The web-site listed votes Ernst missed, stating, "It's important to get the facts out about her record of being AWOL from the Iowa Senate." Research by the

Joni Ernst, as an Iowa Republican Senate candidate, campaigns at the 2014 Iowa State Fair Soapbox in Des Moines, Iowa, on August 8, 2014. *Source:* Photo by Tom Williams, *Congressional Quarterly Roll Call* via AP Images.

Des Moines Register found that Ernst missed a series of votes to fulfill her National Guard duties and attend GOP campaign fund-raising events.[82] Jacobs's approach drove down his favorability ratings and drew rebukes from Republican veterans of war. Senator John McCain sent a statement to the *Des Moines Register* condemning the remarks.[83]

In June 2014, Ernst emerged from the Republican primary with 56.12 percent of the vote, three times the votes received by her closest competitors.[84] She then ran as the Republican nominee against Braley in the November general election, a race that garnered significant national attention: "I was fully aware that it wasn't just my election that was at stake. The Senate was at stake."[85] Republican heavy-hitters such as Romney, Marco Rubio, Rand Paul, and Lindsey Graham visited the Iowa State Fair to stump for Ernst. Graham said of her, "It would be nice to have somebody in the Senate who doesn't talk about boots on the ground but has had her boots on the ground." Many of these Republicans also floated the possibility of a presidential run in 2016; getting a head start introducing themselves to Iowans did not hurt their chances in the early caucus state.

Likewise, Braley received visits and support from Bill and Hillary Clinton, Michelle Obama, and Elizabeth Warren.[86]

Ernst was invited to give the Weekly Republican Address in July 2014, though she had to record the message in advance of leaving for her annual two-week National Guard duty. She began her introduction using a familiar refrain: "I'm a mother and grandmother, a soldier, and proud to be Iowa's Republican nominee for U.S. Senate."[87] She shared her experience in the military, the lessons of growing up in farm country, what she witnessed during her two-week immersion in Ukraine, and her conservative values: "Growing up on that southwest Iowa farm, my family didn't have much. My mother canned our food and made our clothes—teaching us the lessons of not spending what you don't have. In our small town, we relied on each other—our neighbors lent us a helping hand when we needed it, and we would do the same in their time of need."[88]

There could not have been a greater contrast between the candidate image of Ernst and that of Braley. Braley also attended ISU and later went on to earn his law degree. He was a trial attorney before election to the House of Representatives in 2007. Because Ernst positioned herself as a political outsider with humble beginnings, voters in Iowa saw Braley as an extension of the "Washington establishment" and an elitist. Frequent campaign gaffes reinforced this perception and made him appear out of touch. During the federal government shutdown in October 2013, for example, he complained to a reporter, "There's no towel service, and so we're doing our own laundry down here." The comments resurfaced and circulated widely during the 2014 Senate campaign, and it gave Ernst an opening to contrast her own experience: "I took pleasure in talking about how many loads of laundry I did a week, all while serving in the state Senate, drilling for the National Guard, and raising my daughter. (Years later, when the Senate gym was affected the same way, I took the towels home and washed them myself. That's what real Iowans do—at least, Iowa women!)."[89] Braley also made national news when he criticized Senator Chuck Grassley (R-IA). Braley questioned how "an Iowa farmer who never went to law school" could become chair of the Senate Judiciary Committee.[90]

Ernst also believed the Democratic team and Braley targeted her in sexist ways. They ran campaign ads against her featuring a chirping chicken, a message she interpreted as "I was a crazy chick."[91] Leaked film from an October Democratic barbeque showed Senator Harkin saying, "Well, I hear so much about Joni Ernst. She is really attractive, and she sounds nice. Well, I got to thinking about that. I don't care if she's as good looking as Taylor Swift, or as nice as Mr. Rogers, but she votes like Michele Bachmann, she's wrong for the state of Iowa."[92] Ernst's husband also drew attention for sexist comments he made on Facebook. In reference to Secretary of Homeland Security Janet Napolitano, he wrote, "And am I suppose [sic] to give up my guns? As if! Traitorous skank!"[93] Referring to the Benghazi raid, he called Secretary of State Clinton a "lying hag."[94] Ernst made a statement condemning the remarks, and her husband issued an apology. Ernst explains, "Sexism is something women in public life have to contend with, but I've never been willing to let it go unchallenged."[95]

Through October 2014, most election reporting sites predicted the Ernst-Braley Senate race as a tossup because the candidates consistently polled within 3 percent to 5 percent of each other. The final election results showed a much larger margin, with Ernst earning 586,921 votes (52.2 percent) to Braley's 491,708 votes (43.7 percent).[96] In counties across the western and southern portion of Iowa, Ernst defeated Braley by three-to-one or four-to-one margins. Republicans gained her Senate seat as well as House seats across the state. Republicans Steve King, David Young, and Rod Blum were elected in three of the four House districts, and the fourth district went to Democrat Dave Loebsack. In the campaign's final weeks, Ernst hammered on linking Braley, a four-term US representative, with the ills of the federal government. Three out of five Iowa voters said they were either "dissatisfied" or "angry" with Obama's administration, according to CNN's exit polling. Of those voters, nearly four out of five voted for Ernst.[97] In her November 2014 victory speech, Ernst reminded voters of her humble beginnings as an "ordinary Iowan" who has had "extraordinary opportunities."[98] She pledged to remember her roots and "take the Iowa way all the way to Washington, D.C." Though it is a long way "from the biscuit line at Hardee's to the United States Senate,"[99] she promised voters that her values would remain consistent, and she would represent them to the best of her ability in her new public office.

Senator

As a US senator, Ernst defines herself as "a champion for Iowa, a defender of our armed forces, a voice for women, and an advocate for farmers and businesses."[100] Only two members of her first-term Senate class were women—herself and Republican Shelley Moore Capito, a former seven-term US representative from West Virginia. Moving from the Iowa Senate, where she had virtually no staff, to the US Senate meant Ernst needed to recruit a chief of staff, legislative director, staff to handle constituent services, a press secretary, a scheduler, and so on in addition to staffing her state offices in Des Moines, Davenport, Cedar Rapids, Sioux City, and Council Bluffs. Given the turnover of the seat from Democrat to Republican, Ernst also felt the need to do a complete staffing overhaul in the US Senate office. After a meeting in December 2014, she selected Lisa Goeas as her chief of staff based on her previous experience working with Senator Tim Hutchinson, the Small Business Administration, and the National Federation of Independent Businesses.[101]

During Ernst's Senate orientation, Majority Leader Mitch McConnell's (R-KY) office informed her that she had been selected to give the Republican response to President Obama's 2015 State of the Union address. The practice of an opposition response began in 1966, when Senator Everett Dirksen (R-IL) and Representative Gerald Ford (R-MI) appeared on TV to offer a response to the address by President Lyndon B. Johnson. Since 1982, the format and delivery of the opposition response has varied, but the remarks are typically offered by one or more party leaders (almost always senators, representatives, or governors) who are "nationally known or generally considered to be promising, emerging political figures."[102] The invitation to provide the remarks shined a spotlight on the junior senator from Iowa as an emerging party leader for the GOP.

Ernst's speech drew national attention not only for its role as part of the annual opposition response tradition but also for a particular personal story she chose to share. When Ernst was a child, her mother instructed her to wear bread bags over her shoes to protect them from rain puddles. Growing up on a small farm in the 1980s meant Ernst had one "good pair" of shoes, and she was expected to take care of them. News of her "bread bag speech" spread on social media like wildfire. Memes played with her campaign language, mocking "Joni Ernst: Mother, Soldier, Bread Bag Icon," and Twitter users created parody accounts with the names "@SenatorBreadBags" and "@JonisBreadBags," in addition to sharing images with the hashtag "#breadbags." In defense of Ernst, Peggy Noonan authored a piece for the *Wall Street Journal* in which she recalled a similar experience: "I liked what Ernst said because it was real. And it reminded me of the old days. . . . Response on the left to Ernst and the bread bags was snobbish, superior, and dumb to the point of embarrassing."[103] Likewise, Charlotte Allen authored a guest blog for the *Baltimore Sun*, chastising: "It's hard to say what coastal liberals think is funnier: the fact that Republican Sen. Joni Ernst's thrifty mother tied bread bags over her little girl's feet to protect her shoes on muddy days—or the fact that Ernst comes from Iowa, where the untutored rubes do things like that."[104]

The committee assignments Ernst received during her first term as a senator reflected areas of policy relevant to her Iowa constituents: the Armed Services Committee (chair of the Subcommittee on Emerging Threats and Capabilities); Agriculture, Nutrition, and Forestry Committee (chair of the Subcommittee on Rural Development and Energy); Homeland Security and Governmental Affairs Committee, later replaced with Environment and Public Works Committee (relevant to her constituency's interest in ethanol); and Small Business and Entrepreneurship Committee. In 2019, she added the Judiciary Committee, where she and Marsha Blackburn (R-TN) became the first Republican women to serve.

In terms of Ernst's legislative work, she and her staff debated which issues to tackle first. Ultimately, she believed veteran's issues would be the best fit. Because of the story of Richard Miles, a forty-one-year-old Iraq War veteran and father from Des Moines, Iowa, who committed suicide, Ernst chose to introduce legislation expanding access to mental health services for veterans.[105] On March 23, 2015, Ernst made her first floor speech in the Senate. She described her experience serving in the armed forces to provide credibility for her position to advocate on behalf of veterans. She explained the significance of her college study in Ukraine and how it shaped her commitment to serve as a citizen-soldier, and the importance of recognizing the "vital role" members of the Reserves and National Guard play in national security. Transitioning to the bill she planned to introduce, the Prioritizing Veterans Access to Mental Health

Senator Joni Ernst (R-IA) speaks during a hearing to examine US Special Operations Command and US Cyber Command in review of the defense authorization request for fiscal year 2022 and the Future Years Defense Program, on Capitol Hill on March 25, 2021. *Source:* Photo by Andrew Harnik, Pool, AP Photo.

Care Act of 2015, Ernst shared statistics about veteran suicide rates and wait times for accessing mental health care and reminded senators that caring for veterans is "not a conservative or liberal concept; not a Republican or Democratic idea. It's an American value."[106] The bill did not have much success, and Ernst reintroduced it in 2017 with original cosponsors Grassley, Thom Tillis (R-NC), and John Cornyn (R-TX).

The limited progress of her first bill did not prevent Ernst from engaging in legislative work specifically designed to support female veterans and members of the armed forces. In February 2016, Ernst, along with Senators Barbara Boxer (D-CA), Richard Blumenthal (D-CT), Sherrod Brown (D-OH), and US Representative Julia Brownley (D-CA), introduced the Female Veterans Suicide Prevention Act. Research has shown that women veterans are six times as likely as nonveteran women to commit suicide. And women veterans ages eighteen to twenty-nine, many of whom served in Iraq and Afghanistan, are twelve times as likely as nonveteran women to commit suicide.[107] Ernst also worked with another member of the Armed Services Committee, Senator Claire McCaskill (D-MO), to cosponsor a series of bills and amendments tackling sexual assault in the military and on college campuses.[108] The bipartisan team, for example, introduced the PRIVATE Act to guard against "revenge porn" by making such conduct a standard offense across the military.[109]

These bipartisan legislative efforts earned Ernst high marks as a leader among her cohort of senators.[110] She was present for votes, got her bills out of committee often, and received significant cosponsorship for them. This momentum continued into her second year, when she introduced four bills that became law (thirty-four bills or resolutions total), had "powerful" cosponsors on seven pieces of legislation, and more bipartisan collaboration (twenty-two out of thirty-four bills) despite being ranked the tenth most conservative member of the Senate.[111] She primarily sponsored bills dealing with the armed forces and national security policy followed by government operations, health, and taxation. Ernst shares in her memoir that she enjoys collaborating with other female senators and participates in the effort to build community, rapport, and collaboration among the bipartisan group. In one memorable example, she shares stories about themed, bipartisan dinners hosted by women senators. When Ernst had the opportunity to host, she chose the military because she felt that "many of the women don't really engage with the military unless they're on the Armed Services Committee."[112] Her unique background as a woman veteran created an opportunity for other women senators, some of whom had never visited the Pentagon, to become more familiar with the armed services, and it allowed Ernst to showcase an area of policy expertise. She feels so strongly about the positive outcomes of this collaborative effort that she argues the best way to "combat partisanship in Congress" is to "elect more women."[113]

This does not mean that the women senators set aside all partisan and policy differences in the interest of community. Ernst's policy positions sometimes ran afoul of her female colleagues across the aisle. She was caught in a dustup with Democrats over the failed renewal of the Violence Against Women Act between 2018 and 2019. Democrats sought stronger restrictions on access to firearms in the renewal, whereas Ernst and other Republicans resisted changes they believed unduly infringed Second Amendment rights. Ernst blames much of the failure on the leadership of Senator Chuck Schumer (D-NY), with whom she engaged in a brief

Twitter spat. He issued tweets accusing Ernst of abandoning domestic violence victims. Ernst responded, "I do not need to be mansplained to by Chuck Schumer. I am a survivor."[114]

In 2020, Ernst ran unopposed in the Iowa Republican Party primary for her US Senate seat, and in the general election she faced Democratic Party nominee Theresa Greenfield. Polling throughout the race indicated a competitive election, with local media outlets labeling it a "toss-up" throughout summer and fall 2020.[115] Ernst concentrated on enhancing her support from core supporters of President Trump, whereas Greenfield maintained higher levels of support from independent voters and women. At campaign events throughout October, Governor Branstad introduced Ernst by highlighting her close relationship with the president, drawing cheers and applause: "Joni Ernst was there to support the president all the way."[116] Ernst's support for Trump included voting along party lines with his position nearly 90 percent of the time after he was sworn into office in January 2017, including key votes to confirm three Supreme Court justice nominees, voting against conviction of the president for obstruction of Congress, and voting against conviction of the president on charges of abuse of power.[117] In the end, strong support from President Trump's electoral base helped Ernst defeat her Democratic challenger in November 2020 with 51.8 percent of the vote to Greenfield's 45.5 percent.[118]

Conclusion

During her first year in the Senate, Ernst retired from the National Guard, ending her twenty-three-year military career. "I wanted very much to use my platform to help the military and veterans, and I ultimately concluded I could better do that from the outside. . . . The way I see it, I didn't lose a military family when I left the Guard. I just found a new way to serve them." Ernst firmly believes that her "service in the army as a woman" provides her with a unique perspective compared with that of other senators. She refuses to be "bulldozed by others" and understands the military "on a deeper level" than most of her colleagues.[119]

Despite being rated the second most conservative member of the Senate in 2019 and having a voting record that aligned with former president Trump 91 percent of the time, Ernst believes the military is an area where she stood her ground against her own party and the president when necessary.[120] Her campaign website reminds voters, "At a time of extreme partisanship, Joni pushes past the noise to advance Iowa values in Washington. Whether it is working with Democrats or Republicans, Joni has a proven record as an Iowan who works tirelessly to find a path forward toward a brighter future with opportunity for all."[121] To support this claim, she cites her opposition to the Trump administration's all-out ban on transgender people serving in the military and her support for a 2019 amendment opposing Trump's "precipitous withdrawal" of troops from Syria and Afghanistan. She argues, "It is my duty to stand up for the men and women who remain a part of my community—and to do what is necessary to help them protect our freedoms," a vision of service rooted in her observations from a college exchange with Ukraine in 1989.[122]

Ernst also finds that being a woman can be an advantage as long as "you are authentically yourself."[123] Her tagline, which puts her identity as a "mother" first, is a conscious effort to bring all of her experiences to bear on her legislative work, and when she begins to feel worn out by politics, she looks for inspiration in her political heroes, "often women in public service who achieved seemingly impossible feats."[124] As one specific example, she writes in her memoir about Margaret Chase Smith, the indomitable public leader from Maine: "She didn't have much tolerance for self-pity and complaining. For her, service was a high honor, a necessity, and the payment of a debt owed for the privilege of being an American. When I look for renewed energy to serve, I know that I stand on the shoulders of unstoppable women like Smith."[125] Ernst describes how her own commitment to public service likewise aligns with the vision espoused in Smith's often quoted creed: "It must be a complete dedication to the people and to the nation with full recognition that every human being is entitled to courtesy and consideration, that constructive criticism is not only to be expected but sought, that smears are not only to be expected but fought, that honor is to be earned but not bought."[126] This perspective reflects the ethos of the rural community where Ernst was raised; the culture of the US military, where she formed her ideas about leadership; and her philosophy of service.

6

Though most Americans know her as the junior senator from Arizona, Martha McSally grew up on the East Coast. Athletic, hardworking, and determined, she entered the US Air Force Academy (USAFA) just a few years after the first women graduated from the prestigious military school. Her service career is marked by a series of "firsts": the first woman to fly a fighter jet into combat, to command a fighter squadron, and to serve as a full-time pilot instructor for the A-10 Warthog. She gained national attention for her lawsuit against the secretary of defense challenging military regulations on dress code for servicewomen deployed to the Middle East as well as her later public revelation of her status as a survivor of sexual assault and harassment during her years of service. McSally credits her family with instilling in her the values of "service, hard work, and getting an education," all of which drove her interest in public policy and her decision to seek election as the first female Republican to represent Arizona in Congress. As a candidate, she has earned the nickname "Long Shot" in recognition of her limited number of campaign wins by narrow margins. Though McSally explains that she is independent-minded, solution-oriented, mission-focused, and above the politics of Washington, DC, her more recent political positions call this characterization into question.

Quahogging in Matunuck

Born in March 1966 in Warwick, Rhode Island, McSally grew up in what she refers to as a "middle-class" household, spending summers with her family at the beach in Matunuck, digging for clams. She was the youngest of five children, all with names beginning with "M"—Mark, Michael, Martin, Mary Kaitlin, and Martha. Her father, Bernard McSally, was a graduate of Notre Dame University, a recipient of GI Bill support, and a retired officer in the US Navy. After his service in the armed forces, he worked as a lawyer while McSally's mother, Eleanor, managed the household. Her father suffered a heart attack and unexpectedly passed away at the age of forty-nine, when McSally was only twelve years old. Now the sole breadwinner for the family of six, Eleanor returned to school to earn a master's degree and began working full time.

As a teenager, McSally got a job bussing tables at a popular local restaurant and worked the morning shift before school, catering to fishers and other workers who headed out for the day before sunrise. She excelled as both a student and an athlete, maintaining strong grades while competing in running, swimming, and javelin. In high school, she made a deal with her mom: "If I kept a 4.0 GPA, I could skip school when I wanted. So, I was absent a lot."[1]

Beneath her litany of accomplishments and outward confidence, McSally shares that she also struggled internally with grief over losing her father and a beloved family pet, a golden retriever named Casey. In an impulsive suicidal moment, she "downed some pills and ended up in the hospital, drinking charcoal and having my stomach pumped."[2] It was a cry for help. Her struggles were also complicated by an inappropriate relationship with her track coach, who sexually assaulted her. During an interview with the Wall Street Journal in April 2018, she shared that her track-and-field coach pressured her into a sexual relationship during her senior year at St. Mary's Academy–Bay View, an all-girls Catholic school. She said that the coach used "emotional manipulation" to keep her compliant, and, like many victims of assault, she did not reveal the incident to friends or family until years after it occurred.[3]

Accidental Pioneers

McSally chose to apply to the USAFA during her senior year despite receiving recruitment offers from other colleges interested in her athletic abilities. She admits that she "stumbled into" the opportunity.[4] She was conscious of the costs of attending college and wanted to avoid taking on substantial student debt. "Going to a service academy meant that my widowed mother wouldn't have to try to pay for college and medical school."[5] The thought of attending school 2,000 miles from home in Colorado was also appealing: "Although I had been accepted to other universities closer to home, the academy seemed like a great way to have a fresh start."[6] The distance allowed her to set aside the issues she was still navigating at home, including the death of her father and her abusive track coach.

The USAFA began admitting women in 1976, and the class of 1980 was the first graduating cohort to include women cadets, only four years before McSally arrived in Colorado Springs. In interview questionnaires for *Checkpoints* magazine, the USAFA's alumni publication, the "80s Ladies" discussed their first-year experiences as the inaugural cohort of women cadets. Many entered the USAFA because they saw it as an affordable path to a good education. Sue (Henke) Laushine recalled, "Being in the first class of women at the Academy was not a priority for me. I wanted to come to the Academy because I came from a very poor family, and I saw the Academy [as a way] to obtain a first-class education as well as experience many of the other opportunities available."[7] Others joined because the USAFA provided training that would help them advance into careers with the National Aeronautics and Space Administration (NASA) or in science, technology, engineering, and math (STEM) related fields. Anne Martin Fletcher wrote, "I didn't care about being first as much as I cared about wanting to be an astronaut—and the path to becoming an astronaut at that time required being a military test pilot, and that path was most likely to include graduation from USAFA or U.S. Naval Academy."[8] Nearly all of the women interviewed for the special issues acknowledged that they had a limited understanding of how "historic" their enrollment in the USAFA was despite media coverage and requests for interviews in national publications. Former cadet Kathleen Utley Kornahrens described their group as "accidental pioneers."[9]

The young women who entered the USAFA in those first years experienced the gender politics in the military in different ways, navigating the academy's lack of preparedness for integration, hostility from some other cadets, and lack of clear leadership by members of the cadre. In her memoir, *Groundbreaker: Coming of Age in the First Class of Women at the United States Air Force Academy*, Fletcher describes the "ongoing battle" to prove that society and its institutions, including the military, benefit from having a larger, more diverse talent pool. Fletcher writes, "Neither side knew if women would withstand the physical and psychological rigors of male-centric military training. Just as important a question was: Could men bond with women to form a cohesive military unit?"[10]

McSally acknowledges that she knew "very little" about the military when she applied to the USAFA. Although her father had served in the US Navy, she did not grow up listening to stories about his time in the service, and her family did not live on or near a military base. In her book she shares, "I don't recall meeting anyone in uniform before I applied to the academy."[11] She was already a star student and in excellent physical shape because of her athletic training; most of her preparation to attend the USAFA was self-directed. She bought combat boots, paid to have her hair cut extremely short by a professional, and practiced running around her neighborhood in her new footwear to enhance her stamina and conditioning. It was clear she could meet the test of physical readiness by the time she departed for Colorado, but what was less certain was whether she was mentally and emotionally prepared to enter the politically charged, highly competitive institution of the USAFA.

McSally felt that the events of her life (grief, sexual assault, mental discipline from athletic training, growing up with older brothers) gave her a reservoir of experience to draw on during challenging moments at the USAFA. But none of it prepared her or her female classmates for the level of sexual harassment and assault experienced by female and some male cadets. In later interviews and publications, McSally shared, "During my early years in uniform, I was harassed, abused, assaulted, and raped, like countless other women and some men who have served their country. Yes, raped."[12] She shared publicly for the first time during a Senate Armed Services Committee hearing in 2019 that she had been raped by a superior officer, one of multiple times she was sexually assaulted while she served her country.[13] Pausing to maintain her composure, she shared, "I thought I was strong but felt powerless. The perpetrators abused their position of power in profound ways." The issue was personal to her in two respects, both as a commander and as a survivor of assault.[14]

In her later book, *Dare to Fly*, McSally notes that her story is not unique and that she believes the issues of sexual assault are symptomatic of leadership culture in the military, including the institution of the "leadership laboratory," where senior cadets supervise newer cadets at the academies on weekends. Studies of sexual assault in the military present evidence to support McSally's position. Some veterans' studies report numbers as high as one in three women in the US military being victimized, a rate twice as high as that of civilians. Women are also up to ten times more likely to experience sexual assault or harassment than their male counterparts.[15] A Department of Defense (DOD) report for fiscal year 2017 disclosed that the department received 6,769 reports of sexual assault involving servicemembers as either victims or subjects of criminal investigation, a 9.7 percent increase over the 6,172 reports made in fiscal year 2016.[16]

Further, Kelsey E. B. Knoer writes that sexual assault survivors in the military face a Catch-22; of those who do report, nearly two-thirds face some form of retaliation.[17] In both 2012 and in 2014, 62 percent of women who filed a report indicated that they experienced professional retaliation (such as being denied a promotion or training), social retaliation (such as being ignored by coworkers), adverse administrative actions (such as being transferred to a different assignment), or punishments for violations associated with the sexual assault (such as underage drinking or fraternization).[18] In response to the assault and abuse McSally experienced, she chose to remain silent: "Like so many women and men, I did not trust the system at the time. I blamed myself. I was ashamed and confused."[19] She felt that she had to find her own healing, following a pattern of self-reliance she began at a younger age. Instead of leaving the military, she chose to "stay and continue to serve and fight and lead, to be a voice from within the ranks for women."[20]

McSally completed her studies at the USAFA and graduated in 1988 with a bachelor of science degree in biology. Although she had initially applied with the intention of studying medicine, a decision inspired by the contributing factors to her father's death, the opportunity to shadow professionals serving in the US Air Force changed her mind. During the summer between her sophomore and junior year, she spent three weeks at Torrejón Air Base in Madrid, Spain, and got the chance to fly in the backseat of an F-16 during some training flights. She left the experience in Spain knowing she "belonged" as a pilot—any questions she had about her future plans "were answered during that trip."[21]

Many cadets at the service academies aspire to become pilots, but there are strict physical requirements that ensure all candidates are "pilot-qualified." McSally's standing height of five feet and three inches was one inch shorter than the minimum required. She met the sitting height requirements and passed all the other physical screenings to demonstrate her ability and, with support from both a flight surgeon and instructor pilot, applied for a waiver that would allow her to begin training. She was denied without explanation.

McSally's response to this denial set the stage for subsequent challenges to US Air Force policy. Rather than divert to another career and training path, she approached the USAFA's clinic commander, Colonel Christopher Bell, for more information. He resubmitted her materials with a request for reconsideration. Her application was again denied. Bell was able to obtain more information about the denial, which he learned was part of a blanket denial of height waivers for all candidates at that time. Several pilots who had received waivers for their height were more likely to abort takeoffs, skid off runways, and do damage to their planes. Yet, McSally recalled the example of another cadet who, in addition to being a talented football player, failed his cockpit test because he was too tall. When the flight surgeon and instructor pilots recommended "denial of flight clearance," the male cadet's waiver was approved. This moment fomented her perception of "how callous and irrational bureaucracies can be."[22]

Once again, rather than be dissuaded, McSally worked with Bell to conduct an independent study to demonstrate that her athletic strength, particularly her leg strength, was above average compared with that of both male athletes and other pilot-qualified cadets. They applied for a waiver for the third time and, once again, were denied. McSally raged against the "faceless bureaucrats" that were "taking the path of least resistance rather than looking at individual circumstances."[23] Finally, by coincidence, Lieutenant General Charles Hamm learned of her situation and personally delivered McSally's waiver application package with all its supporting documentation to the head of Air Training Command. Her waiver was finally granted; McSally would train to become a pilot.

In 2020, the US Air Force removed the height restrictions that prevented McSally from becoming pilot-qualified to enhance its diversity and in response to a pilot shortage. In a press release, Gwendolyn DeFilippi, assistant deputy chief of staff for Manpower, Personnel, and Services, noted, "We're really focused on identifying and eliminating barriers to serve in the Air Force. This is a huge win, especially for women and minorities of smaller stature who previously may have assumed they weren't qualified to join our team." Lieutenant Colonel Jessica Ruttenber, mobility planner, programmer, and team leader on the Women's Initiative Team, added, "Studies have shown that women's perceptions about being fully qualified for a job makes them less likely to apply, even though there is a waiver option. Modifying the height standard allows the Air Force to accommodate a larger and more diverse rated applicant pool within existing aircraft constraints."[24]

Like McSally, the cadets who applied for waivers found themselves in what she viewed as a struggle between the recommendations of experts and the obstacles presented by bureaucrats. Her desire to change and fix systems, including those that limited her career options, also led McSally to develop an interest in public policy. Being among the top graduates of the USAFA opened opportunities for internships with the North Atlantic Treaty Organization (NATO) and the Pentagon as well as studies at the John F. Kennedy School of Government at Harvard University, where she earned a master's degree in public policy before proceeding to pilot training. The timing of her studies allowed her to deepen her knowledge of national security just at the cold war was coming to an end and a new age of securitization was beginning, and it delayed her enrollment in flight school just long enough to allow the restrictions on female combat pilots to be lifted.[25]

The "A-10 Chick Who Likes to Dip"

McSally's graduating class at the USAFA was only the ninth to include women, and there was just one other woman in her pilot training class.

During her time as a pilot instructor, she was the only woman in her group. Her USAFA education and training introduced McSally to the challenges of being a woman in a male-dominated institution. It was not always a conscious choice, but she learned to be one of the guys, blend in, and prove you belong—a lesson that proved invaluable as she moved forward in her pilot career.[26]

McSally was slated to begin pilot training in August 1990, the same month the Iraqi Army invaded and occupied Kuwait. Less than six months later, Congress authorized the use of force against Iraq, the most explicit authorization of war by Congress since the Tonkin Gulf Resolution approved US military involvement in Vietnam in 1964. The US military deployed more than 37,000 women as part of Operations Desert Shield and Desert Storm, though technically they were listed in "combat support" roles. The capture of two servicewomen and deaths of fifteen servicewomen in the first Iraq War led to fresh debates about the role of women in combat—including female fighter pilots.

In the early 1990s, the US military and federal government were still engaged in heated debates about the combat status of female fighter pilots. McSally notes that one of the primary concerns expressed by those who opposed opening the opportunity to women was that women's presence would "ruin this fighter pilot culture."[27] Given that camaraderie and esprit de corps were critical aspects of "military readiness," detractors raised questions such as: Would women make male colleagues take down the pinup posters behind their desks? Would they stop their male colleagues from visiting strip clubs when deployed to Las Vegas for a training exercise? Would women "ban them from singing songs about rape and lust and big boobs, and making jokes about the carnage of war? Would we file complaints against them for swearing?"[28]

Congress ultimately voted to repeal prohibitions on women becoming combat pilots, though McSally notes, "It did not require any of the military services to change their policies, and they didn't."[29] While undergoing pilot training at the USAFA, McSally and most other female cadets had no desire to engage in revising the culture that existed in the US Air Force. Going by the nickname "Momma Mac," sharing mint Skoal with an instructor pilot, and playing physically aggressive games such as "Crud" were all part of "joining the boys' club."[30] McSally and other female students focused on proving that women were capable of becoming excellent cadets and in McSally's case, fighter pilots. Her approach was to "outstudy, outprepare, and strive to outfly and outshoot" the other cadets.[31] She earned her US Air Force pilot wings in 1991 after completing training at Williams Air Force Base in Arizona, and following graduation, she chose an assignment as a T-37 instructor pilot at Laughlin Air Force Base in Del Rio, Texas.

After the opportunity to train as a combat pilot opened to women, McSally transitioned to fighter planes in 1994. For a time, she was the only woman in a flight suit with the A-10 Thunderbolt patch on her arm. Also known as the Warthog, the A-10 is a rugged workhorse of an attack plane. Originally designed to combat Soviet tanks and provide close air support for ground troops, the plane is uniquely suited for "air-to-ground attack" missions against enemy forces; hence the "A" for "Attack!" in A-10.[32] As a brand-new A-10 pilot who had just completed her training, McSally won an incredibly difficult bombing competition that required a combination of precision flying and real-time, rapid math calculations for weapons targeting. She writes, "No one expected the new girl to post better scores than dozens of highly experienced, veteran pilots."[33] The timing of this demonstration of skill and competence was important because it earned her respect from some of the other pilots, she believes.

McSally was only twenty-eight years old and a freshly minted A-10 pilot when she was assigned to an operation that deployed to Kuwait in January 1995. Their squadron flew combat patrol over Iraq in support of Operation Southern Watch, enforcing the no-fly zone over southern Iraq. During this mission, she became the first female fighter pilot to fly in combat and the first woman to command a fighter squadron. She reported to the Al-Jaber Air Base in southern Kuwait, about seventy-five miles south of the Iraqi border, where active-duty US Air National Guard, Air Force Reserve A-10 Thunderbolt II units, and General Dynamics F-16 Fighting Falcon units monitored airspace and provided support for ground forces.

During her deployment, McSally continued to focus on "working hard, flying well, blending in, and being one of the guys."[34] Unfortunately, the facilities that housed her squadron were not set up to accommodate a female pilot. Men stationed at the base serving in combat support roles were housed in tent cities, whereas women were assigned to live in older dormitories. The pilots lived together in trailers located in one area of the base referred to as "pilot town." When McSally arrived on base, she was dropped off at the dorms instead of pilot town with her squadron. Each day brought new logistical challenges as the base adapted to having a female pilot in residence, including navigating shared bathroom and shower facilities and negotiating the dress code for women working out on base. The last thing she wanted was to complain about a "'female' issue or policy," but eventually McSally reached her breaking point.

A "Female" Issue

Before being deployed to bases across the Middle East, including the Al-Jaber Air Base, women serving in the US military were instructed that they could not show their legs, so they had to wear long pants. They also had to take other measures to adapt their appearance in deference to local cultural customs regarding women's apparel and expectations of modesty. Knowing that she would be on base in Kuwait between January and April, when average temperatures reach well above ninety degrees Fahrenheit, McSally packed workout tights and clothing she believed would allow her to comply with guidelines on apparel. After her first workout at the gym, she was instructed that her attire was inappropriate and too form-fitting; in response to "host nation sensitivities," she donned a pair of large, gray army sweatpants for the duration of her deployment. Whether she was running the eight-mile loop around the base's runway or waterskiing, McSally sported her "shar-pei sweats." As she continued to press her colleagues and contacts for information about the source of the sweatpants policy, she discovered it was a policy instituted by the US military with no specific evidence of a request coming from the host nation of Kuwait. McSally pushed back against these policies. She asked questions and eventually saw results: "A senior general abruptly ended the sweatpants policy one year later in 1996 after I raised it again on my next deployment."[35]

The experience of advocating for herself in response to the sweatpants policy primed McSally for a more public, prolonged, high-profile battle over other regulations on women's attire during deployment. While on base in Kuwait, she happened to observe a photo of an American military woman in an *abaya* on the cover of a US military magazine. The abaya, sometimes referred to as an *aba*, is a loose-fitting garment similar to a robe worn by women in some parts of the Muslim world. Traditional *abayat* are black and cover the whole body except the head, hands, and feet. Some women choose to add gloves or head coverings, such as a *niqāb*. The caption for the magazine cover explained to US military women the proper ways to wear this attire when traveling off base in Saudi Arabia. Though she was not currently serving in Saudi Arabia, the policy shocked McSally and moved her to action. She started by researching the source of the policy and found out that, parallel to the sweatpants policy in Kuwait, servicewomen were required to wear it and comply with other directives because of "the possibility of offending host nation sensitivities."[36] McSally's source informed her that it was part of a status-of-forces agreement between the United States and Saudi Arabia to allow US military forces to be stationed in the Saudi Kingdom. As she dug deeper and reviewed the specific language of the policy, she also discovered that servicemen were not required to wear traditional Muslim attire or clothing in deference to local customs.

At the time she was investigating the abaya policy, Secretary of Defense William J. Perry planned a visit to the base where McSally was stationed. Part of the visit included meetings with various groups of servicemembers and a larger public forum with a question-and-answer session. McSally planned to ask about the policy during her group's private meeting, but it was cancelled. She made the choice to pose a question during the public forum, in front of reporters. "Secretary Perry," she inquired, "I understand you just came from Saudi Arabia, meeting with Saudi leaders. Has there been any consideration to treating our female troops serving there with a little bit more dignity?"[37] Perry gave a measured response: "I will be honest with you. We haven't made a lot of progress in that area, but we won't give up." Reporters present for the session seized on the conversation, and that day, the Associated Press quoted both McSally and Perry on the issue.[38] McSally had received significant media training in preparation for the Pentagon's announcement that it was allowing women to train for combat flying. Her question was not spontaneous but "well thought out and memorized, after a deliberate decision."[39] Officials in the US military were unhappy about her choice to question the policy publicly, though they took no specific retaliatory steps against her.

In 1997, after her deployment concluded, McSally was selected to be a full-time A-10 instructor pilot, becoming the first woman to achieve that role, and promoted to the rank of major two years ahead of schedule.[40] She continued asking questions about the abaya policy as she transitioned into new opportunities for professional development. In 1999, McSally deployed to Europe in support of Operation Allied Force and was selected as one of seven active-duty US Air Force officers for the legislative fellowship program, an opportunity to continue her studies of policy from her time at Harvard. The legislative liaison and fellowship programs were developed to provide servicemembers opportunities to improve their understanding of the functions and operations of the legislative branch and how it affects the military and simultaneously to provide members of the legislature the expertise and perspective of the servicemembers. McSally lived in Washington, DC, and worked as a national security adviser to Senator Jon Kyl (R-AZ).[41]

Finally, in November 2000, McSally received orders to deploy to Saudi Arabia for one year to direct Combat Search-and-Rescue (CSAR) operations for pilots flying inside southern Iraq. She had no desire to deploy to Saudi Arabia, and during her interview with the general in charge, she restated her objection to the abaya policy: "I have a problem with policies that treat servicewomen like property instead of military members. It is wrong on so many levels, demeaning to the troops, bad for good order and discipline, and an abandonment of American values."[42] Through her conversations with military and diplomatic personnel, McSally discovered that the policy was not codified in any official agreements between Saudi Arabia and the United States. Further, the US Department of State had not made the request; it was an "internal U.S. military policy."[43] This solidified her view that the policy was arbitrary and that it was worth continuing her effort to push back against it.

Martha McSally v. Donald Rumsfeld

On Sunday, November 12, 2000, at 10:43 p.m., less than forty-eight hours before her departure to Saudi Arabia, McSally sent an email with the subject line "Potential Problem upon Arrival in Theater," advising the colonel in charge that she did not intend to comply with the abaya policy. She then waited for the response, sitting alongside her packed green duffel bags at her brother's house. It took less than seven hours for the colonel to reply, cc-ing the two-star general in the response: "It would be regrettable if you were to choose to place yourself personally at risk by ignoring force protection measures. It would also be extremely regrettable if you were to place yourself at risk professionally by choosing to violate specific command directives. I encourage you to carefully consider your actions."[44] Faced with the choice between being arrested, court-martialed, and discharged from the US Air Force or complying with a dress policy that conflicted with her deeply held values, McSally resolved to comply with the abaya policy one time. "I would end my career, but not change the policy," she reflected.[45] When she arrived in-country for her deployment, McSally donned the black abaya and head scarf and sat in the backseat of her transport, though she was the highest-ranking military member in the vehicle.

McSally continued to plead her case for ending the abaya policy with US military leadership in Saudi Arabia, though they were unmoved. She was then approached by Edward Pound, a USA Today reporter who heard about the conflict from a congressional staffer. McSally agreed to an interview with Pound and disclosed the meeting to the Air Force Public Affairs Office at the Pentagon. The story ran on the front page, headlined "Saudi Rules Anger Top Air Force Pilot: Female Officer Speaks Out against Muslim Dress for Americans."[46] In the interview, McSally explains, "I've fought and spoken and been patient and worked within the system for so long to try and effect some change in this policy, so the fact that I would just be truthful I would hope wouldn't hurt me and, if it does, then so be it."[47] But her statements were juxtaposed with remarks from other women stationed at Eskan Village Air Base, such as Major Lisa Caldwell, a senior spokesperson for US Armed Forces in the Middle East. Caldwell stated she had no problems with the restrictions, and the policy allowed military women to "show respect for Islamic law and Arabic customs." Captain Richard Johnson, a US Air Force spokesperson based in the United States, reinforced concerns about "force-protection. . . . You always have to be on the alert for terrorist attacks. We just want to blend in with the population, be less of a target to terrorists."[48] McSally's interview received mixed responses—admonitions from military leadership and support from female diplomats serving in the US Embassy in Saudi Arabia. It drew attention from Congress, and a bipartisan group of five senators asked Secretary of

Defense Donald Rumsfeld for a full policy review.[49] John Whitehead of the Rutherford Institute, a nonprofit organization that provides legal support for individuals challenging government rules or regulations they believe violate constitutional rights, offered to represent McSally if she chose to file a lawsuit against the military.

At the time, McSally had never heard of a servicemember filing a lawsuit against the military, but she soon learned of a small number of cases in which servicemembers successfully sued to change military policy. Captain Kathy Bruyere of the US Navy became the first woman tapped as a flag secretary and aide to an admiral in 1975. In her role, she led the admiral's staff and handled all liaisons between his headquarters and the nine Pacific training commands. She acknowledged that in her role, she was not thrilled about the potential for combat but said she "would not like to deny any woman the opportunity to do anything she is capable of doing, including firing a gun."[50] Within one year of assuming her position, Bruyere and five other female sailors helped clear the path for women to serve on ships and aircraft engaged in combat—assignments previously barred to them under the Women's Armed Services Integration Act of 1948. The sailors, who claimed their careers and potential promotions were negatively affected by the policy, filed a class-action lawsuit against the secretary of defense and secretary of the navy in 1977. US District Judge John Sirica ruled in 1978 that the law was unconstitutional. Decades later, in an interview about the decision to sue the US military, Bruyere shared with the *Navy Times*, "I just believe we should all have the same opportunities. There is nothing today's women cannot do—we need them to keep charging ahead."[51] Bruyere continued with a successful military career, serving as special assistant to the chief of naval operations for women's policy, where she was involved in a 1987 study examining career opportunities for women in the US Navy and sexism across the service. Reflecting back on the historical moment, she shares, "Some people thought it was treason—'How dare I try to challenge the system?' But others kept saying, 'Good for you, good for you.'"[52]

A second example came in the case of Captain Susan Struck of the US Air Force, a nurse serving in Vietnam who challenged military policy directed at expectant mothers. After Struck's commanding officer learned of her pregnancy in 1970, he gave her two choices: abortion or resignation from the military. Struck chose neither and sued, retaining the services of the American Civil Liberties Union (ACLU) and future Supreme Court justice Ruth Bader Ginsburg. Representing Struck, Ginsburg argued that the regulation banning pregnant women from service was sex discrimination and that Struck should have the right to choose whether she wanted to have a child; a military directive to the contrary violated Struck's constitutional rights. When the Supreme Court agreed to hear the case, the solicitor general of the United States, Erwin Griswold, convinced the US Air Force to abandon the policy. After the military revised the policy, the case became moot.[53]

Bolstered by the support of the Rutherford Institute and frustrated by the lack of responsiveness from the US military, McSally decided to proceed with filing a lawsuit against the highest-ranking civilian in the chain of command, the US secretary of defense. Though McSally's legal team initially planned to file the lawsuit on September 12, 2001, the events of 9/11 led them to delay filing until December. The war in Afghanistan continued to escalate, and McSally could not help but see hypocrisy in the discussions over women's rights: "Celebrities and other national figures such as First Lady Laura Bush talked about how U.S. forces were freeing the Afghan people from the oppression of the Taliban. Women were no longer being forced to wear the burqa. I remember sitting in the Saudi-based operations center watching news reports and yelling: 'Am I the only one who sees the irony in this?'"[54]

After McSally filed her lawsuit in December 2001, it quickly gained media attention, and McSally received numerous requests for interviews.[55] As a major (O-4), she was the highest-ranking female fighter pilot in the US Air Force, and she argued that the regulations required her to send the message that she believes women are subservient to men. In a *60 Minutes* interview broadcast on CBS on January 20, 2002, she described the discrimination she experienced under the policy: "I have to sit in the back and at all times I must be escorted by a male . . . [who], when questioned, is supposed to claim me as his wife," she said. "I can fly a single-seat aircraft in enemy territory, but [in Saudi Arabia] I can't drive a vehicle."[56] McSally reiterated that her goal was not to be "the ugly American" but to advocate for her constitutional rights.

Popular culture quickly picked up on the national conversation as well, with a special episode of JAG (judge advocate general) focused on the abaya policy. In February 2002, as part of the seventh season of the series, JAG aired the episode "Head to Toe." It featured a story line in which Harm and Mac, two central characters, travel to Saudi Arabia to defend Lieutenant Stephanie Donato, a female naval aviator who flies a C-130 Hercules while serving with the US Air Force but refuses to wear the abaya when off base.

In late January 2002, General Tommy Franks, then commander of the US Central Command, announced that US military servicewomen would no longer be required to wear the abaya, although they would be "strongly encouraged" to do so as a show of respect for local customs.[57] Commenting on the change, US Central Command spokesperson Colonel Rick Thomas denied that the decision was made in response to McSally's lawsuit. In his comments to reporters, Thomas explained, "The policy was under review before the lawsuit was filed, so the change was not a direct result of that."[58] US Representative Jim Langevin (D-RI), who grew up in the same neighborhood as McSally and knew her family, invited her to attend President George W. Bush's State of the Union Address to Congress on January 29, 2002. The Rutherford Institute shared the news about her attendance with the media. When the president referenced cultural sensitivities, women's rights, and equality around the world, cameras spotlighted McSally and flashed her name and rank.[59]

Though the military softened the language of the policy, McSally was unsatisfied and remained determined to see clarification and greater protection through either a judicial ruling or legislative amendment. Using her knowledge of Capitol Hill from her time as a legislative fellow in Senator Kyl's office, McSally set to work building a team to draft and support an amendment to the annual defense spending bill. Representatives Langevin, Heather Wilson (R-NM), and John Hostettler (R-IN) sponsored the bill, which prohibited anyone in the military from "requiring or encouraging servicewomen to put on abayas in Saudi Arabia or to use taxpayers' money to buy them." McSally watched from the gallery as the legislation unanimously passed the House of Representatives in May 2002.[60] Through strategic lobbying, supporters of the bill prevented any changes as the legislation moved through the Senate, and on December 2, 2002, McSally stayed up late to watch C-SPAN from Saudi Arabia, as President Bush signed the annual defense bill into law.

"Kick Him in the Jimmy"

McSally continued to be a success leader in the US Air Force, taking command of the 354th Fighter Squadron at Davis-Monthan Air Force Base in July 2004, then deploying to Afghanistan for Operation Enduring Freedom. Her squadron eventually won the David C. Shilling Award from the Air Force Association "for the most outstanding contribution to the field of flight."[61] By May 2010, McSally was finally ready to retire from the US Air Force, and she accepted a position as a professor at the George C. Marshall European Center for Security Studies in Garmisch-Partenkirchen, Germany. In the early 1990s, the United States and its allies had sought opportunities to build relationships with security and defense professionals in emerging democracies throughout Central and Eastern Europe. The Marshall Center was founded in 1993 with the mission to create a more stable security environment by promoting democratic institutions and strategic relationships, particularly in the field of defense. The faculty is composed of representatives from the United States, Germany, Austria, Italy, Hungary, the United Kingdom, Albania, and other countries across Europe. McSally's background in policy and defense, both from her academic studies and experience as a practitioner, made her an ideal candidate for a faculty position.

Yet her time at the Marshall Center was brief. On January 22, 2012, McSally learned that Gabrielle Giffords (D-AZ) planned to resign her seat in Congress. Giffords was first elected to represent Arizona's Eighth District in 2006, but in January 2011 Giffords was shot in a mass shooting at a public event outside of Tucson.[62] She suffered a severe traumatic brain injury that affected her ability to speak, read, write, and walk. Though Giffords made incredible progress toward regaining these functions, she chose to resign her seat later that year. This triggered a special election, with primaries to be held roughly ninety days from the announcement. The winner of the special election would serve the remainder of Giffords's term and stand for reelection to a full term in November 2012.

McSally broached the subject with her colleagues at the Marshall Center, who supported her interest in returning to Arizona to enter the election. The morning after Gifford's announcement, McSally reached out to US Representative Wilson, whom she met through her advocacy on the military's abaya policy, and Wilson connected McSally with the National Republican Congressional Committee. McSally described the response from the committee chair as "a tough-guy speech" and a warning that she would need to raise $100,000 from her friends and family to even be considered a serious candidate.[63] This was not an option for McSally, who was not independently wealthy and did not have connections that could easily contribute these startup campaign funds. She followed up the conversation with outreach to Kyl, who offered to arrange a series of meetings with people who could share their insights and experience with her, to help inform her decision to run. McSally had to proceed cautiously, however, because she was technically still a federal employee subject to the provisions of the Hatch Act, a law that prohibits civil service employees in the executive branch of the federal government from engaging in some forms of political activity.[64]

Less than four hours after resigning her position with the Marshall Center, McSally met with Kyl's southern Arizona staff. Though they discouraged her from becoming a candidate, telling her not to waste her first attempt at political office on the special election, McSally was resolved: "I laughed and told them I didn't care how I got labeled, I was running."[65] She described her decision as "following my calling, instead of my comfort." Although McSally had a wealth of both academic and practical experience with foreign and defense policy in addition to formal media training in the armed forces, she had no campaign funds or real name recognition in Arizona. But as someone who consistently turned opposition into opportunity, she accepted these circumstances as a challenge and officially announced her candidacy for the special election for Arizona's Eighth District on February 9, 2012. She gained some national attention for her candidacy during a *Fox and Friends* interview when she responded to comments by Senator Rick Santorum (R-PA), a candidate in the Republican primary for the presidential nomination. Santorum objected to the US military's decision to open additional combat positions to women, and when asked about his comments, McSally responded, "You know, I agree with many of the things that Rick Santorum says, but when I heard this, I really just wanted to go and kick him in the jimmy."[66] The candid response went viral.

Despite the series of speaking engagements, meet-and-greets, phone calls, debates, media interviews, and a moment of national notoriety, Mc-Sally placed second in the Republican primary for the special election. Democrat Ron Barber, a political moderate who received Giffords's endorsement, won the special election. Barber served as district director to Giffords during her time in office and was present at the shooting in January 2011, where he suffered gunshot wounds to the thigh and cheek.[67] Barber sought reelection for a full term in November, and McSally once again entered the race, this time winning the Republican nomination. With greater name recognition, she received endorsements from the National Federation of Independent Businesses, the US Chamber of Commerce, the National Association of Wholesalers, and the Associated Builders and Contractors.

After redistricting, the race to represent Arizona's Second District became one of the closest in the nation in 2012.[68] McSally led on Election Day by a few hundred votes, but the race was deemed too close to call because of a large number of provisional ballots in Pima County. By the end of the week, Barber led by 1,400 votes, and the Associated Press analysis determined the gap was too great for McSally to overcome.[69] She conceded the race and posted a congratulatory message to Barber on Facebook.

"Don't Walk by a Problem"

Though she did not have a position in public office, McSally continued to advocate for issues about which she felt strongly. In February 2013, she appeared on a panel, Women in Combat, hosted by the Stockholm Institute and the Service Women's Action Network (SWAN), alongside women representing the Canadian and Norwegian militaries. McSally explained what she viewed as a "leadership issue" in the US military, which failed to provide opportunities for women to successfully integrate into combat or leadership roles, in contrast with policies such as Don't Ask, Don't Tell.[70] She also clarified that the hostility she experienced most frequently was from people she never met, more so than her own teammates or those in her squadron. Strangers still questioned her promotions based on assumptions about lower standards, quotas, or gender.

The next year, McSally decided once again to enter the race for Arizona's Second District. Barber was considered vulnerable, given that he had won the seat by less than 1 percent in the prior election cycle. The district's electoral makeup was evenly split among voters, identifying as "roughly one-third Republican, one-third Democratic, and one-third independent."[71] McSally emerged as the clear winner of the Republican primary against two opponents, taking nearly 70 percent of the vote. She laughs that in this third electoral attempt, even Rumsfeld, the secretary of state she sued over the military's abaya policy, donated to her campaign.[72]

McSally and Barber participated in a series of debates ahead of the general election, and the candidates positioned themselves as independent-minded voices for the district who would be comfortable crossing party lines when needed. McSally leveraged her military experience to establish her leadership credentials: "I have shown that I am going to stand up and speak truth to power. I'm going to do the right thing, and I'm going to show moral courage even if it comes at a personal cost. And these are values that we don't have in Congress now."[73] She reiterated the phrase "Don't Walk by a Problem," in reference to her refusal to walk by the photo of the American military woman in the abaya and allow the dress code policy to go unchallenged. When Barber questioned her on her more conservative policy positions, McSally pivoted to emphasize her "outsider status" in politics, reinforcing that Washington, DC, politics were failing the American people.[74]

More than 4,000 television ads aired during the election cycle, and the candidates raised a combined $8.8 million, the most of any congressional race in Arizona that year and double the amount raised in 2012.[75] Once again, on Election Day, the race was too close to call; it eventually became the last federal election of the 2014 cycle to be decided. With 100 percent of the votes counted, McSally had a 161-vote lead and declared victory on November 12, 2014. Yet because the margin of victory was less than 1 percent, it triggered an automatic recount on December 1. Two weeks later—which seemed like an electoral eternity—the official recount declared McSally the winner by 167 votes.[76] She was only the second Republican ever to represent a southern Arizona district in the US House of Representatives and the first female Republican representative from Arizona. In reflecting on these early campaign experiences, she shared, "All the denigration that I had faced as a woman in the military prepared me well for being attacked, lied about, and smeared on TV."[77]

After she was elected, McSally set to work building her congressional office staff with experienced professionals. For example, she hired C. J. Karamargin, formerly the communications director for Giffords, as her district director. McSally was assigned to committees that fell within her areas of expertise, including the Armed Services Committee, the Education and the Workforce Committee, and the Homeland Security Committee, where she eventually served as the chair of the Subcommittee on Border and Maritime Security and the Subcommittee on Emergency Preparedness, Response, and Communications.

The opportunity to serve as a committee chair in her first term put McSally in an advantageous position to advance legislation. In that term, McSally proposed nine bills, seven of which passed, and among all members of the House, she ranked second in the number of bills she authored that made it through the chamber.[78] Her bills were generally "narrowly drawn proposals to improve homeland security or to help veterans" or focused on border security issues relevant to Arizona constituents.[79] She strongly critiqued the Obama administration on issues of defense and foreign policy; during an interview about the authorization for use of military force (AUMF) in the fight against the Islamic State in Iraq and Syria (ISIL), she called the administration's military strategy "inadequate" and "disgusting," likening it to US engagement in Vietnam.[80] Six months later, while offering the weekly Republican radio address following the terrorist attacks on Paris, she challenged the administration to "step up," "unleash" the force of the US military, and "take off the gloves."[81] At each engagement, she reiterated her "26 years of service" and experience with the Marshall Center to reinforce her credentials and authority on issues of security and defense.

Despite her challenges to the Obama administration, McSally earned a reputation as a political moderate in her first term. "It's easy when you vote for legislation that is 100 percent of what you want," she notes. "It's the 51-to-49 votes that are the tough ones."[82] The Arizona Republic credited her as "one of the most prolific fundraisers among House members not holding a leadership role, while cultivating a reputation as a conscientious and moderate lawmaker."[83] In reflecting on the qualities that made her successful in this role, McSally shares, "I have been a woman in a male-dominated environment for most of my adult life, and so I've learned to

US Representative Martha McSally (R-AZ) speaks during an event on the reinstatement of World War II female pilots at Arlington National Cemetery on Capitol Hill on March 16, 2016. Joining the effort are Terry Harmon, *second from left*, daughter of World War II veteran Women Airforce Service Pilots (WASP) Elaine Harmon and Erin Miller, *third from left*, granddaughter of Elaine Harmon. Arlington National Cemetery approved in 2002 active duty designees, including WASP pilots, for military honors and inurnments. However, in March 2015, then-secretary of the army John McHugh reversed this decision. *Source:* Photo by Molly Riley, AP Photo.

survive and thrive in that environment and be successful and productive in that environment. Being a woman in the military helped prepare me for being in this role in many ways. I certainly had to learn how to have thick skin but also not lose my humanity."[84]

When McSally ran for reelection in 2016, she was unopposed in the Republican primary, and in the general election she defeated her Democratic opponent by a margin of 57 percent to 43 percent. In her second term, she continued to advocate for bills and earmarks that benefited southern Arizona's defense economy. At an American Israel Public Affairs Committee (AIPAC) policy conference in March 2017, she used her speaking time to praise the "David's Sling" interceptor missile defense system being jointly developed between Israeli defense contractor Rafael Advanced Defense Systems and US contractor Raytheon Missiles and Defense for the Israel

US Representative Martha McSally (R-AZ) leaves in a World War II T-6 airplane after speaking at a rally on January 12, 2018, in Phoenix. *Source:* Photo by Matt York, AP Photo.

Defense Forces. Identifying herself as a "proud and vocal" supporter of US assistance to Israel, McSally reiterated the economic benefits of the US-built defense system for her district and home state; the industry employs roughly 10,000 people in Arizona, supports 500 statewide suppliers, and generates $2.1 billion for the state.[85] Working with Senator John McCain (R-AZ), McSally was able to secure an amendment to the National Defense Authorization Act that added millions of dollars in additional funding for A-10 repairs, procure of $2.5 billion worth of weapon systems made by Raytheon Missiles and Defense, and bring home millions of dollars of investments for military installations and expanded defense contracts in southern Arizona.[86]

McSally balanced her security and defense advocacy with promoting opportunities for women and girls in the military and private sector. In March 2017, as chair of the Women in the 21st Century Workforce working group, she convened a panel of business representatives to hear what steps they had taken to support working women and their family commitments. "Women have made great strides and have achieved so much in this country, but the fact remains that so many women and girls still face barriers to achieving their full potential," she explained. "Many women today are struggling to balance the competing demands from their workplace and their families. They are expected to do it all, and they are exhausted."[87] She pressed the group to determine whether the private sector could advance solutions that support women rather than women having to rely on federal regulations. Her experience in the US Air Force, she believed, provided her a unique perspective useful for facilitating these conversations: "I've been in a nontraditional career, I've broken through barriers myself."[88]

She challenged leaders of the US service academies when survivors of sexual assault and harassment testified before the Armed Services Committee's Subcommittee on Military Personnel. Women who attended the US military and naval academies talked about experiences of reporting assaults and harassment to their respective military institutes and the resulting retaliation they faced. Though not known publicly at the time, McSally's private struggles with assaults, harassment, and discrimination made her uniquely sensitive to the stories shared by cadets during the hearing. She continued to cite the culture of the academies' "leadership laboratories" as the source of the problem and advocated greater integration rather than gender segregation in the institutions.[89]

The "Right" Move

On October 24, 2017, Senator Jeff Flake (R-AZ) shared his plans to retire at the conclusion of his term, citing the environment that had become the "new normal" in US politics during Donald Trump's presidency. In an emotional speech, he voiced concerns about "the personal attacks, the threats against principles, freedoms, and institutions, the flagrant disregard for truth or decency, the reckless provocations, most often for the pettiest and most personal reasons."[90] In January 2018 in Tucson, McSally announced her candidacy for the open seat and began crisscrossing the state, from Phoenix to Prescott, to hold rallies. Her campaign posted online video announcements featuring McSally challenging Washington, DC, Republicans "to grow a pair of ovaries."[91] The announcement represented a "sharp right turn" from McSally's more centrist reputation in the House. In the Republican primary, McSally was expected to run as the establishment candidate; her opponents included former state senator

Kelli Ward and former Maricopa County sheriff Joe Arpaio.[92] As a strong fund-raiser, McSally enjoyed support from Governor Doug Ducey at home and high-profile Republicans across the country. Her history of criticizing Trump drew rebukes from conservative groups, specifically her choice not to endorse him in 2016 and her denouncement of his comments about sexual assault as "disgusting" and "unacceptable."[93] But in the lead-up to announcing her candidacy for the Senate, McSally began to embrace Trump, running ads echoing his conservative immigration policy positions: "Martha McSally wants to make one thing clear before she launches an Arizona Senate campaign: She's a big fan of President Donald Trump."[94]

McSally won the August 2018 Republican primary with 53 percent of the vote and faced the Democratic nominee, Kyrsten Sinema, in the November general election. Prior to running for the open seat, Sinema served as a state representative and state senator. She also served three terms as the US representative from Arizona's Ninth District. During her years in the House, Sinema joined the centrist "Blue Dog" Coalition and bipartisan Problem Solvers Caucus, earning a reputation as a political moderate through her voting record. In stark contrast to McSally's campaign, Sinema's team was credited with running "one of the most moderate-sounding and cautious Senate campaigns this year, keeping the media at arm's length and avoiding controversial issues."[95]

The results of the election remained undecided for several days after Election Day, until all ballots were counted in the close contest. McSally's lead narrowed over those days as more ballots were counted. On November 12, with her golden retriever Boomer by her side, McSally conceded to Sinema, congratulating her on becoming Arizona's first female senator.[96] McSally earned the dubious distinction of being the first Republican to lose a Senate race in Arizona in thirty years.[97]

Conclusion

Shortly before the midterm election, in August 2018, Senator McCain passed away from brain cancer. Ducey appointed former senator Kyl to fill his seat, and when Kyl resigned in late 2018, the governor appointed McSally for the remainder of the term, making her the second woman to serve as a US senator from Arizona. In his announcement, Ducey credited

McSally's career in the US Air Force and public service, noting, "All her life, Martha has put service first—leading in the toughest of fights and at the toughest of times."[98] But McSally's appointment was not without controversy. McCain's family criticized the choice and claimed she "didn't earn her seat," disappointed by McSally's decision to align herself with President Trump and offended by her refusal to speak McCain's name during the National Defense Authorization Act named after the former senator.[99]

Nevertheless, McSally was sworn in as the junior senator from Arizona in January 2019. She was assigned to the Senate Armed Services Committee; Banking, Housing, and Urban Affairs Committee; Energy and Natural Resources Committee; Indian Affairs Committee; and Special Committee on Aging. Her early legislative work as a senator closely aligned her with the Trump administration, where she voted more than 90 percent of the time in support of his policies. A special election for the seat was held in November 2020 to determine who would serve the last two years of the term. McSally faced retired US Navy captain and spouse of former US representative Giffords, astronaut Mark Kelly. In the end, McSally lost her bid for the Senate seat by a margin of 48.8 percent (1,637,661) to 51.2 percent (1,716,467) of the vote.

7

Tulsi Gabbard, a military combat veteran serving as the US representative for Hawaii's Second District, entered the race for the Democratic presidential nomination in 2020. Gabbard's career in US politics has been measured by a series of "firsts"—the first state official to voluntarily step down from public office to serve in a war zone, the first woman ever to be awarded and honored by the Kuwait National Guard for her work in their training and readiness program, one of the first two female combat veterans ever to serve in the US Congress, and its first Hindu member. Gabbard is also among the first post-9/11 veterans to run for the White House.

The Aloha Spirit

Born on April 12, 1981, in Leloaloa, on the island of Tutuila, American Samoa, Gabbard was raised in a multicultural home. Her father, Mike, is Samoan and a member of the Hawai'i State Senate, and her mother, Carol, is a practicing Hindu—a faith Gabbard embraced in her teenage years. Unlike many of the women with military and intelligence backgrounds recruited into politics, Gabbard grew up in a politically active family in which "service" was an expectation. Her mother was on the Hawai'i State Board of Education, and her father was a political activist and Honolulu City Council member. As a teenager, Gabbard even founded her own nonprofit, the Healthy Hawaii Coalition (HHC), a grassroots organization whose mission is to protect the environment and improve individual and community health.

Her father's political activism strongly influenced Gabbard's early political identity. Known in Hawai'i for being one of the state's leading opponents of LGBTQ equality, her father founded Stop Promoting Homosexuality, an organization that opposed not only marriage equality but the very idea of tolerance for homosexuality itself. He was born in American Samoa, and his Catholic faith and participation in an obscure sect of the Hare Krishna movement called the Science of Identity Foundation shaped his views on a number of social issues. The group's leader, a self-described guru named Chris Butler, condemns homosexuality, once arguing that it leads to "an increasing number of American women [keeping] dogs for sexual purposes."[1] Gabbard grew up in Butler's movement, which she acknowledges has shaped her Hindu identity, speaking of her "gratitude to him for the gift of this wonderful spiritual practice that he has given to me."[2]

In September 2001, Gabbard worked for the organization Stand Up for America (SUFA), a self-identified "educational non-profit organization" founded by her father. She also was a self-employed martial arts instructor.[3] In 2002, she chose to enlist in the Hawai'i Army National Guard. At the same time, after redistricting, Gabbard also entered the race to represent the Forty-Second District of the Hawai'i House of Representatives as a Democrat. She does not consider herself loyal to any leader or faction within the party: "No one from the D-triple-C"—the Democratic Congressional Campaign Committee—"came and recruited me to run for Congress. So my situation may be different from others who have relied heavily on Party support from the beginning."[4] She won the Democratic primary with a plurality of the vote and went on to defeat Republican Alfonso Jiminez, becoming at the age of twenty-one the youngest legislator in Hawai'ian history and the youngest woman ever elected to a state legislature.[5]

After she became a member of the Hawai'ian legislature, Gabbard strongly opposed a bill that legalized same-sex civil unions.[6] She led demonstrators in a protest on the third floor of the government building, just outside the Judiciary Committee hearings, and became a vocal advocate of the federal marriage amendment, which would have prevented federal law from overriding state laws regulating same-sex marriage.[7] Although she filed for reelection to the Hawai'i House of Representatives in 2004, Gabbard also remained enlisted in the US Army National Guard. With a twelve-month planned deployment to Iraq in July 2004, she chose not to campaign. This decision made her the first Hawai'ian elected official to resign office to go to war.[8]

Gabbard deployed to Iraq from 2004 to 2005, where she served in a field medical unit of the National Guard in a combat zone. This experience shaped her views on the "true cost of war," which she later expressed in her political speeches. Her twelve-month tour in Iraq included serving at Logistical Support Area Anaconda, part of Balad Air Base, as a specialist with the Twenty-Ninth Infantry Brigade Combat Team. When she returned from Iraq in 2006, Gabbard served as a legislative aide for Senator Daniel Akaka (D-HI), the first Native Hawai'ian in the US Senate. Akaka served first in the US House of Representatives and then from 1990 until 2013 in the US Senate, and there are clear parallels between his and Gabbard's experiences in military and public service. Akaka holds strong religious beliefs, served in the US Army Corps of Engineers until receiving an honorable discharge in 1947, and developed a Hawai'ian-style rapport with his colleagues in government. Though he identified as a liberal Democrat and consistently supported his political party on a majority of legislation, Akaka also vocalized strong support for defense legislation that benefitted military bases in his home state of Hawai'i.[9]

Gabbard continued to advance in her dual public service and military careers, graduating from the accelerated officer candidate school at the Alabama Military Academy, the first woman to finish as the distinguished honor graduate in the academy's fifty-year history, and she deployed to Kuwait for a second tour of duty. Gabbard was commissioned as a second lieutenant, serving as an army military police (MP) officer, and she was assigned to the Twenty-Ninth Infantry Brigade Combat Team again. Between 2008 and 2009, she served as a primary trainer for the Kuwait National Guard. As one of the first women ever to enter a Kuwaiti military facility, she earned recognition for her work in that program. Gabbard also graduated from the Hawai'i Pacific University in 2009, earning a bachelor of science degree in business administration, with a concentration in international business.

A Rising Star

Upon returning home from the Middle East, Gabbard entered the crowded ten-candidate race for the Sixth District seat of the Honolulu City Council, the lawmaking body of the city and county of Honolulu. She finished the September 2010 open primary with 33 percent of the vote, and following a runoff election against Sesnita Moepono, emerged with a double-digit electoral victory. Councilwoman Gabbard introduced measures to support local food truck vendors by easing parking restrictions and introduced a controversial bill that allowed city workers to confiscate personal belongings stored on public property, the latter receiving strong opposition from both the American Civil Liberties Union (ACLU) and Occupy Hawai'i.

Less than three years after earning her seat on the Honolulu City Council, Gabbard once again sought opportunities to serve in national office. Representative Mazie Hirono (D-HI), then the US representative for Hawaii's Second District, announced that she would pursue a US Senate seat in the 2012 election, and Gabbard seized on this opportunity to announce her own candidacy for the open seat. Even with endorsements from the Sierra Club, EMILY's List, and VoteVets, she was a clear underdog in the Democratic primary, facing well-known Mayor Mufi Hannermann of Honolulu in a six-way contest. Yet again, Gabbard beat the odds and won with 62,882 votes (55 percent of the total) in a major upset. In fact, the Honolulu *Star-Advertiser* called her candidacy an "improbable rise from a distant underdog to victory."[10] The grassroots support that pushed her candidacy forward in the primary race likewise carried her through the general election in November 2012, where she defeated Republican Kawika Crowley by a four-to-one margin (168,503 to 40,707 votes, 80.6 percent to 19.4 percent, respectively) and became the first Samoan American and first Hindu member of Congress.

Despite this resounding victory, less than one month later, in December 2012, Gabbard applied to be considered for appointment to the US Senate seat upon the death of Senator Daniel Inouye. Though she did have some support from members of the national Democratic Party, she was not one of the three candidates selected by the Democratic Party of Hawai'i. But her electoral victory in 2012 earned her national name recognition and credibility, specifically from party leaders who labeled her a Democrat to

Hawai'i candidate for Congress Tulsi Gabbard is applauded by House members at the Democratic National Convention in Charlotte, North Carolina, on September 4, 2012. *Source:* Photo by Lynne Sladky, File, AP Photo.

watch. Another rising star, Mayor Cory Booker of Newark, New Jersey, told *Vogue* in 2013, "She's one of the leading voices in the party now."[11] The strength of her campaign and her compelling personal story caught the eye of national Democrats seeking to recruit fresh faces and candidates with diverse backgrounds. In summer 2012, Nancy Pelosi invited her to speak at the Democratic National Convention, and Gabbard served as vice chair for the Democratic National Committee from 2013 to 2016.

As a new member of the House, Gabbard was assigned to the Foreign Affairs Committee and the Homeland Security Committee, though she did not hold a leadership position. She vocally supported the Department of Defense (DOD) policy change to allow female troops in ground combat, calling the decision "an overdue, yet welcome change," and championed legislation and initiatives that promoted clean energy and environmental stewardship. Gabbard was a reliable advocate for veterans and women serving in the military.[12] In one of her first legislative acts, she introduced the bipartisan Helping Heroes Fly Act in March 2013 to improve airport security screenings for wounded veterans. Remarkably, her position on same-sex marriage and civil unions also completely shifted by the start of her first term. In a press release on January 30, 2013, Gabbard affirmed that she "strongly disagree[s] with a two-tiered, discriminatory government policy of 'marriage' and 'civil unions.' Government officials, judges, and bureaucrats should not have the power to declare one relationship 'morally' superior to another."[13]

Gabbard ran for reelection to the House in 2014 and won by a significant margin, defeating Crowley and Libertarian Joe Kent with 75.8 percent of the vote. She was assigned to the Armed Services Committee and Foreign Affairs Committee in her second term and continued to advocate on issues she prioritized during her first term. In 2016 her margin of victory widened further when she defeated Republican Angela Kaaihue with 81.1 percent of the vote, and in 2018, she was reelected for a fourth term.[14] During her third and fourth congressional terms, Gabbard introduced legislation to enhance election security and move the United States away from reliance on fossil fuels, and she cosponsored legislation to enhance congressional oversight of war powers. Gabbard also comfortably broke ranks with leading Democrats when she felt at odds with the party. In 2016, she made the choice to resign from the Democratic National Convention and criticized leadership of the Democratic Party while endorsing Senator Bernie Sanders for the 2016 Democratic presidential nomination.

The 2020 Election

On February 2, 2019, Gabbard launched her 2020 presidential campaign, arguing that it was in the "spirit of service above self." The official launch, however, followed weeks of confusion and miscommunication between Gabbard, her staff, and media outlets reporting on her decision to enter the race. Three weeks prior to her formal February announcement, on January 11, 2019, Gabbard sat for an interview with CNN's Van Jones to discuss her political future. When asked about whether she would enter the race for the Democratic nomination, Gabbard answered directly, "I have decided to run and will be making a formal announcement within the next week."[15] Yet Gabbard's campaign website was not fully ready to go live, and her lean campaign team did not have social media posts co-ordinated to accompany this acknowledgment. *Politico* reported that the CNN interview left her aides working "frantically on a Friday night to get everything up online," and even Jones appeared to be caught off guard by her direct response.[16] Following the CNN announcement, Gabbard's Instagram page posted limited content, mostly in the form of campaign-style videos following her travel back and forth between Washington, DC, and Hawai'i, and two weeks later released a "launch video." Gabbard chose not to follow up her announcement with visits to any of the early primary states, a strategy ordinarily adopted by candidates pursuing the nomination.

Gabbard's approach to media relations and campaign strategy are far from those of an ordinary candidate for political office. In an interview for the *Atlantic*, Gabbard emphasized, "We have a small team of very com-mitted people who really believe in this mission and the kind of leader-ship that I bring."[17] Referring to her campaign and media team as small is something of an understatement. Following the departure of campaign manager Rania Batrice, a former deputy campaign manager for Sanders, and her consulting firm Revolution Messaging, Gabbard's 2020 presi-dential campaign team consisted primarily of close family members and freelance consultants. In the first quarter of 2019, her "Tulsi Now" Fed-eral Election Commission (FEC) filings listed only one full-time employee and a single payment of $2,600 to field staffer Amaury Dujardin, whereas all other members affiliated with her campaign were paid as independent contractors and consultants. Gabbard's husband, Abraham Williams, a trained videographer, often used a special camera stabilizer to livestream her events, and her sister, Vrindavan, played an influential role in cam-paign decisions and frequently took to social media as a vocal champion of her sister's candidacy.

After the departure of Batrice, the Gabbard campaign paid Noland Chambliss as a consultant for campaign management services and slowly expanded the team to include Erika Tsuji as chair and communications director, Erin McCallum as a communications consultant, Cullen Tiernan as a press assistant, and Dujardin as organizing director as well as a variety of other policy, writing, and media consultants.[18] A review of Gabbard's campaign press coverage reveals that Tsuji and Tiernan often acted as

US Representative Tulsi Gabbard addresses attendees at the VoteVets Forum before the New Hampshire Democratic Party Convention in Manchester on September 7, 2019. *Source:* Photo by Nikolas Hample, Sipa USA via AP Images.

spokespeople for the campaign unless Gabbard or her sister were directly addressing the media and the public. With respect to the latter, Gabbard and her close-knit team relied heavily on social media to communicate with the public. FEC filings show that between 2019 and 2020, the campaign invested limited resources in print media and billboards (nearly $310,000), significant resources in both television and radio advertising (nearly $3.1 million), and the most in web-based advertising and promotion (nearly $3.3 million).[19] The campaign spent more than $170,564 on Twitter advertising and messaging; more than $940,000 on Facebook advertising, investing significant amounts in January 2020; and more than $1.4 million on Google advertising, with significant buys in November 2019 and January 2020.[20]

Strikingly, with 159,000 subscribers, her YouTube account consistently had more subscribers than that of any other candidate except Sanders (242,000) in 2019. Likewise, viewership of her videos was high, ranging from 9,000 views up to 1.3 million views. The videos with the most significant viewership tended to feature Gabbard expressing views highly critical of the Democratic "establishment" or US foreign policy in the Middle East.

Gabbard saw a sizable increase in followers and subscribers throughout fall 2019, but those increases did not match up with any similar-size news event or in her polling visibility.[21]

Her supporters on these platforms tend to be overwhelmingly male and fall outside of traditional Democratic circles. A significant portion were more likely to have backed Donald Trump in 2016 and hold conservative views, or identify as Republican, compared with voters backing the other Democratic candidates. An early November poll from the *Economist* and YouGov found that 24 percent of Democratic primary voters who voted for Trump in 2016 backed Gabbard. Primary voters who identified as conservative also backed Gabbard in that poll (16 percent)—only Joe Biden and Kamala Harris enjoyed more support from this group (27 percent and 17 percent, respectively).[22]

As a candidate in the Democratic presidential primary, Gabbard drew on her multicultural background and record of military service to demonstrate her qualifications for the nation's highest executive office. She frequently invoked populist language to situate her candidacy and position on issues, consistent with global trends in populist rhetoric recently analyzed by scholars in both North America and Europe.[23] At its simplest, populism is the belief that government policies should be determined by the will of the masses rather than any elite. However, populism has come to mean opposition, often revolutionary opposition, to the elite minority of citizens in any nation who hold most of the economic or political power. Populist rhetoric normally casts the elite who rule as abusing the masses, trampling on their rights, and ignoring their voices. Although left-wing populists generally oppose the power of the wealthy, big business, capitalism, and religious authority, right-wing populists also claim to represent "the common man" in their opposition to what they see as a left-wing intellectual elite.

When expressing her position on issues of both domestic and foreign policy, Gabbard consistently borrowed populist rhetoric. She reminded voters, "We need to decide whether we want to continue as a country to be the world's police . . . or focus on taking care of our people and rebuilding our own communities. We cannot afford to do both."[24] The "we" that underlies Gabbard's sense of connection to community and others, the foundation for her campaign and ideology, is grounded in her spiritual

Democratic presidential candidate US Representative Tulsi Gabbard (D-HI) does an interview before the Labor Day parade in Dubuque, Iowa, on September 2, 2019. *Source:* Jessica Reilly, Telegraph Herald via AP.

beliefs—a blend of Christianity, Hinduism, and "aloha." Hawai'ian officials are directed to "give consideration to the 'Aloha spirit'" as they discharge their duties, and Gabbard takes that directive to heart, explaining on her campaign website, "Aloha is a promise to protect all living things, the earth we inhabit, the air we all breathe, and the water that gives us all life. We are all connected. We are brothers and sisters."[25] She continues, "That's why I have made aloha a central focus of my campaign. Our campaign is motivated by aloha, rooted in aloha, and is an expression of aloha. Aloha is the spirit of deep respect and love for all of God's children— regardless of their race, religion, gender, sexual orientation, economic status, or level of education."[26]

In the latter statement, she links the connective aspects of her spiritual beliefs with the populism expressed in her politics and the principle of "service above self." Whether this service is in the form of volunteering for local civic organizations and cofounding the HHC or campaigning for local office and enlisting in the armed forces, Gabbard expresses a vision of duty and civic engagement for the well-being of humanity.

Moreover, Gabbard's "service above self" approach to representation allowed her to traverse the politics of both left-wing and right-wing populism. She referenced the "common man" and anti-interventionism, which helped her gain traction with antielitist supporters of Trump from the 2016 election as well as more liberal voters concerned about the environmental abuses of corporations and big business. Her description of her campaign as an open space of respect, where Americans of any political background are welcome, appeals to antielitist, right-wing populists who feel disconnected from establishment Republicans and Democrats. "It is my personal commitment to you that I will always treat you, and all my fellow Americans, with respect. Everyone deserves respect no matter their race, religion, or political views or affiliation."[27] And she offers strong critiques of environmental policy, appealing to left-wing populists who feel that establishment Democrats have not taken bold enough action to address climate change issues.

> Whether we like it or not, our fates as human beings in this world are tied together. And the issues that we face—pollution of our air, our waters, oceans, the climate crisis that's before us—these are all issues that require us to sit down, to talk, and to work together. Whether it be with friends or with people who are adversaries or potential adversaries. If we in the United States do all that we can right now to address climate change, it will still not be enough. We cannot solve these problems alone. We have to work together. We have to work together to make sure that our kids today and for generations to come can not only survive, but thrive, and prosper, without fear of toxic and poisonous water, or polluted air, or not enough food to eat.[28]

These themes, "service above self" and "aloha" as a connective populism, flow through her foreign policy positions as well.

The "True Cost of War"

Gabbard expends significant time during her public appearances and in her media, both digital and print, sharing her story of military service and leadership. One of three veterans who pursued the Democratic nomination, including Mayor Pete Buttigieg (D-IN) and US Representative Seth

Moulton (D-MA), Gabbard insisted that her military service distinguished her in an otherwise crowded field. In making her case to Democratic voters and the public, Gabbard emphasized her military service in terms of experience or "credentialing" and a unique ideology or worldview relative to front-runners in the party. She reminded potential voters that she enlisted in the Army National Guard after the terrorist attacks on 9/11 and served as a soldier for more than sixteen years. The language she used to characterize her military career emphasized it as both a calling and a form of service, in line with her campaign motto of "service above self." This language was the cornerstone of her presidential campaign rhetoric; it was used in the media produced by the campaign advertisements and even became an active hashtag (#serviceaboveself) used by her supporters on Twitter. The examples below illustrate not only her campaign's use of this approach but also how the motto inspired and activated her supporters, who frequently retweeted examples of their own acts of "#serviceaboveself."

Beyond service, Gabbard also emphasized the relevance of her experience, including deployment to conflict zones in the Middle East and her choice of specialization on legislative committees. Gabbard explicitly connected her service specifically to qualifications for the presidential role of commander in chief. In a PBS NewsHour interview with Judy Woodruff about why she felt better qualified to be president in 2020 than Sanders, rather than supporting him as she did in 2016, Gabbard responded:

> It's the expertise and experience that I bring to this job. The most important job that a president has is to serve as commander in chief, to keep the American people safe and secure. And so the experience that I bring of serving as a soldier for over sixteen years, of deploying twice to the Middle East, and serving in Congress now for over six years on both the Armed Services and Foreign Affairs Committees, have brought me that experience and understanding about the issues that face our country and our national security and the cost of war, so that I can walk in on day one to do that job, as president and commander in chief.[29]

At times, Gabbard's attempts to showcase her military service have created issues for her campaign. In August 2018, for example, the Honolulu Star-Advertiser reported that the Hawai'i Army National Guard instructed Gabbard that a video of her in uniform on her VoteTulsi Facebook page did not comply with military ethics rules. Gabbard's campaign removed the video and added a disclaimer to the website's banner image of Gabbard in uniform in a veteran's cemetery clarifying that the image does not imply an endorsement from the military. A spokesperson for Gabbard said that her campaign would continue to work closely with the DOD to ensure compliance with all regulations in the future.

Is Today the Day?

In town hall gatherings and campaign media, Gabbard shared a very formative experience, one that fundamentally reshaped her beliefs about war and peace: "The first day Tulsi arrived at her camp in Iraq, she saw a large sign at one of the gates that read, 'Is today the day?' It was a blunt reminder that today may be the day that any of the soldiers would be called to make the ultimate sacrifice for their country. It caused her to reflect on her own life and the reality that each of us could die at any moment."[30]

Her economic policy platform has been described as populist, and her foreign policy platform has been described as anti-interventionist. Her critique of the Bush-era wars in the Middle East is particularly important because she grounds her antiwar arguments in her personal experience witnessing the "cost of war." In some ways, this immunizes her from the "soft on terrorism" charges so many Democrats face, making her a powerful critic of nation-building and "wars of choice."[31] Though a handful of candidates delivered foreign policy speeches, the Democratic primary of 2020 remained focused on domestic issues. Given Gabbard's background of military service and work on foreign policy and veterans issues, she saw a strategic opening for herself in the foreign policy space. She critiqued moderators of Democratic debates for not raising the issue of nuclear weapons or the threat of nuclear war, which she regards as "the most existential threat we face in this country."[32] When discussing the presidency, she specifically emphasized the constitutional role of commander in chief and the president's role in foreign policy. In her mind, these are the foundation for all other areas of policymaking:

> And there are many different issues that we face here domestically, and you will hear a lot of the other candidates talking about that. But what

is often not addressed is the fact that our foreign policy, the cost of these continued wasteful regime change wars that we have been waging now for so long, has a direct connection to our domestic policy and our ability to invest the resources that we need to in things like health care, education, infrastructure, and so on.[33]

Gabbard believes foreign policy and domestic policy are inextricably connected, which aligns with her larger philosophical beliefs about the interconnectedness of the human experience and antielite populist ideology. She openly questions and criticizes members of the political establishment, asking "if those who voted to send soldiers to Iraq really understood why they were there—if lawmakers and the President reflected daily on each death, each injury, and the immeasurably high cost of war?"[34] She refers to "chickenhawks" in both parties and argues that the media and the congressional military industrial complex are promoting wars "for their own power and profit."[35] Weaving populist language throughout her critiques, Gabbard lambasts those she perceives as "elites who direct wars tucked away in hidden bunkers" in contrast with those who serve in the military and engage in active combat on behalf of the United States.[36]

Gabbard's strong views on the relationship between military experience and governmental war-making powers derive from her experiences serving in Iraq and Kuwait, which led her to reflect on the very real dangers of working in a combat zone. Her work in the medical unit involved serving at a base located in a densely populated region of Iraq northwest of Baghdad at the height of the war. She shares that part of her responsibilities included the daily task of going through the list of every injury and casualty for the entire theater of operations, looking to see if any soldiers in her unit were on the list so she could ensure they received the care they needed and their families were notified. These experiences led her to evaluate not only her personal position as a soldier in the larger theater of war but also the impact of conflict on those with whom she served and their families. In this context she began to wonder about the impact, or "true cost," of war, and her field experience became the central focus of her subsequent campaigns for political office—a commitment to preventing the US government from "sending our troops into war without a clear mission, strategy, or purpose."[37]

With these goals in mind, Gabbard is broadly anti-interventionist and argues that the United States should not use its military power to reshape other countries' political systems but rather should use diplomacy to find common ground and avoid war even with the most intransigent adversaries. When Gabbard was once asked about her work on the Council on Foreign Relations (CFR), she noted that many on the CFR did not share her foreign policy views, but she qualified her remarks: "If we only sit in rooms with people who we agree with, then we won't be able to bring about the kind of change that we need to see."[38] Gabbard's team often refers to this example as a way of explaining her approach to controversial issues of foreign policy, and her actions demonstrate she is committed to this principle in theory and in practice. In March 2015, for example, Gabbard broke with members of the Democratic Party and chose not to boycott Benjamin Netanyahu's address to the US Congress, saying at the time that relations "must rise above the political fray, as America continues to stand with Israel as her strongest ally."[39] As a worldview, this belief frames her discussion on three specific areas of international security and foreign policy: ending what she refers to as "regime change wars," deescalating the new cold war, and acknowledging an active nuclear arms race.

When explaining her views across each of these areas, Gabbard emphasizes her military service to convince the audience that she is a credible source and that her words have weight and should be taken seriously. She has the experience and judgment necessary to decide what's right. In each speech, each piece of campaign media, and each town hall or debate, she connects her experience and military status as an Iraq War veteran and a major in the Army National Guard to knowledge and capacity for leadership; she knows the "true cost of war."

Gabbard also appeals to the emotion of potential voters and supporters. Using populist rhetoric and her unique "aloha" worldview, she tries to inspire action or change people's positions on issues. She uses strong language to describe the consequences of "wars of regime change," arguing to her audience that they have "cost our nation trillions of dollars and thousands of lives, simultaneously creating more devastation, human suffering, and refugees in the countries where U.S. regime change war is waged."[40] She believes message like this resonates with voters, who should express concern and take action given that the United States "would be far better off spending the trillions of dollars wasted in interventionist wars on more pressing domestic issues in America, like infrastructure, college debt, healthcare, etc."[41]

To achieve these foreign policy goals and prevent escalating nuclear tensions, Gabbard argues that the United States should "abandon the path to confrontation and war" and "pursue the path of cooperation, diplomacy, and peace."[42] As an extension of these goals and in the spirit of aloha, she believes that the president and US officials should "have the courage to meet with leaders of other countries—whether they be adversaries or potential adversaries—in order to achieve peace and security."[43] Although there is internal consistency in Gabbard's ideology and principled approach to foreign policy, the choices she has made while in Congress have led to significant moments of conflict with the Democratic Party over terrorism and US foreign policy in Iraq, Libya, Syria, and Venezuela.

In 2015, the United States witnessed significant partisan conflicts over terrorism, and President Barack Obama's refusal to adopt the phrase "radical Islam." Democrats supported the president, whereas Republicans argued that the president's commitment to political correctness was preventing him from identifying the root cause of jihadist violence: Islamist theology. As early as January 2015, Gabbard began appearing on cable news channels such as CNN and Fox voicing heavy criticism of the Obama administration's policy on terrorism, echoing many of the positions of her Republican colleagues. In an interview with Wolf Blitzer, she lamented, "What is so frustrating . . . is that our administration refuses to recognize who our enemy is. And unless and until that happens, then it's impossible to come up with a strategy to defeat that enemy. We have to recognize that this is about radical Islam."[44] Later that year she met with US-backed President Abdel Fattah el-Sisi of Egypt to discuss the "threat of ISIS and Islamic extremist groups" two years after he led the August 2013 Rabaa massacre, which killed hundreds of civilians.

Going one step further, Gabbard and a small minority of foreign policy analysts began publicly advocating that the best way to defeat the Islamic State in Iraq and Syria (ISIL) was for the United States to align itself with President Bashar al-Assad of Syria. She argued that the United States should cut funding to the rebels fighting Assad and went as far as sponsoring a bill in Congress to cut off US support.[45] In fall 2015, when Russia began its bombing campaign in Syria, Gabbard celebrated it as a win for counterterrorism and issued a series of tweets to rally her supporters.

Two years later, in one of the more controversial moments of her political career, Gabbard traveled to Syria in January 2017 and met with Assad personally, catching Democratic leadership in Congress off guard. Though she informed the House Ethics Committee of her trip to Syria one month prior to departure, she acknowledges that the meeting with Assad was "unplanned" and was part of a series of meetings with religious leaders, citizens, and activists.[46] Upon returning from her visit, Gabbard expressed the unpopular positions of the Assad regime—including the notion that the anti-Assad rebel groups were no different from ISIL. This led to significant criticism from her own political party, including public statements by Loren DeJonge Schulman, a senior National Security Council (NSC) official in the Obama administration: "Rep. Gabbard loses me and, I think, many others when she claims to support peaceful values and policies that protect civilians and still engages with and even defends a murderous dictator, Bashar al-Assad. There is no excuse for this. The hypocrisy of these actions is astonishing. One can be antiwar without being pro-murderous dictator, a fact that seems obvious."[47] But following Gabbard's logic, she would argue there is no hypocrisy in her positions and statements. She has consistently supported policies that prioritize regional stability. Independent analysts and political leaders have expressed concerns that removing Assad could destabilize the Syrian state. As she reiterates, her views on military "intervention" have been framed in the context of unending post-9/11 wars, and she strongly objects to deploying troops without a "clear mission, strategy, or purpose." That test has not been met for her in Syria, let alone Iraq, Libya, or Venezuela.

This does not mean Gabbard is a pacifist; her rhetoric and issue positioning strongly suggest otherwise. She has sharply criticized inaction on the part of both the Obama administration and Trump administration, particularly when a military response would have excluded a significant group troop presence.[48] In November 2018, after President Trump indicated that the United States would not sanction Saudi Arabia over the killing of Jamal Khashoggi, Gabbard tweeted at Trump, "Being Saudi Arabia's bitch is not 'America First.'"[49] These principles, although controversial, form the basis of an evolving sort of "just war" doctrine she is creating.[50]

Gender Politics

While describing the important military, officeholder, and candidate experiences that form the body of her political career, Gabbard consciously draws attention to the series of "firsts" marked by her work. This includes being one of the first female combat veterans elected to Congress, along with Tammy Duckworth, and the first female combat veteran to run for the presidency. As I discussed previously in this book, Gabbard emphasizes how these experiences not only prepare her to lead the nation as the commander in chief, but also to understand what she will explain is the "true cost of war" to potential Democratic voters. Further, to achieve these milestones and establish herself as a woman candidate who has accomplished a series of "firsts" within the very masculine structure of the US military, she reminds voters she is prepared to achieve another "first" as the first woman president of the United States in an equally masculine political institution.

When Gabbard transitions fluidly between her roles as an active military servicemember and congressional representative, she also adjusts her personal appearance and image to suit each role. Photographs of Gabbard shared on her campaign website and through other media channels depict her in military attire, according to guidelines outlined by the Army National Guard. Political science research has shown that voters tend to assess men as assertive, active, and self-confident, whereas they identify women as compassionate, willing to compromise, and people-oriented.[51] And male candidates are perceived as more competent than women in the areas of military crises, crime, and the economy; women are viewed as more competent on issues of gender equity, education, health care, and poverty.[52] Photographs of Gabbard in uniform and in military service convey that she possesses many of the traits voters might associate with male candidates. These stand in stark contrast to the feminized, softened images of US representative and candidate Gabbard shared on her official congressional website and featured in her campaign media.

Interestingly, potential voters and supporters rarely see images of their elected representatives or candidates in wetsuits and swimwear to the degree we see Gabbard depicted. The *New York Times*, to this author's knowledge, has not invited candidates such as Biden or Sanders to appear in half-zipped wetsuits atop surfboards. Yet, in an in-depth political profile, the *New York Times* chose an image of Gabbard in a form-fitting wetsuit as their banner for the feature. Is it because she is conveying the aloha vibe of Hawai'i, her home state? Perhaps she is showcasing her athleticism and youth? Or is it because she is an attractive woman? The same *New York Times* piece featured two quotes describing her as such:

> On Capitol Hill, she is often regarded as a glamorous anomaly: a Hawaiian action figure, fabulously out of place among her besuited colleagues. "She's almost straight from central casting, if you need a heroine," Van Jones, the progressive activist, says. Trey Gowdy, the South Carolina Republican, is one of her closest friends in Congress. He first spied her on the House floor, sitting on the Republican side of the aisle. "This sounds terrible to say, but it's also true—you know, she's cute."[53]

In contrast, Gabbard's team selected photographs of her in a striking white pantsuit, which she also wore to a series of Democratic debates and posted as the official image for her social media profiles, and 2019 became a banner year for the white pantsuit in politics. The House Democratic Women's Working Group invited women of both political parties to wear white to the 2019 State of the Union address in honor of the legacy of women's suffrage. Commentators noted that the "sartorial choice creates a powerful visual representation of elected women's leadership."[54] Notable Democrats continued to make appearances throughout 2019 in white ensembles, and Gabbard made the choice to participate in this symbolic statement of fashion as well. In November 2019, however, a New York style critic argued that the Hawai'i representative's wardrobe made her look like a "cult leader" full of "combative righteousness." The terrifying white fabric has "connotations of the fringe, rather than the center" and even undermines "community building," Vanessa Friedman wrote.[55] The critique unleashed a firestorm on Twitter when Gabbard supporters pointed to an earlier article published by the same fashion critic praising then-candidate Hillary Clinton for her identical choice of a white pantsuit in 2016. The fact that Gabbard's team elected to use an image of her in this particular piece of fashion is yet another example of her determination to make choices that suit her beliefs and vision for her campaign without

Democratic presidential candidate US Representative Tulsi Gabbard (D-HI) speaks during a Democratic presidential primary debate on November 20, 2019, in Atlanta. *Source*: John Bazemore, AP Photo.

regard for the preferences of the *New York Times* or any other established institution of US politics.

The End of a Campaign

Although Gabbard was the most frequently Googled candidate of the first, second, and fourth Democratic debates, her campaign struggled to gain momentum.[56] She remained skeptical of the Democratic National Committee (DNC) and at one point criticized its criteria for debate qualification as lacking transparency.[57] The Gabbard campaign invested significant energy campaigning in New Hampshire, where voters have a notorious independent streak and the early primary can provide campaigns important momentum in the primary process. However, she finished seventh in the polls and went on to gain only two delegates on Super Tuesday from the caucuses of American Samoa. In a video message posted on March 19, 2020, Gabbard dropped out of the 2020 election and endorsed the leading Democratic candidate, Biden.[58]

Gabbard announced in October 2019 that she would not seek reelection to her House seat while pursuing the presidential nomination, and her congressional term likewise ended on January 3, 2021. Since leaving office, she has leveraged her strong social media presence to start her own podcast, *This Is Tulsi Gabbard*. She continues to make appearances on conservative talk shows and has become highly critical of Democratic Party leadership, including US Representative Adam Schiff, whom she referred to as a "domestic terrorist."[59]

In keeping with congressional tradition, Gabbard filled her office with mementos of her home state, including a plaque at the receptionist's desk bearing a friendly but blunt message: "Aloha spirit required here. If you can't share it today, please visit us some other time." When Gabbard shares her passion for "aloha" and "service," she is speaking the language of politics and the military and faith all at once. In speaking her truth, Gabbard's direct, sometimes blunt approach to discussing domestic and foreign policy issues breaks ranks from the Democratic Party. This often engenders praise from the political right and derision from the political left. Her interest in foreign policy alone sets her apart from other ambitious Democrats, many of whom have difficulty articulating a clear position on Syria and virtually all of whom would rather attach themselves to the kinds of domestic issues—opposition to the Trump administration, reducing inequality and poverty, combatting discrimination—that excite and motivate the Democratic base. In this way, Gabbard's approach "can make her seem unusually principled, or maybe just unusual."[60] Her controversial positions reflect her most authentic convictions, and evidence would suggest that her congressional and presidential campaigns were not based on a series of political calculations but a function of the convictions she holds—a matter of principle. Sometimes this resonates with her supporters, giving them a taste of authenticity they crave in US politics, but it can also generate significant controversy and criticism by creating conflict and costing support of leadership within her own political party— fissures that might inhibit her ability to serve at the highest levels.

It's not about being the first female anything. It's about not wanting to be average.
—Tammy Duckworth

When I originally conceived this book, I was just wrapping up an article on Tulsi Gabbard's 2020 presidential bid. Gabbard was one of several women with a record of active military service or veteran status serving in Congress until 2018. But 2018 was another record-breaking year for women in politics, when women with military backgrounds and intelligence experience were elected in historical numbers. Inspired by their diverse paths to politics, the ways in which they communicated their stories, and their policy positions, I wanted to write a book about the significance of this new cohort of political women. What motivates them to run for office? How do they connect their military service to their careers in public service? Does having a military or intelligence background allow them to overcome documented gendered stereotypes about women candidates and foreign policy?

As I was gathering materials to analyze the communication strategies of these women, I was unable to find secondary literature or scholarly investigations of their lives that could serve as the basis for further analysis. I started writing biographical sketches based on research compiled from a variety of primary sources to lay the foundation for the communications strategy and rhetorical analysis work. Each sketch developed into a fuller story that included the personal background of the candidate/officeholder, her military or intelligence service and achievements, her campaigns for elected office, and her work as a legislator. In the end, I found the significance and complexity of each woman's path from military service to public service a compelling story in its own right. To date, there are no such scholarly treatments of their historic contributions and military or political "firsts."

I began my effort to connect the stories of women with military or quasimilitary backgrounds who served in national office. Some names are more familiar than others, particularly those who have made headlines. Their stories have been told individually by journalists and in some cases scholars before this writing. But there is a familiar saying: "When drinking the water, don't forget who dug the well." As I researched more deeply the stories of women in the headlines, my questions drew me further into the stories of the advocates and mentors who preceded them. Each accolade or "first" was accomplished with support from the well-digging of generations of servicewomen and allies in government before them. The legacy of each servicewoman in this book transcends her specific accomplishments in service or in politics. The whole of this story is greater than the sum of the individual parts. It is crucial to examine the antecedents of these figures; those servicewomen who first contributed to what Margaret Chase Smith called the "natural chapter" of American women's history.

Service as Ambition

What can we learn from this broader view of women in American politics by reading the collective stories of women with military or quasimilitary backgrounds who translated that experience into political ambition? Each servicewoman's story examines the factors that motivated the candidate or Congressmember to seek office, further contributing to the literature on political ambition and participation. This includes the motivations for these women seeking their first elected office (local, state, or national) as well as the factors that influenced their decision to pursue subsequent elected positions, including Tammy Duckworth's rise from the House of Representatives to the US Senate, Joni Ernst's move from Iowa state government to the US Senate, and Gabbard's entry into the Democratic presidential primaries from the US House of Representatives.

Broadly speaking, the pool of eligible servicewomen candidates for political office has been shaped by structural factors, specifically the growth in opportunities for women's service and leadership in the military. As servicewomen and their allies in government fought to institutionalize women's military and quasimilitary roles, as better occupational choices became open to women in the military, and as women assumed leadership positions, increasing numbers of women pursued careers in the US Armed Forces. This advocacy and change were supported by what Jeremy Teigen has called "extant factors" in military and political life—wars, military institutions, and politics.[1] For early servicewomen, the economic, political, and social disruptions of war created opportunities and necessities for their participation in military and quasimilitary work. Legislative initiatives and directives from the executive branch of government lifted barriers for women entering service academies, expanding their eligibility for regular status, combat, and leadership positions.

Most of the women I analyze in *Service above Self* were recruited or encouraged to run for political office, which follows a pattern outlined in recent studies of women and political participation.[2] Carroll and Sanbonmatsu (2013) also argue that a combination of lack of recruitment and beliefs about how officeholding will affect their personal lives and relationships affects women's ambition for public office. Like Lawless and Fox (2005), they see gender as both a political and a social construct that has created a masculinized political sphere that makes women feel less qualified to hold public office. However, this relational paradigm does not neatly align with the experience of the women I analyzed in *Service above Self*, who chose to enter military service, an arguably hypermasculine institution, before seeking public office. The question is whether the bombardments of war adequately prepared them for the bombast of electoral politics.

The narratives I feature in this book reveal how the education, training, and socialization of servicewomen in their military and quasimilitary careers shaped their attitudes about gender and the military as well as gender and politics. In both capacities, these women expressed a desire to be treated as individuals without regard to their gender. Duckworth insisted that her decisions in the military were not based on "being the first female anything. It's about not wanting to be average."[3] When Ernst sought mentorship in her new military leadership role, she reiterated to her commanders that she did not specifically need a woman mentor: "The way I saw it, a soldier is a soldier. It doesn't matter your gender. You still have the same job to do."[4]

Yet, these stories and those of other servicewomen in this project illustrate that their experiences were shaped by gender. The prevalence of sexual assault and discrimination in their lived experiences gave them unique insights when appointed to congressional committees with oversight on military service academies. Martha McSally's challenge to dress code policies for servicewomen in Saudi Arabia, M. J. Hegar's efforts to overturn ground-combat exclusion policies barring women, and several other examples of women who fought against inequitable policies and standards elucidate how gender influenced their experiences and opportunities in the armed services.

Kaitlin Sidorsky's All Roads Lead to Power, which I referenced previously in this work, analyzes the political motivations of women who accept appointed positions. She found that appointed women pursue their positions "for an ambition unrelated to the political career ladder—yet an important ambition all the same."[5] Like many of the women in her book, the women with military and intelligence backgrounds I write about did not seek public office for the sake of gaining political power, advantage, or prestige. Rather, they saw elected political office as a path to fulfilling their sense of civic duty, responsibility, and obligation to serve. Their political careers became an extension of their military careers rather than a break from their prior national service. The oath of enlistment, for example, requires servicemembers to swear (or affirm) that they will "support and defend the Constitution of the United States against all enemies, foreign and domestic" and "bear true faith and allegiance to the same." The congressional oath of office begins with the same refrain, and servicemembers draw a clear line between their oath to defend the country in uniform and their oath in public service. Several members of the "Security Democrats" or "Badasses" in Congress, expressed concern that Donald Trump's administration posed a clear domestic threat to the Constitution and the United States—concern borne out in the Capitol attack on January 6, 2021. Some servicemembers felt that their military or quasimilitary service prepared them to shape US national security or foreign policy, an important perspective because the number of veterans in Congress steadily declined in the twentieth and twenty-first centuries. Others expressed their interest in running for elected office as a calling or duty and simply saw political service as an extension of their prior military service to the country.

Though many of the servicewomen entered politics with a service-oriented or mission-focused approach to public policy making, these candidates struggled to balance that goal with partisan politics. Gabbard's independent positions on foreign policy often put her at odds with Democratic Party leadership. Though Ernst and McSally hoped to maintain independent perspectives on behalf of their respective home states, their voting records aligned with Trump's administration more than 90 percent of the time. Despite strong recruitment efforts and substantial funding support, servicewomen candidates are not always successful, and some veterans did not win their electoral contests. In Kentucky's Sixth District, Democrat Amy McGrath, a veteran US Marine fighter pilot, came within nearly 3 percentage points of unseating her opponent, US Representative Andy Barr (R-KY), who won a fourth term in office. She subsequently lost by an even larger margin to Senate Majority Leader Mitch McConnell (R-KY) in 2020. US Air Force veteran Hegar, a Democrat, also lost a tight race to US Representative John Carter (R-TX) in the Thirty-First District, a conservative swath Trump won in 2016, as well as her senatorial challenge to John Cornyn (R-TX) in 2020.

The chronological structure of the initial chapters of this book also revealed characteristics that differentiate generations of veterans and servicewomen who served prior to 9/11 from those who served during the war on terror and related wars in Afghanistan and Iraq. Veterans from more recent conflicts, for example, have the highest levels of education of any previous cohort of servicemembers. More than three-quarters of post-9/11 and Gulf War veterans had at least some college experience, and more than one-third of Gulf War veterans had a college degree. Post-9/11 veterans also have a 43 percent chance of experiencing a service-connected disability, after accounting for differences in demographic and social characteristics among veterans, significantly higher than that of veterans from other periods. According to the Pew Research Center, roughly three-quarters of post-9/11 veterans were deployed at least once, compared with 58 percent of those who served before them. And post-9/11 veterans are about twice as likely as their pre-9/11 counterparts to have served in a combat zone. Post-9/11 women veterans are also more racially diverse and younger than their male colleagues.[6] The average level of educational attainment, increasing percentage of women, and diversification of servicemembers are reflected in the personal and professional backgrounds of the post-9/11 servicewomen I featured in this book.

Avenues of Future Research

Since 1973, when the US military ended conscription and established an all-volunteer force, the number of women serving in active duty rose dramatically. The share of women among the enlisted ranks increased sevenfold, from 2 percent to 14 percent, and the share among commissioned officers quadrupled, from 4 percent to 16 percent.[7] Women in this decade constituted a much greater share of the active-duty military than at any time in US history. Historical records show that significant waves of women occupied military or quasimilitary roles during times of war and conflict throughout US history. Correspondingly, historians have illustrated how those events became a catalyst for economic, political, and social change in US society. The context of World War I for women's suffrage or World War II for women's labor opportunities are two such examples, and it is becoming increasingly apparent that the terrorist attacks of 9/11 also altered opportunities and motivations for women in military or quasimilitary roles.

Though the number of women with service backgrounds in Congress is at historically high levels, they still represent a small sample that presents challenges for statistical analysis. As the number of women with military experience increases, so does the number of eligible servicewomen candidates to run for political office. It will be interesting to see whether the current trend in their candidacies is an aberration or the beginning of a new generation of veterans in public office. Increasing the numbers of prospective candidates and elected servicewomen or expanding the study to include state and local candidates would allow for further analysis of their legislative behavior.

Likewise, political action committees (PACs), political parties, and private organizations have worked vigorously to recruit "service" and "servant leader" candidates for elected office. Scholars should take note of how these organizations inform the public of their mission and how they promote the importance of support for service candidates. Groups such as New Politics; With Honor Action, a "cross-partisan movement dedicated to promoting and advancing principled veteran leadership in elected public service"; and the Service First Women's Victory Fund, organized by the five "Badasses of Congress," represent a parallel emerging trend.

Future research will continue to measure the political impact of women and veterans who serve in office. In telling their stories, this book identifies shared experiences that bind them together as servicewomen as well as the factors that distinguish them from each other in political life. Whether looking at servicewomen's experiences across history or as individual biographies, it is my hope that *Service above Self* provides a foundational synthesis with insights into the motivations of women who have served their country to broaden this "natural chapter" in US history and politics.

NOTES

1. SERVICE ABOVE SELF

1. Margaret Chase Smith, interview with Janann Sherman, March 9, 1989, Margaret Chase Smith Library, Skowhegan, Maine (hereafter referred to as MCSL).

2. "Women in Congress," *Hartford Courant*, June 1, 1948, scrapbook clipping, 53, MCSL.

3. Margaret Chase Smith, interview with Janann Sherman, October 24, 1992, MCSL.

4. Janann Sherman, *No Place for a Woman: A Life of Senator Margaret Chase Smith* (New Brunswick, NJ: Rutgers University Press, 2001), 4.

5. According to the US Department of Labor, there were nearly 2 million women veterans in the United States in 2019. Women make up almost 10 percent of the overall veteran population. Veterans make up 14 percent of men in the United States but only 1.5 percent of women. There are also age gaps and generational differences, with the median age of male veterans at sixty-five years and the median age of female veterans at fifty-one years. "2019 Gender and Veteran Demographics Webinar" (Washington, DC: US Department of Labor, Veterans' Employment and Training Service, 2020), https://www.dol.gov/agencies/vets/womenveterans/womenveterans-demographics. See also Jonathan Vespa, *Those Who Served: America's Veterans from World War II to the War on Terror*, Report No. ACS-43 (Washington, DC: US Census Bureau, June 2, 2020), https://www.census.gov/content/dam/Census/library/publications/2020/demo/acs-43.pdf.

6. Leo Shane III, "Here Are the 173 Veterans Running for Congress in November," *Military Times*, October 19, 2018, https://www.militarytimes.com/news/pentagon-congress/2018/10/19/here-are-the-172-veterans-running-for-congress-in-november/ (please note that 172 is an error in the URL). The 173 candidates included those who won major party primaries and advanced to the general election. That number does not include candidates from minor parties or those who did not win the nomination of a major political party. See also Leo Shane III, "Here Are the 182 Veterans Running for Congress This Year," *Military Times*, October 21, 2020, https://www.militarytimes.com/news/pentagon-congress/2020/10/21/here-are-the-181-veterans-running-for-congress-this-year/ (please note that 181 is an error in the URL); Leo Shane III, "More Vets Running for Congress This Election, but Numbers on Capitol Hill May Still Drop," *Military Times*, October 21, 2020, https://www.militarytimes.com/news/pentagon-congress/2020/10/21/more-vets-running-for-congress-this-election-but-numbers-on-capitol-hill-may-still-drop/.

7. A. W. Geiger, Kristin Bialik, and John Gramlich, "The Changing Face of Congress in 6 Charts," FactTank, Pew Research Center, February 15, 2019, https://www.pewresearch.org/fact-tank/2019/02/15/the-changing-face-of-congress/; W. T. Bianco and J. Markham, "Vanishing Veterans: The Decline of Military Experience in the US Congress," in *Soldiers and Civilians: The Civil-Military Gap and American National Security*, ed. Peter Feaver and Richard Kohn (Cambridge: Massachusetts Institute of Technology Press, 2001), 275–288; W. T. Bianco, "Last Post for 'The Greatest Generation': The Policy Implications of the Decline of Military Experience in the US Congress," *Legislative Studies Quarterly* 30, no. 1 (February 2005): 85–102; O. R. Holsti, "A Widening Gap Between the US Military and Civilian Society? Some Evidence, 1976–96," *International Security* 23, no. 3 (1999): 5–42; O. R. Holsti, "Of Chasms and Convergences: Attitudes and Beliefs of Civilians and Military Elites at the Start of a New Millennium," in *Soldiers and Civilians: The Civil-Military Gap and American National Security*, ed. Peter Feaver and Richard Kohn (Cambridge: Massachusetts Institute of Technology Press, 2001), 15–100; Richard Kohn, "Out of Control: The Crisis in Civil-Military Relations," *National Interest* 35 (1994): 3–17; Sam C. Sarkesian, John Allen Williams, and Fred B. Bryant, *Soldiers, Society, and National Security* (Boulder, CO: Lynne Rienner, 1995).

8. Stuart Rothenberg, "Republican Recruiting," *Rothenberg Political Report*, October 23, 2007, http://insideelections.com/news/article/republican-recruiting; see also Monika L. McDermott and Costas Panagopoulos, "Be All That You Can Be: The Electoral Impact of Military Service as an Information Cue," *Political Research Quarterly* 68, no. 2 (2015): 293–305, http://www.jstor.org/stable/24371833.

9. Susan Zeiger, *In Uncle Sam's Service: Women Workers with the American Expeditionary Force, 1917–1919* (Ithaca, NY: Cornell University Press, 1999); Lettie Gavin, *American Women in World War I: They Also Served* (Niwot: University Press of Colorado, 1997); Cynthia Enloe, *Does Khaki Become You? The Militarisation of Women's Lives* (Boston: South End, 1983); Margaret Randolph Higonnet, Jane Jenson, Sonya Michael, and Margaret Collins Weitz, eds., *Behind the Lines: Gender and the Two World Wars* (New Haven, CT: Yale University Press, 1987); Claire Duncanson and Rachel Woodward. "Regendering the Military: Theorizing Women's Military Participation," *Security Dialogue* 47, no. 1 (2016): 3–21.

10. Zeiger, *In Uncle Sam's Service*, 2–3. Historians have documented the use of women's labor by the military in every war in US history, but Zeiger notes that until World War I their employment was either limited or the conditions under which they worked were informal, unorganized, or voluntary. See also Nina Bennett Smith, "The Women Who Went to War" (PhD diss., Northwestern University, 1981).

11. Zeiger, *In Uncle Sam's Service*, 161.

12. Zeiger, 170.

13. Joanne Meyerowitz, ed., *Not June Cleaver: Women and Gender in Postwar America, 1945–1960* (Philadelphia, PA: Temple University Press, 1994); William H. Chafe, *The Paradox of Change: American Women in the Twentieth Century* (New York: Oxford University Press, 1991); Sherna Berger Gluck, *Rosie the Riveter Revisited: Women, the War, and Social Change* (Boston: Twayne, 1987); Susan M. Hartmann, *The Home Front and Beyond: American Women in the 1940s* (Boston: Twayne, 1984).

14. "World War II: Women and the War," Women's Memorial, https://www.womensmemorial.org/history/detail/?s=wwii-women-and-the-war.

15. Paula Nassen Poulos, ed., *A Woman's War Too: U.S. Women in the Military in WWII* (Washington, DC: National Archives and Records Administration, 1996).

16. As the percentage of women in service increased and they became more integrated into units serving in combat zones, there was a general lack of clarity on what role women could play in support of combat units and operations. In January 1988, the Department of Defense (DOD) Task Force on Women in the Military described how the varying definitions of a "combat mission" led to inconsistencies between the military departments in the assignment of women to roles and duties. In response to the task force findings, the DOD adopted the Risk Rule in February 1988, which excluded women from noncombat units or missions if the risks of exposure to direct combat, hostile fire, or capture were equal to or greater than the risks in the combat units they supported. See US Government Accountability Office, Gender Issues: Information on DOD's Assignment Policy and Direct Ground Combat Definition, GAO/NSAID-99-7, October 1988, 45; US Government Accountability Office, Women in the Military; More Military Jobs Can Be Opened Under Current Statutes, NSAID-88-222, September 1988, 2; and US Government Accountability Office, Women in the Military: Impact of Proposed Legislation to Open More Combat Support Position and Units to Women, GAO/NSIAD-88-197BR, July 1988. For more information on women in combat and changing restrictions, see Kristy N. Kamarck, "Women in Combat: Issues for Congress," Congressional Research Service (December 13, 2016), https://fas.org/sgp/crs/natsec/R42075.pdf.

17. Jennifer Steinhauer, *Firsts: The Inside Story of Women Reshaping Congress* (Chapel Hill, NC: Algonquin, 2020).

18. Jeremy Teigen, *Why Veterans Run: Military Service in American Presidential Elections, 1789–2016* (Philadelphia, PA: Temple University Press, 2018).

19. Jeane J. Kirkpatrick, *Political Woman* (New York: Basic Books, 1974); R. Darcy, Susan Welch, and Janet Clark, *Women, Elections, and Representation*, 2nd ed. (Lincoln: University of Nebraska Press, 1994).

20. Jennifer Lawless and Richard Fox, *It Takes a Candidate: Why Women Don't Run for Office* (New York: Cambridge University Press, 2005), 6–7.

21. Barbara J. Burt-Way and Rita Mae Kelly, "Gender and Sustaining Political Ambition: A Study of Arizona Elected Officials," *Western Political Quarterly* 45, no. 1 (1992): 23.

22. Lawless and Fox, *It Takes a Candidate*, 10.

23. Susan J. Carroll and Kira Sanbonmatsu, *More Women Can Run: Gender and Pathways to the State Legislatures* (New York: Oxford University Press, 2013), 11; Kaitlin N. Sidorsky, *All Roads Lead to Power: Appointed and Elected Paths to Public Office for US Women* (Lawrence: University Press of Kansas, 2019).

24. Sidorsky, *All Roads Lead to Power*, 2–4.

25. Richard L. Fox and Jennifer L. Lawless, "Gaining and Losing Interest in Running for Public Office: The Concept of Dynamic Political Ambition," *Journal of Politics* 73, no. 2 (2011): 443–462.

26. Carroll and Sanbonmatsu, *More Women Can Run*, 44–45.

27. Curtis Gilroy and Cindy Williams, *Service to Country: Personnel Policy and the Transformation of Western Militaries* (Cambridge: Massachusetts Institute of Technology Press, 2007).

2. The "First" Service above Self Women Candidates

1. Susan Zeiger, *In Uncle Sam's Service: Women Workers with the American Expeditionary Force, 1917–1919* (Ithaca, NY: Cornell University Press, 1999), 2. Historians have documented the use of women's labor by the military in every war in US history, but Zeiger notes that until World War I their employment was either very limited or the conditions under which they worked were informal, unorganized, or voluntary. See also, Nina Bennett Smith, "The Women Who Went to War" (Ph.D. diss., Northwestern University, 1981).

2. Zeiger, *In Uncle Sam's Service*, 3.

3. Arnaldo Testi, "The Gender of Reform Politics: Theodore Roosevelt and the Culture of Masculinity," *Journal of American History* 81 (March 1995): 1509–1533.

4. J. Elliot Ramsey, "Double Helpings of Fame," *Delineator* (January 1937): 11. Also quoted in Dorothy M. Brown, "Rohde, Ruth Bryan Owen," *American National Biography* 18 (New York: Oxford University Press, 1999), 782–783.

5. Hope Chamberlin, *A Minority of Members: Women in the U.S. Congress* (New York: Praeger, 1976), 74.

6. Beverly C. Snow, "The Sappers in Peace and War," *Military Engineer* 47, no. 315 (1955): 43–46, http://www.jstor.org/stable44556720.

7. Karen Foerstel, *Biographical Dictionary of Congressional Women* (Westport, CT: Greenwood, 1999), 213.

8. *Current Biography Yearbook* (New York: H. W. Wilson, 1944), 522–525.

9. *Current Biography Yearbook*, 523.

10. William Atherton Du Puy, "'The Lady from Florida' Works Fast," *Washington Post*, October 20, 1929, SM7.

11. US House, Arguments and Hearings before Elections Committee No. 1, Contested Election Case of William C. Lawson v. Ruth Bryan Owen, from the Fourth Congressional District of Florida, 71st Cong., 2nd sess., 1930 (Washington, DC: Government Printing Office, 1930).

12. David T. Canon et al., *Committees in the United States Congress, 1789–1946*, vol. 1 (Washington, DC: Congressional Quarterly Press, 2002), 572. Political scientist Charles Stewart III rated the committee as the ninth most "attractive" panel of the twenty-nine committees extant between 1875 and the major congressional reorganization in 1947. See Stewart, "Committee Hierarchies in the Modernizing House, 1875–1947," *American Journal of Political Science* 36, no. 4 (November 1992): 835–856.

13. US House, 72nd Congress, 1st sess., January 11, 1932, 1719.

14. US House, 71st Congress, 2nd sess., May 21, 1930, 9314–9323.

15. At the time of this writing, US Representative Marcy Kaptur of Ohio holds the record as the longest-serving woman in Congress. Elected in 1983, she broke the record in 2018 previously held by Edith Nourse Rogers. Senator Margaret Chase Smith was the longest-serving female in the US Senate at twenty-three years upon her retirement in 1973. Her record was surpassed by Senator Barbara Mikulski of Maryland, who served for thirty years, from 1987 to 2017.

16. Rudolf Engelbarts, *Women in the United States Congress, 1917–1972* (Littleton, CO: Libraries Unlimited, 1974), 33.

17. "John Jacob Rogers, Bay State Member of Congress, Dead," *Washington Post*, March 29, 1925, 1; "A Friend of the Foreign Service," *New York Times*, March 31, 1925, 18.

18. Frances Mangum, "Congresswoman Good Friend to War Veterans," *Washington Post*, January 23, 1934, 11.

19. Elisabeth Ellicott Poe, "'Angel of Walter Reed' to Return to Washington as Congresswoman," *Washington Post*, July 12, 1925, SM1.

20. "Mrs. Rogers Seeking Election to Congress on Service Goal," *Christian Science Monitor*, June 26, 1925, 5.

21. According to the Center for American Women in Politics, forty-seven women have been elected or appointed to fill congressional vacancies created by the deaths of their husbands since 1923, eight to the US Senate and thirty-nine to the US House of Representatives. Of the thirty-nine women who filled vacancies in the House, thirty-seven won special elections; the exceptions were Leonor Sullivan and Elizabeth Hawley Gasque (D-SC), who was never sworn in or seated because

Congress was not in session between her special election and the expiration of her term. See http://cawp.rutgers.edu/sites/default/files/resources/widows.pdf.

22. US House of Representatives, Committee on House Administration by the Office of History and Preservation, "Mae Ella Hunt Nolan" in *Women in Congress, 1917–2006* (Washington, DC: Government Printing Office, 2006).

23. After Julius Kahn's passing, Republican leaders in San Francisco, including the city's mayor, recruited Florence Prag Kahn to enter the special election for her husband's seat. She received numerous endorsements from community institutions, such as the Republican newspaper the *San Francisco Bulletin*, which argued that supporting her candidacy was not a matter of sentiment directed toward the late Julius Kahn's widow; rather, she was the best candidate "on the solid ground of character and competence." See Glenna Matthews, "'There Is No Sex in Citizenship': The Career of Congresswoman Florence Prag Kahn," in *We Have Come to Stay: American Women and Political Parties, 1880–1960*, ed. Melanie Gustafson, Kristie Millie, and Elisabeth S. Perry (Albuquerque: University of New Mexico Press, 1999), 131–140.

24. In 1922, Kahn's mother, Mary Prag, received a mayoral appointment as one of the first Jewish women to serve on the San Francisco Board of Education. This came only three years before her daughter's election to Congress. When Florence Kahn's husband, Julius, was first elected to represent the fourth congressional district, she served as his secretary to "economize." In addition, she wrote columns on domestic and foreign policy issues for the *San Francisco Chronicle* and took every opportunity to observe the inner workings of Congress during her time in Washington, DC. As a representative and member of the House Military Affairs Committee, Julius prioritized "military preparedness," introducing the bill that established the draft following US entry into World War I. See Matthews, "'There Is No Sex in Citizenship,'" 131–133.

25. After she was sworn into office, Florence Prag Kahn set to work on legislative projects that represented the interests of her district and the policy priorities she and her husband shared. She was an equally strong supporter of military preparedness, becoming the first woman appointed to the House Military Affairs Committee. In a message to her constituents, she outlined her vision for investment and expansion in military buildup in the Bay Area, a strategically important center for the Pacific region. Acting on this promise, Kahn cosponsored legislation establishing Moffett Field in Sunnyvale, Alameda Naval Air Station, and Hamilton Air Base in North Bay. See Message from Florence Prag Kahn to Her Constituents, BANC MSS 2010/642, Box 1, Folder 14, Kahn (Florence Prag and Julius) Family Papers, Bancroft Library, University of California–Berkeley; *Jewish Tribune (New York)*, December 8, 1928; *San Francisco Examiner*, February 26, 1934.

26. US House of Representatives, History, Art, and Archives, "Full Documentary Transcript," https://history.house.gov/Exhibitions-and-Publications/Florence -Kahn/Full-Text/.

27. "J. J. Rogers' Widow Seeks His House Seat," *Washington Post*, April 8, 1925, 3.

28. "Election of Mrs. Rogers Wins Praise of State Dry League," *Christian Science Monitor*, July 1, 1925, 7; "J. J. Rogers' Widow Nominated for House," *Washington Post*, June 17, 1925, 1.

29. "Women Office Holders Are Now Coming from the Home," *New York Times*, July 12, 1925, X3.

30. Special election statistics from Michael J. Dubin et al., *U.S. Congressional Elections, 1788 to 1997* (Jefferson, NC: McFarland, 1998), 458; "Mrs. Rogers Beats Foss by Two-to-One Vote in Bay State Election for Representative," *New York Times*, July 1, 1925, 1; "Mrs. Rogers Wins Election to House," *Washington Post*, July 1, 1925, 1.

31. Dorothy M. Brown, "Rogers, Edith Nourse," *American National Biography*, vol. 18 (New York: Oxford University Press, 1999), 752–753; "Election of Mrs. Rogers Wins Praise of State Dry League," *Christian Science Monitor*, 7.

32. "Bay State Congress Woman Most Tireless Worker on Hill," *Washington Post*, October 18, 1933, 9.

33. David T. Canon et al., *Committees in the U.S. Congress, 1789–1946*, vol. 3 (Washington, DC: Congressional Quarterly Press, 2002), 894, based on Charles Stewart's relative rankings in "Committee Hierarchies in the Modernizing House, 1875–1947," *American Journal of Political Science* 36, no. 4 (1992): 835–856.

34. Brown, "Rogers, Edith Nourse," 753; "Offers Revisions in Veterans' Care: Mrs. Rogers Suggests Nursing and Physicians Corps as a Permanent Adjunct," *New York Times*, August 7, 1943, 14.

35. "Veteran's Tribute to Representative Edith Nourse Rogers," *Washington Post*, May 15, 1930, 6; Chamberlin, *Minority of Members*, 59.

36. US House, 77th Cong., 1st sess., May 28, 1941, 4531–4533; US House, 77th Cong., 1st sess., December 12, 1941, 9747.

37. In the sixty years after passage of the original GI Bill of Rights, more than 21 million veterans and servicemembers received $75 billion in benefits for education and job training. The Veterans' Administration and Department of Veterans Affairs also had guaranteed nearly 17 million home loans since the program's inception. Department of Veterans Affairs, "V.A. Fact Sheet: Facts about the Department of Veterans Affairs" (April 2003), http://www1.va.gov/opa/fact/vafacts.html.

38. "House Hails 'First G.O.P. Lady,'" *New York Times*, July 1, 1950, 8.

39. Lorraine Nelson Spritzer, *The Belle of Ashby Street: Helen Douglas Mankin and Georgia Politics* (Athens: University of Georgia Press, 1982).

40. Lorraine Nelson Spritzer, "Mankin, Helen Douglas," *American National Biography*, vol. 14 (New York: Oxford University Press, 1999), 415–416.

41. Kimberly Jensen, *Mobilizing Minerva: American Women in the First World War* (Champaign-Urbana: University of Illinois Press, 2008), 107–110.

42. Ellen More, *Restoring the Balance: Women Physicians and the Profession of Medicine, 1850–1995* (Cambridge, MA: Harvard University Press, 1999), 652.

43. "American Medical Women Decorated by the French Government," *American Women's Hospital Bulletin* 1, no. 3 (1919): 7. For more information on the AWH and women physicians serving in France, see Heather Munro Prescott, "'Battalion of Life': American Women's Hospitals and the First World War," *Nursing Clio* (November 21, 2018), https://nursingclio.org/2018/11/21/battalion-of-life-american-womens-hospitals-and-the-first-world-war/#footnote10.

44. *Current Biography* (New York: H. W. Wilson, 1946), 379–381.

45. "Work for Better Legislation Promised Anew by Mrs. Mankin," *Christian Science Monitor*, February 21, 1946, 16; Spritzer, *Belle of Ashby Street*, 67.

46. Chamberlin, *Minority of Members*, 191.

47. US House, Committee on House Administration by the Office of History and Preservation, "Helen Douglas Mankin," in *Women in Congress, 1917–2006* (Washington, DC: Government Printing Office, 2006), 245.

48. Spritzer, "Mankin, Helen Douglas," 415–416.

49. Susan Tolchin, *Women in Congress* (Washington, DC: Government Printing Office, 1976), 50.

50. Lewis H. Hood, "High Court Backs Georgia Unit Rule," *New York Times*, October 2, 1946, 19. See also Mankin's letter to the editors of the *Washington Post*, "Rep. Mankin's Contest," *Washington Post*, January 20, 1947, 6.

51. Spritzer, *Belle of Ashby Street*, 130. Years later, Mankin's chief rival in the 1946 special election, Thomas Camp, confirmed that account: "The people who controlled the situation just didn't want any more of her, and out she went." Quoted in Spritzer, *Belle of Ashby Street*, 73.

52. On parents' employment, see Mary Kaptur, *Women of Congress: A Twentieth-Century Odyssey* (Washington, DC: Congressional Quarterly Press, 1996), 85; "Rep. Clyde H. Smith of Maine Was 63," *New York Times*, April 9, 1940, 29.

53. Anna Price, "Cooking with Congress: Senator Margaret Chase Smith's Recipes from Maine," in *Custodia Legis* (July 2, 2020), https://blogs.loc.gov/law/2020/07/cooking-with-congress-senator-margaret-chase-smiths-recipes-from-maine/.

54. Quoted in Janann Sherman, *No Place for a Woman: The Life of Senator Margaret Chase Smith* (New Brunswick, NJ: Rutgers University Press, 2000), 42.

55. "Mrs. Smith to Seek Place of Husband," *Washington Post*, April 9, 1940, 9; "Clyde Smith's Widow Files," *New York Times*, April 16, 1940, 15.

56. "Rep. Clyde Smith's Widow Nominated by Maine G.O.P.," *Washington Post*, May 14, 1940, 1.

57. Sherman, *No Place for a Woman*, 44–45.

58. "Election Statistics, 1920 to Present," http://clerk.house.gov/member _info/electionInfo/index.aspx.

59. Tolchin, *Women in Congress*, 75.

60. US House, 107th Cong., H. Con. Res. 66, House Document 108-223, in *Women of Congress, 1917–2006* (Washington, DC: Government Printing Office, 2006), 86.

61. "First Woman Elected to Both Houses of Congress," Senate Historical Office, https://www.senate.gov/artandhistory/history/minute/First_Woman_Both _Houses.htm.

62. Patricia Ward Wallace, *Politics of Conscience: A Biography of Margaret Chase Smith* (Westport, CT: Praeger, 1995).

63. David M. Kennedy, *Freedom from Fear* (New York: Oxford University Press, 1999), 776.

64. Patricia Schmidt, *Margaret Chase Smith: Beyond Convention* (Orono: University of Maine Press, 1996), 163.

65. US Senate, Committee on Armed Services, 80th Cong., 1st sess., Women's Armed Services Integration Act of 1947: Hearings before the United States Senate Committee on Armed Services, July 2, 9, 15, 1947 (Washington, DC: Government Printing Office, 1948).

66. Janann Sherman notes, "While one cannot say that without Margaret Chase Smith military women would not have regular status, it is certain that the momentum would have been lost and the fight would have been bitter and protracted." Sherman, "'They Either Need These Women or They Do Not': Margaret Chase Smith and the Fight for Regular Status for Women in the Military," *Journal of Military History* 54 (January 1990): 77.

67. US Senate, 80th Cong, 2nd Sess., Public Law 625: The Women's Armed Services Integration Act of 1948, June 12, 1948, https://www.usmcu.edu/Research /Marine-Corps-History-Division/People/Women-in-the-Marine-Corps/The-Wo mens-Armed-Services-Integration-Act-of-1948/; Harry S. Truman, "Executive Order 9981," Truman Presidential Museum and Library, http://www.trumanlibrary .org/9981.htm.

68. Chamberlin, *Minority of Members*, 143.

69. Helen Henley, "Maine GOP Nominates Mrs. Smith for Senator," *Christian Science Monitor*, June 22, 1948, 5; Josephine Ripley, "Women Hail Smith Victory in Maine," *Christian Science Monitor*, June 23, 1948, 7; see also Schmidt, *Margaret Chase Smith*, 181–182.

70. William Graf, *Statistics of the Presidential and Congressional Election of November 2, 1948* (Washington, DC: Government Printing Office, 1949).

71. "Election Statistics, 1920 to Present."

72. US Senate, 87th Cong., 1st sess., September 23, 1961, 20626.

73. Berkeley Rice, "Is the Great Lady from Maine out of Touch?" *New York Times*, June 11, 1972, 38, https://www.nytimes.com/1972/06/11/archives/is-the-great-lady -from-maine-out-of-touch-great-lady-from-maine.html.

74. Tolchin, *Women in Congress*, 76.

75. Margaret Chase Smith received nearly 25 percent of the vote in Illinois, which earned her delegates at the national convention. "The 1964 Elections," *Congress and the Nation, 1945–1964*, vol. 1-A (Washington, DC: Congressional Quarterly Press, 1965), 54.

76. US House, 79th Cong., 2nd sess., July 24, 1946, A4378–A4379.

77. William T. Bianco, "Last Post for "The Greatest Generation": The Policy Implications of the Decline of Military Experience in the US Congress," *Legislative Studies Quarterly* 30, 1 (2005): 85–102; William T. Bianco and Jamie Markham, "Vanishing Veterans: The Decline of Military Experience in the U.S. Congress," in *Soldiers and Civilians: The Civil-Military Gap and American National Security*, ed. Peter D. Feaver and Richard Kohn (Cambridge: Massachusetts Institute of Technology Press, 2001), 275–288.

78. Susan H. Goodson, *Serving Proudly: A History of Women in the U.S. Navy* (Annapolis, MD: Naval Institute Press, 2001).

79. For more on Huey Long, see Alan Brinkley, *Voices of Protest: Huey Long, Father Coughlin, the Great Depression* (New York: Vintage, 2011).

80. Biography/Historical Note, MS-4051, Catherine S. Long Papers, Louisiana and Lower Mississippi Valley Collections, Hill Memorial Library, Louisiana State University, Baton Rouge, Louisiana, https://www.lib.lsu.edu/sites/all/files/sc/fin daid/4051.pdf.

81. Karl Gerard Brandt, "The Ideological Origins of the New Democrat Movement," *Louisiana History: The Journal of the Louisiana Historical Association* 48, no. 3 (2007): 273–294, http://www.jstor.org/stable/4234284.

82. Joan Cook, "Rep. Gillis Long, 61, Louisiana Liberal, Dies," *New York Times*, January 22, 1985, 22.

83. Suzanne Nelson, "Remembering Her Husband: Louisiana Member Willingly Took Her Spouse's Seat, but She's Glad to Be Out," *Roll Call*, October 5, 2000, 46.

84. Will Scheltema, "Cathy Long: She Carries On," *Roll Call*, May 16, 1985, 8.

85. Nelson, "Remembering Her Husband," 46.

86. Nelson, 46.

87. "Catherine S. Long," in *Associated Press Candidate Biographies*, 1986.

88. "Gillis Long's Widow Seeks Vacant Congress Position," *Minden Press-Herald*, March 25, 1985, 1.

89. "Mrs. Long Goes to Washington," Associated Press, April 1, 1985; Michael J. Dubin et al., *United States Congressional Elections, 1788–1997* (Jefferson, NC: McFarland, 1998), 745.

90. Scheltema, "Cathy Long," 8.

91. Scheltema, 8.

92. Jonathan Fuerbringer, "House Votes Sanctions against South Africa," *New York Times*, June 6, 1985, A1.

93. "Rep. Cathy Long Says She Won't Seek Another Term," Associated Press, October 18, 1985.

94. "Women Enter the Military Academies," Women's Memorial, https://www.womensmemorial.org/history/detail/?s=women-enter-the-military-academies.

95. "Steven H. Schiff, 51, New Mexico Congressman," *New York Times*, March 26, 1998, D19, https://www.nytimes.com/1998/03/26/us/steven-h-schiff-51-new-mexico-congressman.html.

96. John Mercurio, "GOP, Wilson Win in N.M.; Democrats Learn It's Not Easy Beating Green," *Roll Call*, June 25, 1998.

97. Rachel Smolkin, "Rep. Wilson Takes Office with a Little Help from 4-Year-Old Son," *Albuquerque Tribune*, June 26, 1998, A6.

98. "Election Statistics, 1920 to Present."

99. Charles Babington and Juliet Eilperin, "House Votes to Require Assent for Ground Troops," *Washington Post*, April 29, 1999, A1, https://www.washingtonpost.com/wp-srv/politics/daily/april99/house042999.htm.

100. *Politics in America 2002* (Washington, DC: Congressional Quarterly Press, 2001), 660–661; *Almanac of American Politics, 2002* (Washington, DC: National Journal, 2001), 1023–1025.

101. *Congressional Record*, vol. 152, no. 124, September 28, 2006, H7853-H7876, https://www.govinfo.gov/content/pkg/CREC-2006-09-28/html/CREC-2006-09-28-pt2-PgH7853.htm.

102. "2012 New Mexico Senate Results," *Politico*, November 19, 2012, https://web.archive.org/web/20170714113617/http://www.politico.com/2012-election/results/senate/new-mexico/.

103. *Congressional Record*, 115th Cong., 1st sess., March 21, 2017, S1898; *Congressional Record*, 115th Cong., 1st sess., May 8, 2017, S2820; Wesley Morgan, "Air Force Secretary Is Stepping Down," *Politico*, March 8, 2019, https://www.politico.com/story/2019/03/08/heather-wilson-stepping-down-1213085.

3. The "Badasses" of the US House of Representatives

1. Mikie Sherrill, interview with Michael Aron, *On the Record with Michael Aron*, PBS February 17, 2018, https://www.pbs.org/video/congressional-candidate-mikie-sherrill-ht3krh/.

2. "Grandfather," Archives of Women's Political Communication, Iowa State University, September 18, 2017, https://awpc.cattcenter.iastate.edu/2018/08/02/grandfather-sept-18-2017/.

3. Maggie Mallon, "Mikie Sherrill Once Flew Helicopter Mission in the Navy—Now She's Running for Congress," *Glamour*, September 1, 2017, https://www.glamour.com/story/mikie-sherrill-running-for-congress.

4. "Mikie Sherrill," *Biographical Directory of the U.S. Congress*, https://bioguideretro.congress.gov/Home/MemberDetails?memIndex=S001207.

5. Sherrill, interview with Aron.

6. US Senate, 108th Cong., *Congressional Record*, vol. 149, no. 119, September 3, 2003, S11049, https://www.govinfo.gov/content/pkg/CREC-2003-09-03/pdf/CREC-2003-0-03-senate.pdf.

7. "2007 New York Summer Associates," Kirkland and Ellis, https://www.kirkland.com/siteFiles/36AE54C970D8332D087354729422C5D7.pdf.

8. Mikie Sherrill, "Meet Mikie Sherrill," Mikie Sherrill for Congress, https://www.mikiesherrill.com/page/meet/.

9. Sherrill, "Meet Mikie Sherrill."

10. Mallon, "Mikie Sherrill Once Flew Helicopter Mission in the Navy."

11. Sherrill, interview with Aron.

12. Sherrill, interview with Aron.

13. Editorial Board, "Opinion: Mikie Sherrill for New Jersey Democrats," *New York Times*, May 28, 2018, https://www.nytimes.com/2018/05/28/opinion/mikie-sherrill-new-jersey-democrats.html.

14. Mallon, "Mikie Sherrill Once Flew Helicopter Mission in the Navy."

15. David Weigel, "House Appropriations Chairman to Retire, Giving Boost to Democrats," *Washington Post*, January 29, 2018, https://www.washingtonpost.com/politics/house-appropriations-chairman-to-retire-giving-boost-to-democrats/2018/01/29/204131f2-0f3e-42b7-8a33-a14f65509174_story.html?utm_term=.64c6cb3f7aa1& itid=lk_interstitial_manual_12.

16. Herb Jackson, "Is Rep. Rodney Frelinghuysen Really Vulnerable in 2018?" *North Jersey*, May 22, 2017, https://www.northjersey.com/story/news/new-jersey/2017/05/22/rep-rodney-frelinghuysen-really-vulnerable-2018/332993001/.

17. Sherrill, interview with Aron.

18. Sarah Almukhtar, "New Jersey Primary Election Results," *New York Times*,

June 5, 2018, https://www.nytimes.com/interactive/2018/06/05/us/elections/re
sults-new-jersey-primary-elections.html.

19. Center for Responsive Politics, "New Jersey District 11 2018 Race," https://
www.opensecrets.org/races/summary?cycle=2018&id=NJ11; Herb Jackson, "Shattering NJ Record, Mikie Sherrill Raises $1.9 Million for House Race," *North Jersey*,
July 16, 2018, https://www.northjersey.com/story/news/new-jersey/2018/07/16
/mikie-sherrill-shatters-record-1-9-million-n-j-house-race/788177002/.

20. Melissa Golden, "40 Under 40: New Civic Leaders," *Time*, October 2010, http://
content.time.com/time/specials/packages/article/0,28804,2023831_2023829,00
.html.

21. Michael Walsh, "The New Jersey Race That Could Be Key to Democrats
Retaking the House," *Yahoo! News*, July 10, 2018, https://www.yahoo.com/news
/new-jersey-race-key-democrats-retaking-house-140913687.html?guccounter=1.

22. "New Jersey's 11th Congressional District Election, 2018," Ballotpedia,
https://ballotpedia.org/Mikie_Sherrill.

23. Mikie Sherrill, "Why I'm Running," Mikie Sherrill for Congress, https://
www.mikiesherrill.com/page/why-im-running/.

24. "7 National Security Democrats; If True, Trump's Actions Are Impeachable," *Washington Post*, September 23, 2019, https://www.washingtonpost.com
/opinions/2019/09/24/seven-freshman-democrats-these-allegations-are-threat
-all-we-have-sworn-protect/.

25. Michael Kruse, "It Feels Like a 1776 Kind of Fight," *Politico*, September
27, 2019, https://www.politico.com/magazine/story/2019/09/27/trump-impeach
ment-national-security-house-democrats-moderate-mikie-sherrill-228430.

26. Center for Responsive Politics, "New Jersey District 11 2020 Race."

27. Ana Marie Cox, "Space the Nation: Chrissy Houlahan Could Handle the
Millennium Falcon, No Problem," *SyFy*, April 28, 2018, https://www.syfy.com/sy
fywire/space-the-nation-chrissy-houlahan-could-handle-the-millennium-falcon
-no-problem.

28. JTA, "Inspired by Trump, These Jewish Women Have Decided to Run for
Office," *Haaretz*, November 8, 2017, https://www.haaretz.com/us-news/inspired
-by-trump-these-jewish-women-have-decided-to-run-for-office-1.5442162.

29. Jeffrey Mervis, "How a Pennsylvania Industrial Engineer Became the Odds-
on Favorite to Win a Seat in Congress," *Science*, May 8, 2018, https://www.science
mag.org/news/2018/05/how-pennsylvania-industrial-engineer-became-odds
-favorite-win-seat-congress.

30. Cox, "Space the Nation."

31. Mervis, "How a Pennsylvania Industrial Engineer Became the Odds-on Favorite to Win a Seat in Congress."

32. Mervis.

33. Mervis.

34. Chrissy Houlahan, "Meet Chrissy," Chrissy Houlahan for Congress, https://www.chrissyhoulahanforcongress.com/meetchrissy.

35. Mervis, "How a Pennsylvania Industrial Engineer Became the Odds-on Favorite to Win a Seat in Congress."

36. John Latimer, "Air Force Vet Challenges Rep. Ryan Costello," *Lebanon Daily News*, April 11, 2017, https://www.ldnews.com/story/news/politics/candidates/2017/04/11/air-force-vet-challenges-rep-ryan-costello/100282870/.

37. Mervis, "How a Pennsylvania Industrial Engineer Became the Odds-on Favorite to Win a Seat in Congress."

38. Center for Responsive Politics, "Pennsylvania District 06 2018 Race," https://www.opensecrets.org/races/summary?cycle=2018&id=PA06.

39. "Chrissy Houlahan," Ballotpedia, https://ballotpedia.org/Chrissy_Houlahan.

40. Chrissy Houlahan, "Representative Houlahan Launches Historic Servicewomen and Women Veterans Congressional Caucus," press release, May 15, 2019, https://houlahan.house.gov/news/documentsingle.aspx?DocumentID=1154.

41. "Chrissy Houlahan," Ballotpedia.

42. Ben Fractenberg, "Navy Vet Represents Wave of Female Jewish Candidates," *Forward*, October 3, 2018, https://forward.com/news/411060/navy-vet-represents-fresh-wave-of-jewish-women-running-for-congress/.

43. Fractenberg, "Navy Vet Represents Wave of Female Jewish Candidates."

44. Terri Denison, "For Elaine Luria, It's Ships to Mermaids," *Jewish News*, April 28, 2017, http://www.jewishnewsva.org/for-elaine-luria-its-ships-to-mermaids/.

45. Gregory Schneider, "Democrats Wexton, Luria, and Spanberger Unseat Taylor and Brat, Which Kaine Cruises in Virginia," *Washington Post*, November 7, 2018, https://www.washingtonpost.com/local/virginia-politics/virginias-most-important-midterm-elections-could-turn-the-state-blue/2018/11/06/7e22bbce-deb6-11e8-85df-7a6b4d25cfbb_story.html.

46. Harry Minium, "ODU Graduate Elaine Luria Wins Tight Election for Seat in U.S. Congress," Old Dominion University, November 7, 2018, https://www.odu.edu/news/2018/11/odu_alum_wins_seat_i#.X7vKthNKii5.

47. Denison, "For Elaine Luria, It's Ships to Mermaids."

48. Denison.

49. Elaine Luria, "Meet Elaine," Elaine Luria for Congress, https://elaineforcongress.com/about/.

50. Fractenberg, "Navy Vet Represents Wave of Female Jewish Candidates."

51. Denison, "For Elaine Luria, It's Ships to Mermaids."

52. Minium, "ODU Graduate Elaine Luria Wins Tight Election for Seat in U.S. Congress."

53. In addition to Violette, Robert Blondin is father to two adult children, Chloe and Claiborne.

54. Luria, "Meet Elaine."

55. Denison, "For Elaine Luria, It's Ships to Mermaids."

56. Luria, "Meet Elaine."

57. Fractenberg, "Navy Vet Represents Wave of Female Jewish Candidates."

58. "In US House Race, Former Navy Commander Targets Former SEAL," WBOC.com, May 24, 2018, http://www.wboc.com/story/38270509/in-us-house-race-former-navy-commander-targets-former-seal.

59. JulieGrace Brufke, "Dem Elaine Luria Defeats GOP's Scott Taylor in Virginia," The Hill, November 6, 2018, https://thehill.com/homenews/campaign/415348-dem-elaine-luria-defeats-gops-scott-taylor-in-virginia.

60. Meagan Flynn, "Virginia's Era as a Swing State Appears to Be Over," Washington Post, September 18, 2020, https://www.washingtonpost.com/local/virginia-politics/virginia-not-a-swing-state/2020/09/18/9741e2e4-f843-11ea-89e3-4b9efa36dc64_story.html.

61. Matt McClain, "Why Analysts Say Democrats Will Keep Majority in Virginia," Washington Post, October 26, 2020, https://www.washingtonpost.com/local/virginia-politics/mccartney-region-virginia-democratic-dominance/2020/10/25/9e4bbf32-1554-11eb-bc10-40b25382f1be_story.html.

62. Luria, "Meet Elaine."

63. Center for Responsive Politics, "Virginia District 02 2018 Race," https://www.opensecrets.org/races/summary?cycle=2018&id=VA02.

64. "Virginia House Results 2018," CNN.com, https://www.cnn.com/election/2018/results/virginia/house.

65. "Congresswoman Elaine Luria Secures Seat on the House Armed Services Committee," Congresswoman Elaine Luria, January 15, 2019, https://luria.house.gov/media/press-releases/congresswoman-elaine-luria-secures-seat-house-armed-services-committee; "Congresswoman Elaine Luria Appointed to Two Subcommittees on House Armed Services Committee," Congresswoman Elaine Luria, January 28, 2019, https://luria.house.gov/media/press-releases/congresswoman-elaine-luria-appointed-two-subcommittees-house-armed-services; "Congresswoman Elaine Luria to Serve as Vice Chair of Seapower and Projection Forces Subcommittee," Congresswoman Elaine Luria, February 1, 2019, https://luria.house.gov/media/press-releases/congresswoman-elaine-luria-serve-vice-chair-seapower-and-projection-forces; "Congresswoman Elaine Luria

Joins House Committee on Veterans Affairs," Congresswoman Elaine Luria, January 30, 2019, https://luria.house.gov/media/press-releases/congresswoman -elaine-luria-joins-house-committee-veterans-affairs; "Congresswoman Elaine Luria to Lead Veterans' Subcommittee," Congresswoman Elaine Luria, January 31, 2019, https://luria.house.gov/media/press-releases/congresswoman-elaine -luria-lead-veterans-subcommittee.

66. "7 National Security Democrats; If True, Trump's Actions Are Impeachable," *Washington Post*.

67. "Elaine Luria." Ballotpedia.

68. Patrick Wilson, "Abigail Spanberger's Passion for Languages Led Her to the CIA," *Richmond Times-Dispatch*, May 12, 2018, https://richmond.com/news/vir ginia/government-politics/abigail-spanberger-s-passion-for-languages-led-her -to-the/article_d99787c8–8f5a-5e99-946c-be207565f62f.html.

69. Abigail Spanberger, "Meet Abigail," Abigail Spanberger for Congress, https://abigailspanberger.com/about-abigail/.

70. Spanberger, "Meet Abigail."

71. Wilson, "Abigail Spanberger's Passion for Languages Led Her to the CIA."

72. Wilson.

73. Rich Griset, "The Operative: Abigail Spanberger," *Chesterfield Observer*, June 6, 2018, https://www.chesterfieldobserver.com/articles/the-operative-abigail -spanberger/.

74. "Abigail Spanberger," EMILY's List, https://web.archive.org/web /20180717212946/https://www.emilyslist.org/candidates/abigail-spanberger.

75. "Abigail Spanberger," EMILY's List; "Abigail Spanberger," Emerge America, https://emergeamerica.org/alumna/abigail-spanberger/.

76. Laura Barrón-López, "This Former CIA Officer Says She Can Beat Virginia Rep. Dave Brat," *Washington Examiner*, May 30, 2018, https://www.washing tonexaminer.com/news/campaigns/abigail-spanberger-the-former-cia-officer -challenging-rep-dave-brat.

77. Eric Linton, "House Majority Leader Eric Cantor Defeated by Tea Party Challenger David Brat in Virginia GOP Primary," *International Business Times*, June 10, 2014, http://www.ibtimes.com/house-majority-leader-eric-cantor-defeated -tea-party-challenger-david-brat-virginia-gop-1597736.

78. Barrón-López, "This Former CIA Officer Says She Can Beat Virginia Rep. Dave Brat."

79. Barrón-López.

80. Patrick Wilson, "Abigail Spanberger Easily Defeats Dan Ward In 7th District Democratic Primary," *Richmond Times-Dispatch*, June 12, 2018, https://www .richmond.com/news/virginia/government-politics/abigail-spanberger-easily

-defeats-dan-ward-in-7th-district-democratic/article_8fb56fc7-89da-54b6-92b0
-6274ed458f3f.html.

81. Center for Responsive Politics, "Virginia District 07 2018 Race," https://
www.opensecrets.org/races/summary?cycle=2018&id=VA07.

82. Sarah Almukhtar, "Virginia's 7th House District Election Results," New
York Times, November 7, 2018, https://www.nytimes.com/elections/results/vir
ginia-house-district-7.

83. Center for Responsive Politics, "Virginia District 07 2020 Race," https://www
.opensecrets.org/races/summary?cycle=2020&id=VA07; "Abigail Spanberger,"
Ballotpedia.

84. Elissa Slotkin, "Meet Elissa," Elissa Slotkin for Congress, https://elissafor
congress.com/meet-elissa-2/.

85. Slotkin, "Meet Elissa."

86. Linda Copman, "Two Cornell Women Who Are Changing the Face of Congress," Cornell University, November 11, 2019, https://alumni.cornell.edu/article
/two-cornell-women-who-are-changing-the-face-of-congress/.

87. "Elissa Slotkin," Jewish Virtual Library, https://www.jewishvirtuallibrary
.org/elissa-slotkin.

88. "Elissa Slotkin," Jewish Virtual Library.

89. Ron Kampeas, "These Jewish Women Are Running for Office Because of
Donald Trump," Jewish Telegraph, August 10, 2017, https://www.jta.org/2017/08/10
/politics/these-jewish-women-are-running-for-office-because-of-donald-trump.

90. Copman, "Two Cornell Women Who Are Changing the Face of Congress."

91. Jack Lessenberry, "Hot Dogs, the CIA, and Congress," Metro Times, April
25, 2018, https://www.metrotimes.com/detroit/hot-dogs-the-cia-and-congress
/Content?oid=11490298.

92. Slotkin, "Meet Elissa."

93. Lessenberry, "Hot Dogs, the CIA, and Congress."

94. Lessenberry.

95. "Michigan Primary Election Results," New York Times, September 24, 2018,
https://www.nytimes.com/interactive/2018/08/07/us/elections/results-michigan
-primary-elections.html.

96. Center for Responsive Politics, "Michigan District 08 2018 Race," https://
www.opensecrets.org/races/summary?cycle=2018&id=MI08.

97. Secretary of State, 2018 Michigan Election Results, November 6, 2018,
https://mielections.us/election/results/2018GEN_CENR.html.

98. "Meet Paul Junge," Paul Junge for Congress, https://pauljunge.com/.

99. Center for Responsive Politics, "Michigan District 08 2020 Race."

100. Associated Press and Abigail Censky, "Democrat Elissa Slotkin Wins

Reelection to U.S. House in Michigan's 8th Congressional District," Michigan Radio, November 4, 2020, https://www.michiganradio.org/post/democrat-elissa -slotkin-wins-reelection-us-house-michigans-8th-congressional-district.

101. Amy McGrath, "Call Sign: 'Krusty,'" in *Band of Sisters: American Women at War in Iraq*, ed. Kirsten Holmstedt (Mechanicsburg, PA: Stackpole, 2007), 93.

102. Eleanor Clift, "Marine Fighter Pilot, War Vet—and Woman and Democrat," *Daily Beast*, October 16, 2017, https://www.thedailybeast.com/marine-fighter-pilot -war-vetand-woman-and-democrat.

103. Aviation Museum of Kentucky, "Lt. Col. Amy McGrath, USMC," YouTube, November 13, 2016, https://www.youtube.com/watch?v=uMNNCXdRLOk&t=148s.

104. McGrath, "Call Sign: 'Krusty,'" 97.

105. McGrath, 97.

106. McGrath, 97.

107. McGrath, 97.

108. McGrath, 99.

109. McGrath, 99.

110. Daniel Desrochers, "These Veterans Are Questioning Amy McGrath's Military Record: Here's What She Did," *Lexington Herald Leader*, October 18, 2018, https://www.kentucky.com/news/politics-government/article220056895.html.

111. Political Science Department, "Lieutenant Colonel Amy 'Krusty' McGrath, U.S. Marine Corps," US Naval Academy, archived from the original on April 29, 2017, https://www.usna.edu/PoliSci/facultybio/mcgrath.php.

112. Political Science Department, "Lieutenant Colonel Amy 'Krusty' McGrath."

113. Jeffrey Lee Puckett, "Kentucky Combat Veteran Amy McGrath Is Going Viral with a Video Announcing Congressional Run," *Courier Journal*, August 3, 2017, https://www.courier-journal.com/story/news/politics/2017/08/03/kentucky -combat-veteran-amy-mcgrath-going-viral-political-video/536522001/.

114. Alex Roarty, "Rising Dem Star Moulton Grants Seal of Approval to Three House Candidates," *News and Observer*, August 9, 2017, https://www.newsobserver .com/news/politics-government/article166228167.html; "VoteVets PAC Endorses Amy McGrath for Congress," VoteVets.org, n.d., https://www.votevets.org/press /votevets-pac-endorses-amy-mcgrath-for-congress; Michael Tackett, "In Conservative Kentucky, Power of Female Candidates Is Tested in Key House Race," *New York Times*, June 16, 2018, https://www.nytimes.com/2018/06/16/us/politics /kentucky-house-race-mcgrath.html. See also, Tackett, "From Annapolis to Congress? These Three Women Known Tough Missions," *New York Times*, January 29, 2018, https://www.nytimes.com/2018/01/29/us/politics/women-annapolis-dem ocrats-congress-trump.html.

115. "Kentucky's Sixth House District Election Results: Andy Barr vs. Amy

McGrath," *New York Times*, May 15, 2019, https://www.nytimes.com/elections /results/kentucky-house-district-6.

116. Eric Bradner, "Who Is Amy McGrath, the Kentucky Democrat Challenging Senate Majority Leader Mitch McConnell?" CNN, July 9, 2019, https://www .cnn.com/2019/07/09/politics/who-is-amy-mcgrath-kentucky-senate-candidate /index.html.

117. "Gov. Beshear Endorses Fellow Democrat Amy McGrath for U.S. Senate," Lex18.com, September 14, 2020, https://www.lex18.com/news/election-2020/gov -beshear-endorses-fellow-democrat-amy-mcgrath-for-u-s-senate; Editorial Board, "After 36 years, Kentucky Can Do Better Than Mitch McConnell. We Endorse Amy McGrath," *Lexington Herald Leader*, October 12, 2020, https://www.ken tucky.com/opinion/editorials/article246227300.html.

118. Center for Responsive Politics, "Kentucky Senate 2020 Race Summary Data: Total Raised and Spent," November 9, 2020, https://www.opensecrets.org /races/summary?cycle=2020&id=KYS1.

119. "Kentucky U.S. Senate Election Results," *New York Times*, November 3, 2020, https://www.nytimes.com/interactive/2020/11/03/us/elections/results-ken tucky-senate.html.

120. Gina Ortiz Jones, "Meet Gina," Gina Ortiz Jones for Congress, November 10, 2020, https://ginaortizjones.com/about.

121. Tim Teeman, "Woman, Lesbian, Filipina-American, Iraq Veteran: How Gina Ortiz Jones Could Make Texas Political History," *Daily Beast*, May 24, 2018, https://www.thedailybeast.com/woman-lesbian-filipina-american-iraq-veteran -how-gina-ortiz-jones-could-make-texas-political-history.

122. Sarah Ruiz-Grossman, "These Candidates Could Make History in November," *Huffington Post*, June 27, 2018, https://www.huffpost.com/entry/candi dates-make-history-november_n_5b340dbce4b0cb56051edf87.

123. Jones, "Meet Gina."

124. Jones.

125. Jennifer Bendery, "She Quit Working for Trump. Now She's Running for Congress to Fight Him," *Huffington Post*, January 6, 2018, https://www.huff post.com/entry/gina-ortiz-jones-will-hurd-texas-2018_n_5a4c069ce4b0b0e5a7a 94c48.

126. Bendery, "She Quit Working for Trump."

127. Patrick Svitek, "U.S. Rep. Will Hurd Gets First Major Democratic Challenger for 2018," *Texas Tribune*, August 2, 2017, https://www.texastribune.org/2017 /08/02/hurd-gets-first-democratic-challenger-2018/.

128. Svitek, "U.S. Rep. Will Hurd Gets First Major Democratic Challenger for 2018."

129. "Gina Ortiz Jones," Ballotpedia, https://ballotpedia.org/Gina_Ortiz_Jones.

130. Center for Responsive Politics, "Texas District 23 2018 Race," https://www.opensecrets.org/races/summary?cycle=2018&id=TX23&spec=N.

131. "Gina Ortiz Jones," Ballotpedia.

132. Jessica Taylor, "Texas Rep. Will Hurd, House's Only Black Republican, Won't Seek Reelection in 2020," NPR.org, August 1, 2019, https://www.npr.org/2019/08/01/747471451/texas-rep-will-hurd-houses-only-black-republican-won-t-seek-reelection-in-2020.

133. Center for Responsive Politics, "Texas District 23 2020 Race."

134. "Gina Ortiz Jones," Ballotpedia.

135. Mary Jennings Hegar, *Shoot Like a Girl: One Woman's Dramatic Fight in Afghanistan and on the Home Front* (New York: Berkley, 2017), 15.

136. Hegar, *Shoot Like a Girl*, 17.

137. Hegar, 18.

138. M. J. Hegar, in discussion with the author, January 2020.

139. Hegar, *Shoot Like a Girl*, 19–21.

140. Hegar, 39–41.

141. Hegar, 72–81.

142. Hegar, Chapter 4. See also Frederika Schouten, "A War Hero Is Running for Congress and She Just Dropped the Best Political Ad," *USA Today*, June 22, 2018, https://www.usatoday.com/story/news/politics/2018/06/22/war-hero-and-democrat-m-j-hegar-draws-attention-house-ad-texas-john-carter/725512002/; Jessica Green, "Airman Returns Home with a Purple Heart," *Air National Guard*, December 10, 2009, https://www.ang.af.mil/Media/Article-Display/Article/436067/airman-returns-home-with-a-purple-heart/.

143. Hegar, *Shoot Like a Girl*, Chapter 6.

144. Terry Gross, "A Purple Heart Warrior Takes Aim at Military Inequality in 'Shoot Like a Girl': Audio Interview with MJ Hegar," *Fresh Air*, March 2, 2017, https://www.npr.org/2017/03/02/517944956/a-purple-heart-warrior-takes-aim-at-military-inequality-in-shoot-like-a-girl.

145. Hegar, *Shoot Like a Girl*, Chapter 8. See also Gross, "A Purple Heart Warrior Takes Aim at Military Inequality in 'Shoot Like a Girl'"; Jessica Green, "Airman Helps Rescue 3 Injured Warriors during Battle in Afghanistan," *Air National Guard*, December 11, 2009, https://www.af.mil/News/Article-Display/Article/118300/airman-helps-rescue-3-injured-warriors-during-battle-in-afghanistan/; Jessica Green, "Heroes Recognized for Lives Saved," *Air National Guard*, November 9, 2011, https://www.ang.af.mil/Media/Article-Display/Article/435809/heroes-recognized-for-lives-saved/.

146. "Mary Jennings Hegar: Follow Your Heart Because It Knows You Best,"

video, TEDxGreatHills Women, April 28, 2018, https://www.youtube.com/watch ?v=zGnjlHbhnmg.

147. Hegar, *Shoot Like a Girl*, 272.

148. Hegar, Chapter 10.

149. Thomas Gillian and Vania Leveille, "*Hegar, et al. v. Panetta*: The Legal Challenge to the Combat Exclusion Policy," American Civil Liberties Union, April 4, 2017, https://www.aclu.org/sites/default/files/field_document/combat_exclusion _factsheet-plaintiffs-4-4-17-final.pdf; Peter Henderson, "ACLU Sues over Policy Barring Women from Combat," *Chicago Tribune*, November 27, 2012, https://www .chicagotribune.com/nation-world/ct-xpm-2012–11–27-sns-rt-us-usa-military -womenbre8aq11j-20121127-story.html.

150. Elisabeth Bumiller and Thorn Shanker, "Pentagon Set to Lift Ban on Women in Combat Roles," *New York Times*, January 23, 2013, https://www.nytimes .com/2013/01/24/us/pentagon-says-it-is-lifting-ban-on-women-in-combat.html; Megan H. MacKenzie, *Beyond the Band of Brothers: The U.S. Military and the Myth That Women Can't Fight* (Cambridge, UK: Cambridge University Press, 2015), 58–63.

151. Hegar, in discussion with the author.

152. Hegar, in discussion with the author.

153. "MJ Hegar—Doors," video, M. J. for Texas, June 20, 2018, https://www.you tube.com/watch?v=Zi6v4CYNSIQ; see also Rachel Cohrs, "Texas Democratic U.S. House Candidate MJ Hegar's Life Story as Campaign Ad Goes Viral," *Dallas Morning News*, June 25, 2018, https://www.dallasnews.com/news/politics/2018/06/25 /texas-democratic-u-s-house-candidate-mj-hegars-life-story-as-campaign-ad -goes-viral/; Ainara Tiefenthäler et al., "These Ads Reveal How Women Candidates Are Changing Campaigns," *New York Times*, July 14, 2018, https://www .nytimes.com/video/us/politics/100000005994805/these-ads-reveal-how -women-candidates-are-changing-campaigns.html; Kate Zernike, "Forget Suits. Show the Tattoo. Female Candidates Are Breaking the Rules," *New York Times*, July 14, 2018, https://www.nytimes.com/2018/07/14/us/politics/women-candidates -midterms.html.

154. "MJ Hegar—Doors," M. J. for Texas.

155. Center for Responsive Politics, "Texas District 31 2018 Race," https:// www.opensecrets.org/races/summary?cycle=2018&id=TX31.

156. "M. J. Hegar," Ballotpedia, https://ballotpedia.org/M.J._Hegar.

157. Center for Responsive Politics, "Texas Senate 2020 Race," https://www .opensecrets.org/races/summary?cycle=2020&id=TXS1.

158. Secretary of State, "Texas Election Results," https://results.texas-election .com/contestdetails?officeID=1003&officeName=U.%20S.%20%20SENATOR &officeType=FEDERAL%20OFFICES&from=race.

159. Kaitlin N. Sidorsky, *All Roads Lead to Power: Appointed and Elected Paths to Public Office for US Women* (Lawrence: University Press of Kansas, 2019), 2.

4. LT. COLONEL DUCKWORTH GOES TO WASHINGTON

1. Mark Lytle, *America's Uncivil Wars: The Sixties Era from Elvis to the Fall of Richard Nixon* (New York: Oxford University Press, 2006), 264–265.

2. Richard A. Ruth, "Why Thailand Takes Pride in the Vietnam War," *New York Times*, November 7, 2017, https://www.nytimes.com/2017/11/07/opinion/thailand -vietnam-war.html.

3. Marlene Wagman-Geller, *Still I Rise: The Persistence of Phenomenal Women* (Coral Gables, FL: Mango, 2017), 239.

4. Tammy Duckworth, "What I Learned at War," *Politico* (July/August 2015), https://www.politico.com/magazine/story/2015/06/tammy-duckworth-what-i -learned-at-war-119243.

5. Wagman-Geller, *Still I Rise*, 239–240.

6. Rebecca Johnson, "Senator Tammy Duckworth on the Attack That Took Her Legs—and Having a Baby at 50," *Vogue*, September 12, 2018.

7. Johnson, "Senator Tammy Duckworth on the Attack That Took Her Legs."

8. Susan Zeiger, *Entangling Alliances: Foreign War Brides and American Soldiers in the Twentieth Century* (New York: New York University Press, 2010), 7.

9. Zeiger, *Entangling Alliances*, 9.

10. Johnson, "Senator Tammy Duckworth on the Attack That Took Her Legs."

11. Duckworth, "What I Learned at War."

12. "Tammy Duckworth on Her Military Service and Medical Treatment at Walter Reed Army Medical Center," C-SPAN, March 10, 2005, https://www.c-span.org /video/?c4628301/tammy-duckworth-military-service-medical-treatment-walter -reed-army-medical-center&playlist=91c1b821716a85e09f107916507ddd41.

13. Wagman-Geller, *Still I Rise*, 240.

14. "Tammy Duckworth on Her Military Service and Medical Treatment at Walter Reed Army Medical Center," C-SPAN.

15. Rudi Williams, "Women Aviators Finally Fill Cockpits of Military Aircraft," *DOD News*, March 19, 2003, https://archive.defense.gov/news/newsarticle.aspx?id= 29276.

16. Les Aspin, "Policy on the Assignment of Women in the Armed Forces," Memorandum to the Secretaries of the Military Department, Chairman of the Joint Chiefs of Staff, Assistant Secretary of Defense (FM&P) and Assistant Secretary of Defense (RA), Washington, DC, 1993.

17. Margaret C. Harrell and Laura L. Miller, *New Opportunities for Military Women:*

Effects upon Readiness, Cohesion, and Morale (Santa Monica, CA: RAND Corporation, 1997), xvii.

18. Harrell and Miller, *New Opportunities for Military Women*, 12.

19. Tammy Duckworth, "Foreword," in *Band of Sisters: American Women at War in Iraq*, ed. Kirsten Holmstedt (Mechanicsburg, PA: Stackpole, 2007), viii.

20. Duckworth, viii.

21. "Tammy Duckworth on Her Military Service and Medical Treatment at Walter Reed Army Medical Center," C-SPAN.

22. Adam Weinstein, "Nobody Puts Tammy Duckworth in a Corner," *Mother Jones* (September/October 2012), https://www.motherjones.com/politics/2012/08/tammy-duckworth-versus-joe-walsh-congress/.

23. Duckworth, *Band of Sisters*, viii.

24. "Tammy Duckworth on Her Military Service and Medical Treatment at Walter Reed Army Medical Center," C-SPAN.

25. Leo Shane, "The Pedals Were Gone, and So Were My Legs," *Stars and Stripes*, June 14, 2005, https://www.stripes.com/news/the-pedals-were-gone-and-so-were-my-legs-1.34578.

26. Shane, "The Pedals Were Gone, and So Were My Legs."

27. Wagman-Geller, *Still I Rise*, Chapter 22; Kathy MacMillan and Manuela Bernardi, *She Spoke: 14 Women Who Raised Their Voices and Changed the World* (Sanger, CA: Familius, 2019).

28. Wagman-Geller, *Still I Rise*, Chapter 22.

29. Senators John McCain, Daniel Inouye, and Bob Dole share common traits; they were decorated veterans who suffered serious injuries in the course of combat, and they were established leaders in their respective political parties, viewed as effective legislators and statesmen. Until the inauguration of Senator Kamala Harris as vice president in 2021, Senator Inouye was the highest-ranking Asian American politician in US history. "Illinois Sen. Tammy Duckworth on Her First Meeting with Senator John McCain," *All Things Considered*, August 27, 2018, https://www.npr.org/2018/08/27/642356449/illinois-sen-tammy-duckworth-on-her-first-meeting-with-sen-john-mccain.

30. "Tammy Duckworth on Her Military Service and Medical Treatment at Walter Reed Army Medical Center," C-SPAN.

31. Shane, "The Pedals Were Gone, and So Were My Legs."

32. "Secretary Rumsfeld Interview with Laura Ingraham," US Department of Defense, June 1, 2005, http://www.freerepublic.com/focus/f-news/1414807/posts.

33. Quoted in Weinstein, "Nobody Puts Tammy Duckworth in a Corner."

34. "Three Years Later with Tammy Duckworth," C-SPAN, August 11, 2008, https://www.c-span.org/video/?280404-5/years-tammy-duckworth.

35. Jennifer E. Manning, "Membership of the 112th Congress: A Profile," Congressional Research Service, August 1, 2012, https://www.documentcloud.org/documents/406644-membership-of-the-112th-congress.html#document/p11/a66561.

36. "The Frontlines of Democracy," *Fighting Dems*, June 7, 2006, https://web.archive.org/web/20060607232029/http://www.democrats.org/page/content/fightingdems/index/.

37. "Three Years Later with Tammy Duckworth," C-SPAN.

38. "Illinois 6th Congressional District Debate," C-SPAN, October 23, 2016, https://www.c-span.org/video/?195060-1/illinois-6th-congressional-district-debate.

39. "Illinois District 06 2006 Race," Open Secrets, https://www.opensecrets.org/races/candidates?cycle=2006&id=IL06&spec=N.

40. Aaron Chambers, "Partisan Playbook: Political Parties Playing Offense and Defense in Three IL Congressional Districts," NPR Illinois, October 1, 2006, https://www.nprillinois.org/post/partisan-playbook-political-parties-playing-offense-defense-three-il-congressional-districts#stream/0.

41. Chambers, "Partisan Playbook."

42. "VFW Group Snubs Iraq Vet and Endorses Her Opponent in Congressional Race," *Daily Journal*, November 4, 2006, https://www.daily-journal.com/news/local/vfw-group-snubs-iraq-vet-and-endorses-her-opponent-in-congressional-race/article_dad72a05-58c4-5b03-a953-e298a25c1fe3.html.

43. "Three Years Later with Tammy Duckworth," C-SPAN.

44. Tiffany Blackstone, "Women of the Year 2006: The Patriot," *Glamour*, October 27, 2006, https://www.glamour.com/gallery/2006-women-of-the-year.

45. "Illinois—6," Real Clear Politics, https://www.realclearpolitics.com/epolls/writeup/illinois_6-28.html.

46. Frank James, "The Swamp," *Chicago Tribune*, November 7, 2006, https://newsblogs.chicagotribune.com/news_theswamp/2006/11/democrats_exper.html.

47. Federal Election Commission, *Federal Elections 2006: Election Results for the U.S. Senate and the U.S. House of Representatives* (Washington, DC: Federal Election Commission, 2007), 62, https://www.fec.gov/resources/cms-content/documents/federalelections2006.pdf.

48. Jeremy Teigen, "Invoking Military Credentials in Congressional Elections 2000–2006," in *Inside Defense: Understanding the U.S. Military in the 21st Century*, ed. D. Reveron and Judith Stein (New York: Palgrave MacMillan, 2008), 115–125.

49. Weinstein, "Nobody Puts Tammy Duckworth in a Corner."

50. "Three Years Later with Tammy Duckworth," C-SPAN.

51. Terri Tanielian, Lisa H. Jaycox, Terry L. Schell, Grant N. Marshall, M.

Audrey Burnam, Christine Eibner, Benjamin Karney, Lisa S. Meredith, Jeanne S. Ringel, and Mary E. Vaiana, *Invisible Wounds: Mental Health and Cognitive Care Needs of America's Returning Veterans* (Santa Monica, CA: RAND Corporation, 2008), https://www.rand.org/pubs/research_briefs/RB9336.html.

52. "Three Years Later with Tammy Duckworth," C-SPAN.

53. John Chase, "Duckworth's Record: Few Legislative Successes, Some Veterans Programs Sputtered," *Chicago Tribune*, October 19, 2016, https://www.chicagotribune.com/politics/ct-tammy-duckworth-veterans-affairs-met-20161018-story.html.

54. Chase, "Duckworth's Record."

55. Weinstein, "Nobody Puts Tammy Duckworth in a Corner."

56. "Three Years Later with Tammy Duckworth," C-SPAN.

57. Katherine Skiba, "Walsh Defense Remarks on Whether Duckworth Is True Hero," *Chicago Tribune*, July 3, 2012, https://www.chicagotribune.com/news/ct-xpm-2012-07-03-ct-met-walsh-duckworth-0704-20120704-story.html.

58. Monique Garcia and Rick Pearson, "Duckworth, Walsh Debate for 1st Time," *Chicago Tribune*, May 12, 2012, https://www.chicagotribune.com/news/ct-xpm-2012-05-12-ct-met-duckworth-walsh-debate-20120512-story.html.

59. "Illinois District 08 2012 Race," Open Secrets, http://www.opensecrets.org/races/summary?cycle=2012&id=IL08&spec=N.

60. "Illinois House Election Results 2012—Map, District Results, Live Updates," *Politico*, July 9, 2013, https://www.politico.com/2012-election/results/house/illinois/.

61. Katherine Skiba, "Illinois Democrats Join Sit-in to Demand U.S. House Votes on Gun Control," *Chicago Tribune*, June 22, 2016, https://www.chicagotribune.com/news/ct-house-sit-in-gun-control-illinois-20160622-story.html.

62. Rick Pearson and Katherine Skiba, "Kirk, Duckworth Headed for Bitter, Expensive Fall Fight," *Chicago Tribune*, March 16, 2016, https://www.chicagotribune.com/politics/ct-illinois-us-senate-race-kirk-duckworth-met-0316-20160315-story.html.

63. "Three Years Later with Tammy Duckworth," C-SPAN.

64. Pearson and Skiba, "Kirk, Duckworth Headed for Bitter, Expensive Fall Fight."

65. "Mark Kirk Questions Opponent Tammy Duckworth's American Heritage at Illinois Debate," NBC News, October 28, 2016, https://www.youtube.com/watch?v=lOnkZ9Um5ic.

66. Rebecca Morrin, "Human Rights Campaign Revokes Mark Kirk Endorsement," *Politico*, October 29, 2016, https://www.politico.com/story/2016/10/human-rights-campaign-revokes-mark-kirk-endorsement-230495.

67. "Illinois Senate 2016 Race," Open Secrets, https://www.opensecrets.org/races/outside-spending?cycle=2016&id=ILS2&spec=N.

68. "Illinois U.S. Senate Results: Tammy Duckworth Wins," New York Times, August 1, 2017, https://www.nytimes.com/elections/2016/results/illinois-senate-kirk-duckworth.

69. Brandon Carter, "Duckworth Slams Trump: I Won't Be Lectured on Military Needs by a 'Five-Deferment Draft Dodger,'" The Hill, January 20, 2018, https://thehill.com/homenews/senate/369960-dem-slams-trump-i-wont-be-lectured-on-military-needs-by-a-five-deferment.

70. Johnson, "Senator Tammy Duckworth on the Attack That Took Her Legs."

71. Johnson.

72. Laurel Wamsley, "Tammy Duckworth Becomes First U.S. Senator to Give Birth While in Office," NPR, April 9, 2018, https://www.npr.org/sections/thetwo-way/2018/04/09/600896586/tammy-duckworth-becomes-first-u-s-senator-to-give-birth-while-in-office.

73. Sheryl Gay Stolberg, "'It's about Time': A Baby Comes to the Senate Floor," New York Times, April 19, 2018, https://www.nytimes.com/2018/04/19/us/politics/baby-duckworth-senate-floor.html

74. Elise Viebeck, "A Duckling Onesie and a Blazer: The Senate Floor Sees Its First Baby, but Many Traditions Stand," Washington Post, April 19, 2018, https://www.washingtonpost.com/powerpost/a-duckling-onesie-and-a-blazer-the-senate-floor-sees-its-first-baby-but-many-traditions-stand/2018/04/19/451ea160-43e0-11e8-ad8f-27a8c409298b_story.html; "Senator Duckworth on Floor with Infant," C-SPAN, April 19, 2018, https://www.c-span.org/video/?444290-8/senator-duckworth-floor-infant.

75. US Senate, 115th Cong., 1st Sess., "S.1110 Friendly Airports for Mothers Act of 2017," https://www.congress.gov/bill/115th-congress/senate-bill/1110.

76. Craig Volden, "Highlights from the New 115th Congress Legislative Effectiveness Scores," Center for Legislative Effectiveness, February 27, 2019, https://thelawmakers.org/legislative-effectiveness-scores/highlights-from-the-new-115th-congress-legislative-effectiveness-scores.

77. Rebecca Nelson, "The Dark Humor of Tammy Duckworth, Iraq War Hero and Gun Control Advocate," GQ, September 29, 2016, https://www.gq.com/story/tammy-duckworth-iraq-war-hero-and-gun-control-advocate-interview.

78. Jon Soucy, "Combat Veteran Provides Insight at Guard Bureau Women's History Event," DOD News, March 19, 2009, https://archive.defense.gov/news/newsarticle.aspx?id=53558.

79. Claudia Grisales, "Tammy Duckworth's Stock Rises as a Possible VP Choice after High-Profile Weeks," NPR Morning Edition, July 21, 2020, https://www.npr

.org/2020/07/21/892585038/tammy-duckworths-stock-rises-as-a-possible-vp
-choice-after-a-high-profile-few-we.

80. Soucy, "Combat Veteran Provides Insight."

81. B. A. Haller, "VA Assistant Secretary Tammy Duckworth Tells of Her Second Chance at a Fulfilling Life as an Amputee," *Media Dis&Dat*, March 28, 2010, http://media-dis-n-dat.blogspot.com/2010/03/va-assistant-secretary-tammy -duckworth.html.

5. MOTHER, SOLDIER, CONSERVATIVE: SENATOR JONI ERNST

1. C. Zulauf, J. Coppess, N. Paulson, and G. Schnitkey, "U.S. Corn, Soybean, Wheat Exports and USSR Grain Embargo: Contemporary Implications," *Farmdoc Daily* 8, no. 129 (2018).

2. "Chapter Eight: Banking and the Agricultural Problems of the 1980s," in *An Examination of the Banking Crises of the 1980s and Early 1990s*, vol. 1 (Washington, DC: Federal Deposit Insurance Corporation, 1997), https://www.fdic.gov/bank /historical/history/259_290.pdf.

3. Joni Ernst, *Daughter of the Heartland: My Ode to the Country That Raised Me* (New York: Simon and Schuster, 2020), 25.

4. Ernst, *Daughter of the Heartland*, 26.

5. Mike Rosman, "Depression: Common for Farm People," Mental Health and the Impact for Farm Families, https://nasdonline.org/7122/d002366/depression -common-for-farm-people.html.

6. Larry Dreiling, "Baldwin, Ernst over Bill to Provide Mental Health Support to Agricultural Communities," *High Plains Journal*, May 13, 2018, https://www.hpj .com/ag_news/baldwin-ernst-over-bill-to-provide-mental-health-support-to-ag ricultural-communities/article_ocfb7a05-8080-5241-bf66-3db568bb39f0.html.

7. Ernst, *Daughter of the Heartland*, 31.

8. Ernst, 26.

9. Ernst, 35.

10. Ernst, 36.

11. US House, 100th Cong., 2nd sess., Committee on Appropriations, Subcommittee on Rural Development, Agriculture, and Related Agencies, "Rural Development, Agriculture, and Related Agencies Appropriations for 1989" (Washington, DC: US Government Printing Office, 1988), 409.

12. US House, "Rural Development, Agriculture, and Related Agencies Appropriations for 1989," 884.

13. US House, 884.

14. Ernst, *Daughter of the Heartland*, 36.

15. David Marples, "1989: A Look Back," *Ukrainian Weekly*, December 31, 1989, http://www.ukrweekly.com/old/archive/1989/538917.shtml.

16. James Risen, "Ukraine Turns to Food as a Political Weapon," *Los Angeles Times*, October 25, 1991, https://www.latimes.com/archives/la-xpm-1991-10-25 -mn-253-story.html.

17. Timothy N. Ash, "Land and Agricultural Reform in Ukraine," in *Land Reform in the Former Soviet Union and Eastern Europe*, ed. Stephen K. Wegren (New York: Routledge, 1998), 62–86.

18. Ash, "Land and Agricultural Reform in Ukraine," 62–86.

19. The May 1st Collective Farm is named in honor of May Day, also called Workers' Day or International Workers' Day. Observed in many countries on May 1, the day was designated to commemorate the historic struggles and gains made by workers and the labor movement. In the United States, an international federation of socialist groups and trade unions designated May 1 as Workers' Day, a day in support of workers, in commemoration of the Haymarket Riot in Chicago (1886). In 1894, President Grover Cleveland signed legislation to make Labor Day—already held in some states on the first Monday of September—the official US holiday in honor of workers and divorce the commemoration from the broader socialist movement. See Michael Kazin and Steven J. Ross, "America's Labor Day: The Dilemma of a Workers' Celebration," *Journal of American History* 78, no. 4 (1992): 1294–1323.

20. Ernst, *Daughter of the Heartland*, 41.

21. Ernst, 43.

22. Ernst, 47–48.

23. Ernst, 50.

24. Rich Morin, "The Difficult Transition from Military to Civilian Life," Pew Research Center, December 8, 2011, https://www.pewsocialtrends.org/2011/12/08 /the-difficult-transition-from-military-to-civilian-life/.

25. Ernst, *Daughter of the Heartland*, 53.

26. Ernst, 57.

27. Ernst, 59.

28. Ernst, 59.

29. A company is a military unit that typically consists of 100 to 250 soldiers, often organized into three or four smaller units called platoons. The exact organization of a company varies by country, service, and unit type.

30. For more on the gender double bind, see Kathleen Hall Jamieson, *Beyond the Double Bind: Women and Leadership* (New York: Oxford University Press, 1995); Robin Romm, ed., *Double Bind: Women on Ambition* (New York: Liveright, 2017);

Mia Costa, "He Said, She Said: The Gender Double Bind in Legislator-Constituent Communication," *Politics and Gender* (2020): 1–24.

31. Aida Alvinius, Clary Krekula, and Gerry Larsson, "Managing Visibility and Differentiating in Recruitment of Women as Leaders in the Armed Forces," *Journal of Gender Studies* 27, no. 5 (2018): 534–546; Frida Linehagen, "Conforming One's Conduct to Unwritten Rules: Experiences of Female Military Personnel in a Male-Dominated Organization," *Res Militaris* 8, no. 1 (2018): 1–25; Veronika Marenčinová, "Gender and Leadership in the Military," *Science and Military Journal* 13, no. 1 (2018): 44–49.

32. Ernst, *Daughter of the Heartland*, 60.

33. Ernst, 61.

34. Ernst, 61.

35. Ernst, 60.

36. Ernst, 61.

37. Ernst, 62.

38. Kirsten Holmstedt, ed., *Band of Sisters: American Women at War in Iraq* (Mechanicsburg, PA: Stackpole, 2007), 217.

39. Ernst, *Daughter of the Heartland*, 65.

40. Meltem Müftüler-Bac, "Turkey and the United States: The Impact of the War in Iraq," *International Journal* 61, no. 1 (2005): 61–81.

41. Frank Bruni, "A Nation at War: Ankara; Turkey Sends Army Troops into Iraq, Report Says," *New York Times*, March 22, 2003, https://www.nytimes.com/2003/03/22/world/a-nation-at-war-ankara-turkey-sends-army-troops-into-iraq-report-says.html.

42. Gregory Fontenot, E. J. Degen, and David Tohn, *On Point: The United States Army in Operation Iraqi Freedom* (Annapolis, MD: Naval Institute Press, 2005).

43. Ernst, *Daughter of the Heartland*, 71.

44. Ernst, 67.

45. Ernst, 77.

46. Ernst, 77.

47. Ernst, 77–78.

48. Ernst, 71.

49. Ernst, 80.

50. Ernst, 81.

51. Ernst, 93.

52. Ernst, 84.

53. Brien T. Boyce, "Montgomery Auditor Charged with Assault," *Daily Non-Pareil*, March 21, 2003, https://www.nonpareilonline.com/news/montgomery

-auditor-charged-with-assault/article_3458c0ef-2b89-5c7a-9f8c-e4b6664dcfaf
.html.

54. Ernst, *Daughter of the Heartland*, 89. At the time, Kim Reynolds was a four-term Clarke County treasurer. She would be elected to the Iowa Senate, the position of lieutenant governor alongside Terry Branstad, and assume the position as Iowa's first female governor in 2017, when Branstad resigned.

55. Ernst, *Daughter of the Heartland*, 85.

56. "Joni Ernst Announces Bid for Kim Reynolds' Iowa Senate Seat," *Iowa Republican*, November 18, 2010, https://web.archive.org/web/20150115181318 /http://theiowarepublican.com/2010/joni-ernst-announces-bid-for-kim-rey nolds-iowa-senate-seat/.

57. Ernst, *Daughter of the Heartland*, 96–99.

58. Ernst, 93.

59. Ernst, 101.

60. Iowa Secretary of State, "Official Statewide Results: January 4, 2011, Election Canvass Results Summary," https://sos.iowa.gov/elections/pdf/2011/SD48of ficialcanvass.pdf.

61. Democrat Brian H. Schoenjahn was the incumbent for the Twelfth District of the Iowa Senate, but after redistricting, he won reelection in the Thirty-Second District of the Iowa Senate in the 2012 election.

62. In 2012, the US Supreme Court, in *United States v. Alvarez* (567 U.S. 709), struck down a portion of the Stolen Valor Act. The federal law criminalized false statements about having a military medal, and the Supreme Court ruled in a 6–3 decision that this conflicted with first amendment protection of free speech. See https://www.supremecourt.gov/opinions/11pdf/11-210d4e9.pdf.

63. Rod Boshart, "Stolen Valor' Measure Debate on Hold," *Courier*, March 17, 2011, https://wcfcourier.com/news/local/govt-and-politics/stolen-valor-measure -debate-on-hold/article_8e569baf-90db-5b3e-a102-cbd2788c4aa6.html.

64. Boshart, "Stolen Valor' Measure Debate on Hold."

65. Boshart.

66. Ernst, *Daughter of the Heartland*, 110.

67. Ernst, 111.

68. The other men entering the Republican primary were Sam Clovis, Mark Jacobs, Scott Schaben, and Matthew Whitaker. Paul Lunde and David Young withdrew their candidacies. The Democrats nominated Bruce Braley, who won his primary unopposed.

69. Annika Neklason, "The 2018 Midterms and the Rise of Motherhood," *Atlantic*, July 23, 2018, https://www.theatlantic.com/family/archive/2018/07/midterms -2018-mothers/565703/.

70. Neklason, "The 2018 Midterms and the Rise of Motherhood."

71. Ernst, *Daughter of the Heartland*, 113.

72. "Iowa Senate Debate 2014," C-SPAN, October 16, 2014, https://www .c-span.org/video/?322118-1/iowa-senate-debate.

73. Ernst, *Daughter of the Heartland*, 114.

74. "Bright Prospects for GOP in 2016," *Colbert Report*, March 26, 214, http:// www.cc.com/video-clips/q8pyub/the-colbert-report-bright-prospects-for-the -gop-in-2016.

75. Ernst, *Daughter of the Heartland*, 114.

76. Ernst, 112.

77. Tal Kopan, "Palin Endorses 'Pork-Cutting' Ernst," *Politico*, March 26, 2014, https://www.politico.com/story/2014/03/sarah-palin-endorses-joni-ernst -iowa-105059.

78. Phillip Rucker and Dan Balz, "How Joni Ernst's Ad about 'Castrating Hogs' Transformed Iowa's U.S. Senate Race," *Washington Post*, May 11, 2014, https://www.washingtonpost.com/politics/how-joni-ernsts-ad-about-castrating -hogs-transformed-iowas-us-senate-race/2014/05/11/c02d1804-d85b-11e3-95d3 -3bcd77cd4e11_story.html.

79. James Hohmann, "Joni Ernst Focused on Primary in Final Iowa Debate," *Politico*, May 29, 2014, http://www.politico.com/story/2014/05/joni-ernst-election -iowa-debate-107237.html.

80. James Hohmann, "Romney Backs Ernst in Iowa Race," *Politico*, March 5, 2014, https://www.politico.com/story/2014/03/mitt-romney-joni-ernst-iowa-sen ate-104288; Katrina Lamansky, "Romney Visits QC to Endorse Joni Ernst," *WQAD*, May 29, 2014, https://www.wqad.com/article/news/politics/romney-visits-qc-to -campaign-with-joni-ernst/526-b188ca48-67ee-4ee9-a6fb-181539a30929; Tal Kopan, "Palin Endorses 'Pork-Cutting' Ernst," *Politico*, March 26, 2014, https://www.politico.com/story/2014/03/sarah-palin-endorses-joni-ernst-iowa -105059.

81. Jennifer Jacobs, "GOP Fight Breaks Out over Accusation about Joni Ernst Being 'AWOL' from Votes," *Des Moines Register*, May 2, 2014, https://www.desmoines register.com/story/news/politics/elections/2014/05/02/ernst-iowa/8643825/.

82. Jacobs, "GOP Fight Breaks Out over Accusation about Joni Ernst Being 'AWOL' from Votes."

83. Jennifer Jacobs, "John McCain: Iowa GOP Candidate's AWOL Jab Is 'Inex-cusable,'" *Des Moines Register*, May 6, 2014, https://www.desmoinesregister.com /story/news/politics/elections/2014/05/06/john-mccain-iowa/8758349/.

84. Iowa Secretary of State, "Iowa Election Results," June 3, 2014, https://web .archive.org/web/20140608014224/http://electionresults.sos.iowa.gov/Views

/TabularData.aspx?TabView=StateRaces%5EFederal%20%2F%20Statewide%20
Races%5E83&ElectionID=83.

85. Ernst, *Daughter of the Heartland*, 115.

86. Ernst, 119.

87. "Weekly Republican Address," C-SPAN, July 12, 2014, https://www.c-span
.org/video/?320425-2/weekly-republican-address.

88. "Weekly Republican Address," C-SPAN.

89. Ernst, *Daughter of the Heartland*, 118.

90. Sarah Wheaton, "Representative Apologizes for Criticizing Iowa Senator,"
New York Times, March 25, 2014, https://www.nytimes.com/2014/03/26/us/politics
/representative-apologizes-for-criticizing-iowa-senator.html.

91. Ernst, *Daughter of the Heartland*, 121.

92. Ernst, 122; William Petroski, "Harkin Says He 'Regrets' Remarks about
Ernst," *Des Moines Register*, November 1, 2014, https://www.desmoinesregister.com
/story/news/elections/2014/11/02/iowa-harkin-senate-ernst/18389193/; Kendall
Breitman, "Ernst: 'Very Offended' by Harkin," *Politico*, November 3, 2014, https://
www.politico.com/story/2014/11/joni-ernst-tom-harkin-taylor-swift-112444.

93. Jennifer Jacobs, "Democrats Pounce on Inflammatory Remarks by Joni
Ernst's Husband," *Des Moines Register*, June 9, 2014, https://www.desmoinesregis
ter.com/story/news/politics/elections/2014/06/10/gail-ernst-remarks/10302971/.

94. Jacobs, "Democrats Pounce on Inflammatory Remarks by Joni Ernst's
Husband."

95. Ernst, *Daughter of the Heartland*, 123.

96. "Iowa Election Results," *New York Times*, December 17, 2014, https://www
.nytimes.com/elections/2014/iowa-elections#house.

97. Erin Murphy, "Voter Data Shows How Ernst Beat Braley," *Quad-City Times*,
November 6, 2014, https://qctimes.com/news/local/government-and-politics
/elections/voter-data-shows-how-ernst-beat-braley/article_dc43ece0-0cad-506b
-8400-de2bb2b8451a.html.

98. "Joni Ernst Victory Speech," C-SPAN, November 4, 2014, https://www
.c-span.org/video/?322480-1/joni-ernst-victory-speech.

99. "Joni Ernst Victory Speech," C-SPAN.

100. Ernst, *Daughter of the Heartland*, 127.

101. "Politico Playbook Power List 2019: Lisa Goeas," *Politico*, https://www
.politico.com/interactives/2018/politico-power-list-2019/lisa-goeas/.

102. Maria Kreiser and Michael Greene, "History, Evolution, and Practices of
the President's State of the Union Address," *Congressional Research Service*,
January 29, 2020, https://fas.org/sgp/crs/misc/R44770.pdf.

103. Ernst, *Daughter of the Heartland*, 136; Peggy Noonan, "Bread Bags," *Wall Street Journal*, January 26, 2015, https://peggynoonan.com/page/26/?email=495.

104. Charlotte Allen, "In Mocking Sen. Joni Ernst's 'Bread Bags,' Aren't Liberals Being Hypocritical?" *Baltimore Sun*, January 22, 2015, https://www.baltimore sun.com/maryland/carroll/la-ol-joni-ernsts-bread-bags-20150122-story.html.

105. Ernst, *Daughter of the Heartland*, 143.

106. US Senate, "Statements on Introduced Bills and Joint Resolutions," *Congressional Record* 161, no. 48 (March 23, 2015): S1716, https://www.congress.gov /congressional-record/2015/03/23/senate-section/article/S1710-1.

107. Alan Zarembo, "Suicide Rate of Female Military Veterans Is Called 'Staggering,'" *Los Angeles Times*, June 8, 2015, https://www.latimes.com/nation/la-na-female -veteran-suicide-20150608-story.html.

108. See, for example, the Military Retaliation Prevention Act (2016) and Campus Accountability and Safety Act (2018).

109. In 2017, news surfaced about an active Facebook group called Marines United, with thousands of members, some active duty, who distributed hundreds of photos of nude female servicemembers.

110. "Senator Joni Ernst's 2016 (2018, 2019) Report Card," GovTrack, https:// www.govtrack.us/congress/members/joni_ernst/412667/report-card/2016.

111. "Senator Joni Ernst's 2016 (2018, 2019) Report Card," GovTrack.

112. Ernst, *Daughter of the Heartland*, 151.

113. Ernst, 153.

114. Ernst, 160; James Q. Lynch, "Ernst Says No 'Mansplaining' Necessary on Domestic Abuse Legislation," *Sioux City Journal*, November 21, 2019, https:// siouxcityjournal.com/news/state-and-regional/ernst-says-no-mansplaining -necessary-on-domestic-abuse-legislation/article_7a786f1f-0028-55c6-9bf4 -aba14a2db89d.html.

115. Brianne Pfannenstiel, "Iowa Poll: Republican Joni Ernst Pulls Ahead of Democrat Theresa Greenfield in Closing Days of Senate Race," *Des Moines Register*, October 31, 2020, https://www.desmoinesregister.com/story/news/poli tics/iowa-poll/2020/10/31/election-2020-iowa-poll-greenfield-ernst-us-senate -race-voters/6055545002/.

116. Brianne Pfannenstiel, "Joni Ernst Has Embraced President Donald Trump. Will That Hurt Her or Help Her as She Runs for a Second Term?" *Des Moines Register*, October 13, 2020, https://www.desmoinesregister.com/story/news/politics/2020 /10/13/joni-ernst-intertwined-donald-trump-hurt-her-president-senate/597163 7002/.

117. "Tracking Congress in the Age of Trump: Joni Ernst," FiveThirtyEight,

January 13, 2021, https://projects.fivethirtyeight.com/congress-trump-score/joni -ernst/.

118. "2020 Iowa U.S. Senate Election Results," *Des Moines Register*, November 3, 2020, https://www.desmoinesregister.com/elections/results/race/2020-11-03 -senate-IA-17247/.

119. Ernst, *Daughter of the Heartland*, 147.

120. "Senator Joni Ernst—2019 Report Card," GovTrack, https://www.gov track.us/congress/members/joni_ernst/412667/report-card/2019.

121. Joni Ernst, "Meet Joni," Joni for Iowa, https://joniernst.com/meet-joni/.

122. Ernst, *Daughter of the Heartland*, 147.

123. Ernst, 161.

124. Ernst, 211.

125. Ernst, 212.

126. As quoted by Susan Collins, "The Ethics of Conscience: Continuing the Legacy of Margaret Chase Smith," *Portland Press Herald*, March 30, 2006, https://www.pressherald.com/2006/03/30/the-ethics-of-conscience-continuing -the-legacy-of-margaret-chase-smith/.

6. MARTHA MCSALLY, THE "LONG-SHOT" CANDIDATE

1. Martha McSally, *Dare to Fly: Simple Lessons in Never Giving Up* (New York: HarperCollins, 2020), 164.

2. McSally, *Dare to Fly*, 165.

3. Kristina Peterson, "Arizona Rep. Martha McSally Alleges Sexual Abuse by High-School Coach," *Wall Street Journal*, April 23, 2018, https://www.wsj.com /articles/arizona-rep-martha-mcsally-alleges-sexual-abuse-by-high-school -coach-1524518307.

4. Martha McSally, "Dare to Fly," interview with Peter Slen for C-SPAN Books, June 24, 2020, https://www.c-span.org/video/?473123-1/dare-fly.

5. McSally, *Dare to Fly*, 6.

6. McSally, 167.

7. US Air Force Academy, "'80s Ladies Recall First Year Experiences at USAFA," *Checkpoints* (June 2016), https://www2.usafa.org/Images/Checkpoints/2016-June /80sLadiesResponses.pdf.

8. US Air Force Academy, "'80s Ladies Recall First Year Experiences at USAFA." See also Anne Martin Fletcher, "Groundbreaker," in *Calling Down the Mountain: Writing from the Jane's Stories Press Foundation Women into Print Retreat* (Fremont, IN: Jane's Stories Press Foundation, 2008), 5–8, https://annemartinfletcher.word press.com/about/groundbreaker-description/.

9. Fletcher, "Groundbreaker."

10. Fletcher.

11. McSally, *Dare to Fly*, 6.

12. McSally, 168.

13. Emily Cochrane and Jennifer Steinhauer, "Senator Martha McSally Says Superior Officer in the Air Force Raped Her," *New York Times*, March 6, 2019, https://www.nytimes.com/2019/03/06/us/politics/martha-mcsally-sexual-assault.html.

14. US Senate, "Senate Armed Services Hearing on Sexual Assault in the Military," C-SPAN, March 6, 2019, https://www.c-span.org/video/?458475-1/senate-armed-services-subcommittee-holds-hearing-military-sexual-assault-prevention.

15. Kelsey E. B. Knoer, "The Catch-22 of Females Reporting Sexual Assault in the Military: A Cause for Holistic International Intervention," *Nebraska Law Review* 95, no. 4 (2017): 1160–1190, http://digitalcommons.unl.edu/nlr/vol95/iss4/7.

16. Lisa Ferdinando, "DOD Releases Annual Report on Sexual Assault in Military," *DOD News*, May 1, 2018, https://www.defense.gov/Explore/News/Article/Article/1508127/dod-releases-annual-report-on-sexual-assault-in-military/.

17. Knoer, "The Catch-22 of Females Reporting Sexual Assault in the Military."

18. Knoer.

19. US Senate, "Senate Armed Services Hearing on Sexual Assault in the Military."

20. US Senate.

21. McSally, *Dare to Fly*, 7.

22. McSally, 10.

23. McSally, 11.

24. Brian W. Everstine, "Air Force Removes Height Requirement for Pilot Applicants," *Air Force Magazine*, May 22, 2020, https://www.airforcemag.com/air-force-removes-minimum-height-requirement-for-pilot-applicants/.

25. Eric Schmitt, "Senate Votes to Remove Ban on Women as Combat Pilots," *New York Times*, August 1, 1991, A1, https://www.nytimes.com/1991/08/01/us/senate-votes-to-remove-ban-on-women-as-combat-pilots.html.

26. McSally, "Dare to Fly," interview with Slen.

27. McSally, *Dare to Fly*, 44.

28. McSally, 45.

29. McSally, 17.

30. McSally, 48–49.

31. McSally, 45.

32. McSally, 82.

33. McSally, 52

34. McSally, 124.

35. McSally, 126.

36. McSally, 128.

37. McSally, 132.

38. "Perry Expects Extended U.S. Presence in Gulf."

39. McSally, *Dare to Fly*, 134.

40. McSally, 52.

41. Senator Kyl was first elected as a US representative from Arizona in 1986 and to the Senate in 1994.

42. McSally, *Dare to Fly*, 142.

43. McSally, 135.

44. McSally, 143.

45. McSally, 145.

46. Edward T. Pound, "Saudi Rules Anger Top Air Force Pilot: Female Officer Speaks Out against Muslim Dress Code for Americans," *USA Today*, April 18, 2001, 1.

47. Pound, "Saudi Rules Anger Top Air Force Pilot."

48. Pound.

49. Peter Grier, "Female USAF Fighter Pilot Slams Dress Rules in Saudi Arabia," *Air Force Magazine* (June 2001), 14, https://www.airforcemag.com/PDF/Maga zineArchive/Magazine%20Documents/2001/June%202001/0601world.pdf.

50. Diana Stancy Correll, "Retired Navy Captain and Trailblazer for Women's Equality in the Service Dies at 76," *Navy Times*, September 10, 2020, https://www .navytimes.com/news/your-navy/2020/09/10/retired-navy-captain-and-trail blazer-for-womens-equality-in-the-service-dies-at-76/.

51. Correll, "Retired Navy Captain and Trailblazer for Women's Equality in the Service Dies at 76."

52. Anne Groer, "New Trainer Undaunted by NTC's Uncertain Fate," *Orlando Sentinel*, June 25, 1991, https://www.orlandosentinel.com/news/os-xpm-1991-06 -25-9106250635-story.html.

53. Blake Stilwell, "How Ruth Bader Ginsburg Helped End the Military's Forced Abortion Policy," Military.com, https://www.military.com/history/how -ruth-bader-ginsburg-helped-end-militarys-policy-of-forced-abortion.html; Todd S. Albright, Alan P. Gehrich, Johnnie Wright Jr., Christine F. Lettieri, Susan G. Dunlow, and Jerome L. Buller, "Pregnancy during Operation Iraqi Freedom /Operation Enduring Freedom," *Military Medicine* 172, no. 5 (2007): 511–514.

54. McSally, *Dare to Fly*, 153.

55. "Female Officer Presses Suit on U.S. Military Rules in Saudi Arabia," CNN, January 24, 2002, http://edition.cnn.com/2002/US/01/24/airforce.suit.saudi.cnna /index.html?related.

56. "Women in Combat," CBS, November 26, 2008, https://www.youtube.com/watch?v=pTDolvRZZ_Y.

57. "U.S. Military Women Cast Off Abayas," *CBS News*, January 22, 2002, https://www.cbsnews.com/news/us-military-women-cast-off-abayas/.

58. "U.S. Military Women Cast Off Abayas," *CBS News*.

59. "State of the Union Address 2002," Politics 101, https://www.youtube.com/watch?v=OzLDlTAgYJc. McSally appears at 46:55.

60. US House, 107th Cong., 2nd sess., "Prohibiting Members of Armed Forces in Saudi Arabia from Being Required or Compelled to Wear the Abaya," *Congressional Record*, May 14, 2002, 148, 61, https://www.congress.gov/congressional-record/2002/05/14/house-section/article/H2422-1, H2422-H2427.

61. "Air, Space, and Cyber Awards," Air Force Association, https://www.afa.org/membership/awards.

62. Marc Lacey and David M. Herszenhorn, "In Attack's Wake, Political Repercussions," *New York Times*, January 8, 2011, https://www.nytimes.com/2011/01/09/us/politics/09giffords.html.

63. McSally, *Dare to Fly*, 229.

64. Exceptions exist for the president and vice president. An Act to Prevent Pernicious Political Activities, Public Law 76-252, U.S. *Statutes at Large*, 410 (August 2, 1939), 1147–1149, https://govtrackus.s3.amazonaws.com/legislink/pdf/stat/53/STATUTE-53-Pg1147.pdf.

65. McSally, *Dare to Fly*, 230.

66. M.J. Lee, "GOP Candidate Wants to Kick Rick," *Politico*, February 17, 2012, https://www.politico.com/story/2012/02/gop-candidate-wants-to-kick-rick-073024.

67. "Ron Barber Defeats Martha McSally in Race for Giffords's Former Seat," *Washington Post*, November 17, 2012, https://www.washingtonpost.com/politics/ron-barber-defeats-martha-mcsally-in-race-for-giffordss-seat/2012/11/17/f276e570-30f9-11e2-9f50-0308e1e75445_story.html.

68. The Arizona Independent Redistricting Commission redrew congressional districts for the state. The new district map was finalized and adopted for the 2012 elections. Arizona's Eighth District was redrawn and labeled the Second District. See Colleen Mathis, Daniel Moskowitz, and Benjamin Schneer, "The Arizona Independent Redistricting Commission: One State's Model for Gerrymandering Reform," Harvard Kennedy School, Ash Center for Democratic Governance and Innovation, September 2019, https://ash.harvard.edu/files/ash/files/az_redistricting_policy_brief.pdf.

69. "Ron Barber Defeats Martha McSally in Race for Giffords's Former Seat," *Washington Post*.

70. "Women in Combat, Past Integration Efforts," C-SPAN, February 1, 2013,

https://www.c-span.org/video/?310750-2/women-combat-past-integration-efforts#.

71. Ted Robbins, "2nd Congressional District Seat May Be up to Convincing Independents," Arizona Public Media, October 11, 2014, https://www.azpm.org/s/24221-2nd-congressional-district-seat-may-be-up-to-convincing-independents/.

72. McSally, Dare to Fly, 234.

73. Editorial Board, "McSally's Time: A GOP Talent Rises," Arizona Republic, October 1, 2014, https://www.azcentral.com/story/opinion/editorial/2014/10/01/martha-mcsally-congress-endorsement/16565955/.

74. "Arizona 2nd Congressional District Debate," C-SPAN, October 7, 2014, https://www.c-span.org/video/?321922-1/arizona-2nd-congressional-district-debate.

75. With respect to advertising, see Ben Kamisar, "Group Expects More Than $1B in Political Ads by End of 2014 Cycle," The Hill, October 14, 2014, https://thehill.com/blogs/blog-briefing-room/220780-group-expects-more-than-1-billion-in-political-ads-by-end-of-2014. On fund-raising totals, see Center for Responsive Politics, "Arizona Congressional Races: 2014 Election Cycle," https://www.opensecrets.org/races/election?cycle=2014&id=AZ. US Representative Ron Barber raised $4,029,501, and Martha McSally raised $4,808,014, for a combined $8,837,515 in the race for Arizona's Second District.

76. Tarini Parti, "Republican McSally Wins Last House Race of 2014," Politico, December 17, 2014, https://www.politico.com/story/2014/12/martha-mcsally-arizona-second-113640.

77. McSally, Dare to Fly, 233.

78. Cristina Marcos, "Vulnerable House Freshmen Passed Most Bills in Decades, Analysis Finds," The Hill, October 24, 2016, https://thehill.com/blogs/floor-action/house/302533-vulnerable-gop-lawmakers-outpace-other-freshmen-in-productivity#.WA5_DRZ3uvA.twitter.

79. Ronald Hansen, "Arizona Congresswoman's GOP-Leaning District Is Drifting Leftward," Arizona Republic, May 20, 2017, https://www.azcentral.com/story/news/politics/azdc/2017/05/20/arizona-congresswomans-gop-leaning-district-drifting-leftward/333744001/.

80. "Authorization for Use of Military Force Request: Interview with Martha McSally," C-SPAN, Washington Journal, February 11, 2015, https://www.c-span.org/video/?324241-4/washington-journal-representative-martha-mcsally-r-az.

81. Martha McSally, "Weekly Republican Radio Address," C-SPAN, November 21, 2015, https://www.c-span.org/video/?401096-101/weekly-republican-address.

82. Robert O'Neill, "Fighter: Congresswoman Martha McSally MPP 1990, Defiant, Pragmatic, and in Congress," Harvard Kennedy School (Summer 2017), https://www.hks.harvard.edu/faculty-research/policy-topics/politics/fighter-congresswoman-martha-mcsally-mpp-1990-defiant.

83. Hansen, "Arizona Congresswoman's GOP-Leaning District Is Drifting Leftward."

84. O'Neill, "Fighter."

85. "AIPAC Policy Conference, Members of Congress," C-SPAN, March 28, 2017, https://www.c-span.org/video/?426089-3/aipac-policy-conference-members-congress.

86. David Wichner, "Defense Bill Will Extend Life of A-10, Boost Raytheon Programs," *Arizona Daily Star*, August 13, 2018, https://tucson.com/news/local/defense-bill-will-extend-life-of-a-10-boost-raytheon-programs/article_489f32cb-32cc-5ad2-b67e-57348751d5a5.html.

87. Eliza S. Collins, "Arizona Rep. Martha McSally Aims to Be Republican Voice on Women's Issues," *Arizona Republic*, April 5, 2017, https://www.azcentral.com/story/news/politics/arizona/2017/04/05/arizona-rep-martha-mcsally-aims-republican-voice-women-issues/100079834/.

88. Collins, "Arizona Rep. Martha McSally Aims to Be Republican Voice on Women's Issues."

89. "Military Academy Sexual Harassment Report," C-SPAN, May 2, 2017, https://www.c-span.org/video/?427730-1/victims-testify-sexual-assaults-military-academies.

90. "Jeff Flake's Full Speech Announcing He Won't Run for Reelection," CNN, October 24, 2017, https://www.cnn.com/2017/10/24/politics/jeff-flake-retirement-speech-full-text/index.html.

91. Dan Nowicki, "'Grow a Pair of Ovaries,' Martha McSally Says in Trumpian Campaign Video," *Arizona Republic*, January 12, 2018, https://www.azcentral.com/story/news/politics/elections/2018/01/12/martha-mcsally-senate-says-grow-pair-ovaries-gop-campaign-video-trump-sharia-law/1028071001/.

92. Ed Kilgore, "GOP Establishment Favorite Martha McSally Will Run for Senate as a Sharia-Hating Trump Ally," *New York Magazine*, January 12, 2018, https://nymag.com/intelligencer/2018/01/establishment-fave-mcsally-will-run-for-senate-as-trump-ally.html.

93. Martha McSally for U.S. Senate on Twitter, @MarthaMcSally, "Trump's Comments Are Disgusting. Joking about Sexual Assault Is Unacceptable. I'm Appalled," October 8, 2016, https://twitter.com/marthamcsally/status/784615339053215744?lang=en.

94. Maggie Severns, "McSally Embraces Trump Ahead of Arizona Senate Run," *Politico*, November 29, 2017, https://www.politico.com/newsletters/morning-score/2017/11/29/mcsally-embraces-trump-ahead-of-arizona-senate-run-035211.

95. Jonathan Martin, "A Senate Candidate's Image Shifted. Did Her Life Story?" *New York Times*, September 24, 2018, https://www.nytimes.com/2018/09/24/us/politics/kyrsten-sinema-arizona.html.

96. Martha McSally, "'I Wish Her Success': McSally Concedes Arizona Senate Race to Sinema," *Washington Post*, November 12, 2018, https://www.washingtonpost.com/video/politics/i-wish-her-success-mcsally-concedes-arizona-senate-race-to-sinema/2018/11/12/2ce8fe80-e6e0-11e8-8449-1ff263609a31_video.html.

97. Li Zhou, "Kyrsten Sinema Is the First Democrat to Win an Arizona Senate Seat in 30 Years," *Vox*, November 12, 2018, https://www.vox.com/2018/11/12/18056978/senate-midterm-results-arizona-kyrsten-sinema-winner.

98. Jessica Taylor, "Republican Martha McSally Picked to Fill Senate Seat Formerly Held by John McCain," NPR, December 18, 2018, https://www.npr.org/2018/12/18/677766098/republican-martha-mcsally-picked-to-fill-senate-seat-formerly-held-by-john-mccain.

99. Taylor, "Republican Martha McSally Picked to Fill Senate Seat Formerly Held by John McCain."

7. TULSI GABBARD AND THE "TRUE COST OF WAR"

1. Zack Beauchamp, "Tulsi Gabbard, the Controversial, LongShot Democratic 2020 Candidate, Explained," *Vox*, June 26, 2019, https://www.vox.com/policy-and-politics/2019/1/16/18182114/tulsi-gabbard-2020-president-campaign-policies.

2. Kelefa Sanneh, "What Does Tusli Gabbard Believe?" *New Yorker*, October 30, 2017, https://www.newyorker.com/magazine/2017/11/06/what-does-tulsi-gabbard-believe?subId1=xid:fr1584360188772gja.

3. SUFA allegedly propelled the right-wing meme of a "war on Christmas" by those who did not respect Christmas's Christian origins. Its goal is to promote patriotism and aims to "increase our awareness of our identity as citizens of one nation under God." Catherine Toth, "Ewa Candidates Talk Traffic," *Honolulu Advertiser*, September 13, 2002, B3.

4. "State House Candidates," *Honolulu Advertiser*, September 16, 2002, https://www.newspapers.com/image/265839952/.

5. "Hawaii Primary Elections, 2002," Hawaii Office of Elections, September 28, 2002, https://elections.hawaii.gov/election-result/primary-election/.

6. Gordon Pang, "Civil-Union Hearing Packed," *Honolulu Advertiser*, February 20, 2004, 1.

7. Gordon Pang, "Bill to Allow Civil Unions May Be Stalled in House," *Honolulu Advertiser*, February 20, 2004, http://the.honoluluadvertiser.com/article/2004/Feb/20/ln/ln09a.html.

8. Bret LoGiurato, "Meet Tulsi Gabbard, the Unlikely Rising Star of the Democratic Party," *Business Insider*, September 6, 2012, https://www.businessinsider.com/tulsi-gabbard—dnc-democratic-party-rising-star-convention-speech-2012-9.

9. For more information on Daniel Akaka's political career and personal biography, see US House of Representatives, History, Art, and Archives, "AKAKA, Daniel Kahikina," https://history.house.gov/People/Listing/A/AKAKA,-Daniel-Kahikina-(A000069)/.

10. Gordon Pang, "Gabbard Triumphs," *Star Advertiser*, August 12, 2012, https://www.staradvertiser.com/2012/08/12/hawaii-news/gabbard-triumphs/.

11. John Powers, "Making a Splash: Is Tulsi Gabbard the Next Democratic Star?" *Vogue*, June 24, 2013, https://www.vogue.com/article/making-a-splash-is-tulsi-gabbard-the-next-democratic-party-star.

12. "Rep. Tulsi Gabbard Statement on Defense Department Allowing Female Troops in Ground Combat," press release, January 23, 2013, https://gabbard.house.gov/news/press-releases/photos-video-rep-tulsi-gabbard-conducts-hawai-i-island-agriculture-and-farm-tou?page=137.

13. "Rep. Tulsi Gabbard Statement on Same-Sex Marriage," press release, January 30, 2013, https://gabbard.house.gov/news/press-releases/photos-video-rep-tulsi-gabbard-conducts-hawai-i-island-agriculture-and-farm-tou?page=137.

14. "2016 Hawaii House Election Results," *Politico*, December 13, 2016, https://www.politico.com/2016-election/results/map/house/hawaii/.

15. Caroline Kelly, "Tulsi Gabbard Says She Will Run for President in 2020," CNN, January 12, 2019, https://www.cnn.com/2019/01/11/politics/tulsi-gabbard-van-jones/index.html.

16. Daniel Strauss, "Tulsi Gabbard Campaign in Disarray," *Politico*, January 29, 2019, https://www.politico.com/story/2019/01/29/tulsi-gabbard-2020-election-1134055.

17. Edward-Isaac Dovere, "The Enduring Mystery of Tulsi Gabbard," *Atlantic*, September 5, 2019, https://www.theatlantic.com/politics/archive/2019/09/tulsi-gabbard-2020-candidate/597226/.

18. "Disbursements for Tulsi Now, 2019–2020," Federal Election Commission, https://www.fec.gov/data/disbursements/?committee_id=C00693713&two_year_transaction_period=2020&two_year_transaction_period=2018&line_number=F3P-23&data_type=processed.

19. "Disbursements for Tulsi Now, 2019–2020," Federal Election Commission.

20. "Disbursements for Tulsi Now, 2019–2020," Federal Election Commission.

21. Bill Frischling, "Tulsi Gabbard's Social Media Stats ≠ Sense," *Factbl.og*, October 26, 2019, https://blog.factba.se/2019/10/26/tulsi-gabbards-social-media-stats-%E2%89%A0-sense/.

22. "*The Economist/YouGov* Poll," November 3–5, 2019, https://d25d2506sfb94s.cloudfront.net/cumulus_uploads/document/cseozthmrp/econTabReport.pdf.

23. Team Populism was formed by a group of scholars from Europe and the Americas with the purpose of studying the causes and consequences of populism. Recent scholarship from the group can be found on the organization's website, https://populism.byu.edu/.

24. Tulsi Gabbard, as quoted in Jackson Truesdale, "Representative Gabbard Talks Presidential Campaign, Focuses on Cost of War," *Brown Daily Herald*, April 23, 2019, https://www.browndailyherald.com/2019/04/23/representative-gabbard-talks-presidential-campaign-tactics-students/.

25. "About Tulsi Gabbard—Service above Self," Tulsi 2020, n.d. accessed January 10, 2020, https://www.tulsi2020.com/about/tulsi-gabbard-service-above-self.

26. "About Tulsi Gabbard—My Spiritual Path," Tulsi 2020, n.d., accessed January 10, 2020, https://www.tulsi2020.com/about/about-tulsi-gabbard-my-spiritual-path.

27. Tulsi Gabbard, "To Respect You—That Is My Personal Commitment," video, November 26, 2019, https://youtu.be/pzBwjtNj9X4.

28. "Congresswoman Tulsi Gabbard—Build, Don't Bomb: A New American Foreign Policy," video, Brown University, Watson Institute for International and Public Affairs, April 23, 2019, https://www.youtube.com/watch?v=dKDuLdPFyto.

29. Judy Woodruff, "Tulsi Gabbard on Why She Wants to Prioritize Foreign Policy," PBS *NewsHour*, May 17, 2019, https://www.pbs.org/newshour/show/tulsi-gabbard-on-why-she-wants-to-prioritize-foreign-policy.

30. "About Tulsi Gabbard—Military Service—the Cost of War," Tulsi 2020, n.d., accessed January 10, 2020, https://www.tulsi2020.com/about/tulsi-gabbard-military-service.

31. "How My Military Experience Helps Me Fight for Vets in Congress," *Time*, October 15, 2014, https://time.com/collection-post/3501808/veterans-tulsi/.

32. Tom Nichols, "How Hillary Clinton Boosted Tulsi Gabbard," *Atlantic*, October 20, 2019, https://www.theatlantic.com/ideas/archive/2019/10/hillary-clinton-elevating-tulsi-gabbard/600370/.

33. Woodruff, "Tulsi Gabbard on Why She Wants to Prioritize Foreign Policy."

34. "About Tulsi Gabbard—Military Service—the Cost of War." See also Tyler Olsen, "Tulsi Gabbard: 5 Things to Know," *Fox News*, February 19, 2020, https://www.foxnews.com/politics/tulsi-gabbard-5-things-to-know.

35. Chickenhawk is a political term used in the United States to describe a

person who strongly supports war or other military action yet who actively avoids or avoided military service when of age. "Tulsi Gabbard—Trump's Chickenhawk Cabinet," Tulsi 2020, n.d., accessed January 10, 2020, https://www.tulsi2020 .com/splash/chickenhawks.

36. "Congresswoman Tulsi Gabbard," Brown University.

37. "About Tulsi Gabbard—Military Service—the Cost of War."

38. "Candidate Tracker—Tulsi Gabbard's Foreign Policy," Council on Foreign Relations, https://www.cfr.org/election2020/candidate-tracker/tulsi-gabbard.

39. Will Caron, "Gabbard's Supposed Progressive Alignment Questioned by Hawaii Lawmaker," *Hawaii Independent*, November 21, 2016, https://theha waiiindependent.com/story/gabbards-supposed-progressive-alignment-ques tioned-by-hawaii-lawmaker/.

40. "Tulsi Gabbard on Regime Change Wars," Tulsi 2020, n.d., https://www .tulsigabbard.org/tulsi-gabbard-on-regime-change-war.

41. "Tulsi Gabbard on Regime Change Wars," Tulsi 2020.

42. "Issues—War and Waste," Tulsi 2020, n.d., https://www.tulsi2020.com /issues/war-waste.

43. "Issues—War and Diplomacy," Tulsi 2020, n.d., https://www.tulsi2020 .com/issues/war-diplomacy-international-trade.

44. "Rep. Gabbard: Obama Refuses to Say Enemy Is 'Islamic,'" CNN, January 16, 2015, https://www.youtube.com/watch?v=RC67E_3KOJQ&app=desktop.

45. The Stop Arming Terrorists Act (H.R. 608) would have prohibited any federal agency from using taxpayer dollars to provide weapons, cash, intelligence, or any support to al-Qaeda, ISIL, and other terrorist groups and prohibited the government from funneling money and weapons through other countries directly or indirectly supporting terrorists. The legislation was cosponsored by Representatives Peter Welch (D-VT), Barbara Lee (D-CA), Walter B. Jones (R-NC), Thomas Massie (R-KY), Ted Yoho (R-FL), and Garrett Thomas (R-VA).

46. "Rep. Gabbard: Obama Refuses to Say Enemy Is 'Islamic,'" CNN.

47. Beauchamp, "Tulsi Gabbard, the Controversial, Long-Shot Democratic 2020 Candidate, Explained."

48. "Rep. Tulsi Gabbard: The Democrat That Republicans Love and the DNC Can't Control," *Washington Post*, October 15, 2015, https://www.washingtonpost .com/news/the-fix/wp/2015/10/15/rep-tulsi-gabbard-the-democrat-that-republi cans-love-and-the-dnc-cant-control/.

49. Tulsi Gabbard (@TulsiGabbard). 2018. "Hey @realdonaldtrump: being Saudi Arabia's bitch is not 'America First.'" Twitter, November 21, 2018, 12:01 p.m., https://twitter.com/TulsiGabbard/status/1065289231977738240.

50. Just war theory deals with the justification of how and why wars are fought.

The justification can be either theoretical or historical. For more information, see Alexander Mosley, "Just War Theory," *Internet Encyclopedia of Philosophy*, https://www.iep.utm.edu/justwar/.

51. Barbara Burrell, "Campaign Finance: Women's Experience in the Modern Era," in *Women and Elective Office*, ed. S. Thomas and C. Wilcox (New York: Oxford University Press, 2014), 26–37; Leonie Huddy and Nayda Terkildsen, "Gender Stereotypes and the Perception of Male and Female Candidates," *American Journal of Political Science* 37, no. 1 (1993): 119–147; Jennifer Lawless, "Women, War, and Winning Elections: Gender Stereotyping in the Post September 11th Era," *Political Research Quarterly* 53, no. 3 (2004): 479–490; Mark Leeper, "The Impact of Prejudice on Female Candidates: An Experimental Look at Voter Inference," *American Politics Quarterly* 19, no. 2 (1991): 248–261; Shirley M. Rosenwasser and Norma G. Dean, "Gender Roles and Political Office: Effects of Perceived Masculinity/Femininity of Candidate and Political Office," *Psychology of Women Quarterly* 13 (June 1989): 77–85.

52. Deborah Alexander and Kristi Andersen, "Gender as a Factor in the Attribution of Leadership Traits," *Political Research Quarterly* 46, no. 3 (1993): 527–545.

53. Sanneh, "What Does Tulsi Gabbard Believe?"

54. Brittany Shoot, "Why Democratic Women Are Wearing White to Tuesday Night's State of the Union Address," *Fortune*, February 5, 2019, https://fortune.com/2019/02/05/state-of-the-union-sotu-2019-house-democrat-women-wearing-suffragette-white/.

55. Vanessa Friedman, "Tulsi Gabbard's White Pantsuit Isn't Winning," *New York Times*, November 21, 2019, https://www.nytimes.com/2019/11/21/style/tulsi-gabbard-democratic-debate-white-pantsuit.html.

56. Joe Concha, "Gabbard Is Most Searched on Google after Democratic Debate," *The Hill*, June 27, 2019, https://thehill.com/homenews/media/450601-gabbard-is-most-searched-on-google-after-democratic-debate; "Gabbard, Again Most Googled Candidate, Slams 'Despicable' CNN, NYT Coverage of Her Syria Policy," *Haaretz*, October 16, 2019, https://www.haaretz.com/us-news/gabbard-again-most-googled-candidate-slams-despicable-cnn-nyt-1.7993106.

57. Jeanine Santucci, "Tulsi Gabbard Tells Fox News Host Tucker Carlson That DNC Debate Criteria Isn't Transparent," *USA Today*, August 29, 2019, https://www.usatoday.com/story/news/politics/2019/08/29/tulsi-gabbard-didnt-make-3rd-debate-tells-tucker-carlson-no-transparency/2152483001/.

58. Meg Kinnard, "Gabbard Ends Long-Shot 2020 Presidential Bid, Throws Support to Biden," *Orange County Register*, March 19, 2020, https://www.ocregister.com/2020/03/19/gabbard-ends-long-shot-2020-bid-throws-support-to-biden/.

59. Yael Halon, "Gabbard Doubles Down on Slam of Schiff, Brannan as Greater Dangers to America Than Capitol Rioters," Fox News, January 29, 2021. https://web.archive.org/web/20210129110353/https://www.foxnews.com/politics/tulsi-gabbard-brennan-schiff-domestic-terror-capitol-rioters.

60. Sanneh, "What Does Tulsi Gabbard Believe?"

CONCLUSION: DIGGING THE WELL

Epigraph: Tammy Duckworth, "Foreword," in Band of Sisters: American Women at War in Iraq, ed. Kirsten Holmstedt (Mechanicsburg, PA: Stackpole, 2007), x.

1. Jeremy Teigen, Why Veterans Run: Military Service in American Presidential Elections, 1789–2016 (Philadelphia, PA: Temple University Press, 2018), 239.

2. For example: Jennifer Lawless and Richard Fox, It Takes a Candidate: Why Women Don't Run for Office (New York: Cambridge University Press, 2005); Richard Fox and Jennifer Lawless, "If Only They'd Ask: Gender, Recruitment, and Political Ambition," Journal of Politics 72, no. 2 (2010): 310–326; Jennifer Lawless, Becoming a Candidate (New York: Cambridge University Press, 2012); Susan J. Carroll and Kira Sanbonmatsu, More Women Can Run: Gender and Pathways to the State Legislatures (New York: Oxford University Press, 2013); Kelly Dittmar, Navigating Gendered Terrain: Stereotypes and Strategy in Political Campaigns (Philadelphia, PA: Temple University Press, 2015); Kelly Dittmar, Kira Sanbonmatsu, and Susan J. Carroll, A Seat at the Table: Congresswomen's Perspectives on Why Their Presence Matters (New York: Oxford University Press, 2018); Kaitlin Sidorsky, All Roads Lead to Power: Appointed and Elected Paths to Public Office for U.S. Women (Lawrence: University Press of Kansas, 2019).

3. Duckworth, "Foreword," x.

4. Joni Ernst, Daughter of the Heartland: My Ode to the Country That Raised Me (New York: Simon and Schuster, 2020), 61.

5. Sidorsky, All Roads Lead to Power, 2.

6. Kim Parker, Ruth Igielnik, Amanda Barroso, and Anthony Cilluffo, "The American Veteran Experience and the Post-9/11 Generation," Pew Research Center, September 10, 2019, https://www.pewsocialtrends.org/2019/09/10/the-american-veteran-experience-and-the-post-9-11-generation/; National Center for Veterans Analysis and Statistics, "Profile of Post-9/11 Veterans: 2014," US Department of Veterans Affairs, May 2016, https://www.va.gov/vetdata/docs/SpecialReports/Post_911_Veterans_Profile_2014.pdf.

7. Eileen Patten and Kim Parker, "Women in the U.S. Military: Growing Share, Distinctive Profile," Pew Research Center, March 2011, https://www.pewresearch.org/wp—content/uploads/sites/3/2011/12/women-in-the-military.pdf.

Reconstructing the "natural chapter" of American servicewomen's history and politics necessitates the inclusion of a diverse range of research materials. Chapter 2 draws heavily on archival research, including the Edith Nourse Rogers papers at Harvard University; Florence Prag Kahn papers at the University of California–Berkeley; Catherine Small Long papers at Louisiana State University; and the Margaret Chase Smith papers, recordings, and ephemera at the Margaret Chase Smith Library in Skowhegan, Maine. The perspectives of these significant women in their own words are essential to understanding the history of women in the armed forces as well as women in US politics. For those elected to office, I used the *Congressional Record* to explore their political careers qualitatively and the Center for American Women and Politics for quantitative data. Coverage of these historical figures and the issues they fought for or against, in national media such as the *Washington Post* and *New York Times* as well as local newspapers from San Francisco to Baton Rouge, and politically focused outlets such as *Roll Call*, the *Christian Science Monitor*, or more recently *Politico* are crucial to interpreting these women and the impact of their careers in service and politics. For secondary source material on women in the US military, Susan Zeiger's *In Uncle Sam's Service* and Kimberly Jensen's *Mobilizing Minerva* provide excellent historical and theoretical frameworks. Further biographical information on some of the women featured in Chapter 2 can be found in Janaan Sherman's *No Place for a Woman: A Life of Senator Margaret Chase Smith*, Glenna Matthews's "'There Is No Sex in Citizenship': The Career of Congresswoman Florence Prag Kahn," and Lorraine Nelson Spitzer's *The Belle of Ashby Street: Helen Douglas Mankin and Georgia Politics*.

For the recent campaigns and careers of the women I discuss in Chapter 3, I also drew on local and national media as well as the *Congressional Record*, but the research was enhanced significantly by fund-raising data from the Center for Responsive Politics and a wealth of digital sources. Specifically, the campaign advertisements and interviews from the C-SPAN archives, on PBS.com, and on the websites of the women campaigning and serving in office are all treasure troves of sources for political researchers. Exemplary secondary sources also informed Chapter 3: Megan H. MacKenzie's *Beyond the Band of Brothers* for women in the military, and Kaitlin Sidorsky's *All Roads Lead to Power* for women in politics. The perspective of women I discuss in this chapter, those who gained military experience before political experience, are invaluable firsthand accounts. *Band of Sisters:*

American Women at War in Iraq, is an edited collection that captures many of those stories, whereas M. J. Hegar's *Shoot Like a Girl* is a rich and detailed memoir. Interviews with Hegar were also essential to gaining more information and insight related to these "badasses," who parlayed their military service into political campaigns.

Senator Tammy Duckworth's remarkable military and political careers have engendered a great deal of primary source material in national newspapers and the vibrant Illinois media (particularly the *Chicago Tribune* and Chicago Public Media) as well as military and political websites. Secondary sources such as Susan Zeiger's *Entangling Alliances* and Mark Lytle's *America's Uncivil Wars* establish the context to understand Duckworth's journey. Like other servicewomen who entered the political arena, government documents and records as well as C-SPAN's archives preserve Duckworth's history of campaigns and legislation. These are enhanced by data from the Center for Legislative Effectiveness as well as the Center for Responsive Politics. But because of Duckworth's powerful story and the national attention it has received, research on her also includes popular national media such as *Vogue* and *GC* magazine articles, unique to Chapters 4 and 7.

The starting point for research on Joni Ernst is her memoir, *Daughter of the Heartland*, released in the midst of her reelection campaign in 2020. Some of her recollections can be corroborated by local reporting, for example in the *High Plains Journal*, *Iowa Republican*, *Des Moines Register*, and *Sioux City Journal*, as well as election results from the Iowa secretary of state. But her specific experiences with domestic farming and foreign exchange led to agricultural publications such as NASD Online and US Department of Agriculture reporting as well as international sources such as the *Ukrainian Weekly*. As with the other women in this book, national media from the *Los Angeles Times*, the *New York Times*, the *Atlantic*, and *Politico* followed Ernst's political campaigns and legislative work. Campaign advertisements appeared on Ernst's YouTube channel, and other materials are archived on C-SPAN. For analysis of Ernst's work in the Senate, the *Congressional Record*, GovTrack Report Card, and *Pew Researcher* remain indispensable and accessible sources for historical analyses of a contemporary senator.

Like that of Ernst, Martha McSally's autobiography, *Dare to Fly*, was published during her campaign to win the Senate seat to which she had been appointed. Because that hotly contested campaign garnered national attention, my research for Chapter 6 drew on major newspapers as well as digital publications that focus on politics such as *Politico*, *The Hill*, and *Vox*. Coverage from Arizona media on McSally's time in office and her campaign also informed this chapter. Finally, considering McSally's unique position both in service and in forwarding challenges to the armed services, military periodicals such as *Air Force Magazine* and *Navy Times* contained more information for McSally than for some of the other women I studied for this book.

As Hawai'i's most recognizable national politician, Tulsi Gabbard inspired research from sources in Hawai'i and on the mainland. Specifically, the *Honolulu Advertiser* covered her campaigns and legislative career, and the Hawai'i Office of Elections provided results. After Gabbard announced her bid for the Democratic nomination for president, national media such as the *Atlantic*, *Time*, *Fortune*, *Business Insider*, *Politico*, and CNN covered her career. Gabbard's own YouTube channel and social media profiles preserved many of her campaign videos and direct messages to voters and were rich sources for Chapter 7. Secondary sources included articles from academic journals that provided theoretical grounding. Jeremy Teigen's *Why Veterans Run* was crucial for understanding Gabbard and many of the women servicemembers I discussed throughout this book who sought to transition their military service into electoral politics.